CAMBRIDGE STUDIES IN PHILOSOPHY

Judgement and Justification

CAMBRIDGE STUDIES IN PHILOSOPHY

General editor SYDNEY SHOEMAKER

Advisory editors J. E. J. ALTHAM, SIMON BLACKBURN,
GILBERT HARMAN, MARTIN HOLLIS, FRANK JACKSON,
JONATHAN LEAR, JOHN PERRY, BARRY STROUD

Judgement and Justification

William G. Lycan

University of North Carolina, Chapel Hill

The right of the
University of Cambridge
to print and sell
all manner of books
was granted by
Henry VIII in 1534.
The University has printed
and published continuously
since 1584.

Cambridge University Press

Cambridge

New York   New Rochelle   Melbourne   Sydney

Published by the Press Syndicate of the University of Cambridge
The Pitt Building, Trumpington Street, Cambridge CB2 1RP
32 East 57th Street, New York, NY 10022, USA
10 Stamford Road, Oakleigh, Melbourne 3166, Australia

First published 1988

Printed in the United States of America

Library of Congress Cataloging-in-Publication Data
Lycan, William G.
Judgment and justification.
(Cambridge studies in philosophy)
Bibliography: p.
1. Belief and doubt.   2. Justification (Theory of
knowledge)   I. Title.   II. Series.
BD215.L92   1988   121'.6   87–12490

ISBN 0 521 34047 0 hard covers
ISBN 0 521 33580 9 paperback

British Library Cataloging in Publication applied for

121.6
L98j

For our foster son
Devin Thompson
wherever he may be

Contents

vii

Preface

Thanks to the kaleidoscopic yet clarificatory powers of the home computer, this volume is neither a straightforward collection of previously published essays nor an entirely new book. Most of the material it contains has appeared before in one form or another (typically in very obscure places). But most of it has been greatly rearranged, updated, augmented, and supplemented, to a particular corporate end, and there are several new chapters. The volume's purpose is to present a coherent ontology of belief and believing and then, far more urgent, a global theory of epistemic warrant for beliefs. It is primarily an epistemological work, set though it is on a metaphysical and psychological foundation. My main concern is to defend a version of epistemological explanationism against more fashionable theories of epistemic justification and to display what I think is the natural ground of epistemic value.

Following three previous books – *Logical Form in Natural Language* (1984), *Knowing Who* (with Steven Boër, 1986), and *Consciousness* (1987) – this essay completes the presentation of my view of cognition; that is, it is the last piece in my overall puzzle of language, mind, and knowledge. I am not dogmatically confident that my picture is the right one; indeed, I doubt that it is right. But if it is not right, then I have not the faintest idea of what cognition is, and I do not think anyone else has either.

Acknowledgments

For discussion, criticism, and generous comments on individual chapters I am grateful to many people: D. M. Armstrong, David Austin, Lynne Rudder Baker, William Bechtel, John Biro, Ned Block, Steven Boër, Jim Bogen, Paul Churchland, Dan Dennett, Michael Devitt, Fred Dretske, Ray Elugardo, Ken Gemes, Clark Glymour, Gilbert Harman, James Hudson, John Josephson, Murray Kiteley, Robert Kraut, Larry Laudan, Ron Laymon, Jarrett Leplin, Gary Letchinger, Don Loeb, Peter Machamer, Ausonio Marras, Alan Musgrave, Andrew Oldenquist, George Pappas, Phil Peterson, Joe Pitt, Tim Potts, Robert Richardson, Bernard Rosen, David Sanford, Geoff Sayre McCord, Fred Schmitt, Elliott Sober, Jan Srednicki, Michael Stack, Stephen Stich, Rick Suiter, Marshall Swain, Bill Tolhurst, Joe Tolliver, Michael Tye, Robert Vishny, David Williams, and the late Herbert Heidelberger. My special thanks also to Jonathan Sinclair-Wilson for suggesting, supporting and encouraging this project.

Most of the chapters are based on previously published essays, but all have been substantially edited and revised; some have been mixed with others to the point of unrecognizability, although (for no very good reason) I have kept most of the original titles. Here are the original sources:

Chapter 1: "Toward a Homuncular Theory of Believing." *Cognition and Brain Theory* 4 (1981):139–59.
Chapter 2: "Psychological Laws." *Philosophical Topics* 12 (1981):9–38.
Chapter 3: "Tacit Belief." In R. J. Bogdan, ed., *Belief* (Oxford: Oxford University Press, 1986), pp. 61–82. Reprinted by permission.
Chapter 4, "Representation and the Semantics of Belief-Ascription," contains a bit of material from "The Paradox of Naming," in B.-K. Matilal and J. L. Shaw, eds., *Analytical Philosophy in*

Comparative Perspective (Dordrecht: Reidel, 1985), pp. 81–102 (copyright © 1985 by D. Reidel Publishing Company; reprinted by permission), and a section from "Thoughts about Things," in M. Brand and R. M. Harnish, eds., *The Representation of Knowledge and Belief* (Tucson: University of Arizona Press, copyright 1986), pp. 160–86.

Chapter 5, "Reliabilism," is based on my earlier "Armstrong's Theory of Knowing," in R. J. Bogdan, ed., *Profile: D. M. Armstrong* (Dordrecht: Reidel, 1984), pp. 139–60. Copyright © 1984 by D. Reidel Publishing Company. Reprinted by permission.

Chapter 6: "Occam's Razor." *Metaphilosophy* 7 (1976):223–37.

Chapter 7: "Epistemic Value." *Synthese* 64 (1985):137–64. Copyright © 1985 by D. Reidel Publishing Company. Reprinted by permission.

Chapter 8: "Conservatism and the Data Base." In Nicholas Rescher, ed., *Reason and Rationality in Natural Science* (Lanham, Md.: University Press of America, 1985), pp. 103–25.

Chapter 9, "Induction and Best Explanation," appears here for the first time.

Chapter 10, "Reality," appears here for the first time.

Chapter 11: "Moral Facts and Moral Knowledge." In *Proceedings of the 1985 Spindel Conference on Moral Realism, Southern Journal of Philosophy* 24 (suppl.) (1986):79–94.

PART ONE

Judgment

1

Toward a homuncular theory of believing

For years and years, philosophers took thoughts and beliefs to be modifications of incorporeal Cartesian egos. Happily, since early in the present century it has become clearer that thinkers are complex organisms embedded in natural, physical environments and are nothing (metaphysically) more that that; materialism in one form or another has prevailed ever since. Yet the mere rejection of spookstuff has done little or nothing to illuminate the positive nature of thought and belief. We have heard it said (in effect) that to believe such and such, say, that P, is to act or be disposed to act as if one believed that P (that was in the 1940s), or perhaps to have one's B_P-fibers firing (1950s), or to be in some state or other that instantiates square B_P of whatever Turing Machine table applies (1960s), or for the belief that P to be predictively attributable to one (1970s). Only with the comparatively recent resurgence of interest in intentionality itself and with the attending of philosophy to "cognitive science" have we begun to see where to look for a more substantive idea of what a belief might be and to detail the ontological anatomy of believing. Part One of this book is a modest contribution to the anatomical project.

I   THE REALITY OF BELIEFS

Traditional philosophy of mind joins common sense in characterizing beliefs as being inner states of individual persons. According to this common portrayal, a belief occurs in someone typically as the result of sensory input, or as the product of a reasoning process generated by already existing beliefs, or through some combination of the two. Existing beliefs interact with the person's desires and with other physiological states in such a way as to result in action. Beliefs commonly give rise, in an especially direct way, to characteristic verbal behavior that "expresses" them.

Unstartling as these truisms may seem, they have been denied

3

by some distinguished contemporary philosophers. Quine (1960) and Putnam (1978), in particular, maintain that when I ascribe a specific belief (such as the belief that Ronald Reagan won the 1980 election) to a fellow creature, my ascription is not a true or false statement of fact concerning any genuine inner state of the creature but is, rather, a bit of convenient but entirely subjective interpretation on my part – a mere calculational device that I use in predicting, but not genuinely explaining, the creature's future behavior. A consequence of this nihilistic view is that no cognitive psychology that makes essential use of "believe" as a theoretical term is a genuine factual science; even if such psychology could be formulated at all, it could not in principle be correct to the exclusion of apparently competing interpretive schemes but would have the factual status of something like an inspired piece of literary criticism.

The arguments for the nihilistic view are difficult and obscure, and I doubt that they alone have garnered many converts. I discuss some of them in Chapter 10 of *Logical Form in Natural Language* [Lycan 1984a], and I shall take up some more in the next chapter of the present volume. But the consequence of this view for cognitive psychology has recently attracted any number of prominent adherents on its own, among philosophers at any rate: Donald Davidson (1970, 1974), D. C. Dennett (1978, 1981a, 1981b), Stephen Stich (1978a, 1983), Paul Churchland (1979, 1982), Patricia Churchland (1980), Churchland and Churchland (1983), and other doxastophobes have all vigorously challenged the ideal that a mature and genuinely scientific psychology could make use of propositional-attitude notions such as those of belief and desire (or, presumably, intention, memory, learning, or fear). Typically their arguments take the form: "Common sense characterizes beliefs [say] as having each of the following properties: F, G, H, ... But nothing that will be mentioned by any respectable future psychology will have all or even very many of those properties; therefore, beliefs will not figure in a mature psychology."

My purpose in this chapter is to show how the model for psychology that I favor does accommodate a notion of belief that provides for all the important sorts of properties that common sense ascribes to beliefs. I begin by sketching the model, which I have defended at length (1981a, 1987), locating beliefs within it and summarizing the advantages of the resulting account; in what space

4

remains, I shall then answer some of the main objections put by the doxastophobes aforementioned and others.

The model I have in mind is the one I have called Homuncular Functionalism, (Lycan, 1981a). It owes its philosophical articulation primarily to Jerry Fodor (1968a) and D. C. Dennett (1978); see also Cummins (1975) and Haugeland (1978). The Homuncular Functionalist sees a human being or any other sentient creature as a kind of corporate entity – as an integrated system of intercommunicating "departments" that cooperatively go about the business of interpreting the stimuli that impinge on the corporate organism and of producing appropriate behavioral responses. In this model, a psychological description of a human being will consist of a set of flowcharts, nested hierarchically. The top or "master" flowchart will depict the person's immediate subsystems or departments. Each of these will be represented by a black box on the chart, and each of their routes of communicative access to the others will be represented by an arrow of one kind or another, with accompanying commentary. The subsystems will be characterized in terms of their respective corporate responsibilities: "Executive Unit," "Perceptual Analyzer," "Speech Center," "Buffer Memory," and the like. Now, each of the subsystems will itself be described by a lower-level flowchart that breaks it down into its own component departments or agencies (sub-subsystems of the containing person), which corporately produce its various outputs given inputs, and so forth. The psychologist will also characterize each of the sub-subsystems, and all the ensuing sub–. . . subsystems, in terms of their respective tasks or responsibilities. As these tasks become more specialized, so will the characterizations: The psychologist will speak of "receptors," "pathways," "stores," "triggers," "filters," "damping mechanisms," "inhibitors," and so forth. When these more specialized components have been broken down by further flowcharting into their own components and this process has been continued at some length, characterization will become more recognizably biological, though still job-descriptive – and finally, neuroanatomical. Thus, the psychologist will first explain the behavior and behavioral capacities of the whole person in terms of the joint

5

behavior and capacities of the person's immediately subpersonal departments, and if deeper and more detailed explanation is desired, the psychologist will explain the behavior of the departments in terms of the joint behavior and capacities of their own components, and so on down as far as anyone might care to go.

The homuncular model has many virtues, both technical and philosophical; see Dennett (1978) and Lycan (1981a, 1987) for the beginnings of a compendium. My task here, however, is not to praise the model further but to use it as the basis for a psychologically credible account of belief.[1] The homunctionalist philosopher's accounts of particular mental state-types take the form: "To be in mental state M is to have a sub– . . . subpersonal ϕ-er that is in its characteristic state $S(\phi)$." What is it, then, to believe that P?

To think of belief is to think of information storage, and it is a version of the information-storage paradigm that I shall defend against the doxastophobes. Let us begin by concentrating on the core class of occurrent beliefs, or judgments – if you like, episodes of mental affirmation. (I distinguish these from merely tacit beliefs, which I shall discuss in Chapter 3.) Now, I suggest, occurrent beliefs are sentencelike representations stored and played back in our brains, where by "sentencelike" I mean just that our psychological theory will characterize them in the same sorts of syntactic/ semantical terms that linguists use in characterizing sentences of natural languages. Homunctionally: To judge or believe occurrently that P is to have a storage-and-playback mechanism that in a certain distinctive way harbors a representation whose syntactic/semantic structure is analogous to that of the sentence that replaces "P." What makes such a state of affairs a case of believing *that* P is the syntactic/semantical properties that the representation shares with the (here, English) sentence in question; what makes it a case of *believing* that P is the distinctive mode of "harboring" or storage-and-playback. This distinctive mode of storage is what we might otherwise call the type of functional role played by a belief qua belief – the characteristic contribution that a "believed" represen-tation makes to the believer's ongoing institutional order of busi-

<hr>

1 Here I diverge sharply from Dennett, who is concerned precisely to *exclude* beliefs from the homuncular model and from science (and perhaps reality) tout court. See his (1978, 1981a, 1981b, 1981c), and for criticism, Fodor (1981b), Stich (1981, 1983), and my Chapter 2. I shall take issue with several more of Dennett's specific doxastophobic points in what follows.

6

ness. Thus, it is this mode of storage or type of functional role that distinguishes beliefs from other propositional attitudes. And a full specification of the mode of storage would contain parameters whose values would determine such interesting features as belief-strength; I take belief-strength to be a matter of the use of the belief in explanatory inference, the amount and type of causal sustenance that it receives from its basing reason(s), and its authority in interacting with other beliefs and desires in determining action.

The account I have sketched comes essentially from the works of Wilfrid Sellars (1956, 1967, 1973), who has done more than anyone else to promote the idea that thoughts and occurrent beliefs are internal representings, inner tokenings, utterances *in foro interno* that play certain distinctive representational and behavior-causing roles. More recently, other versions of this view have been carefully formulated and ably defended by Gilbert Harman (1973), Jay Rosenberg (1974), Jerry Fodor (1975, 1978), Christopher Hill (1976), Hartry Field (1978), and others; I believe my homuncular version inherits all or most of the advantages of theirs and has a few of its own in addition. I shall summarize the advantages, passing quickly over those I or any of the authors just mentioned have bruited elsewhere.

III THE ADVANTAGES OF REPRESENTATIONALISM

1. *The representational account squares with a plausible semantics for belief-ascriptions.* Sellars, Hill, and also Davidson (1968) have argued that the sentential complement of a belief-ascription serves as a sort of exemplar of what is said to be believed, the semantical function of the complementizer "that" being to ostend or demonstrate this exemplar.[2] Thus:

(1) Jones believes that broccoli causes erysipelas.

is to be understood along the lines of

(2) Jones believes some •Broccoli causes erysipelas•

---

2 I am here presenting what I take to be the common core of these authors' proposals; probably none of them would accept the doctrine in precisely the form in which I am stating it. For a full, formal working-out, see Chapters 3 and 4 of Boër and Lycan (1986).

where the Sellarsian dot quotes are common-noun–forming operators that also serve to ostend the linguistic token that they enclose. A slight variation would be to express the force of (1) as

(3) Jones believes one of those.

> Broccoli causes erysipelas.

Thus, in this approach, belief is constructed as a dyadic relation that a person bears to a linguistic or quasi-linguistic token that falls into a certain category. (The original proponents of this semantical hypothesis have already touted its virtues, and Steven Boër and I (1986) have gone into them at length; but I shall say just a bit more in Chapter 4.)

Now, how are we to determine the extension of the predicate "is a •Broccoli causes erysipelas•"? Alternatively, how are we to tell when some linguistic or quasi-linguistic token of some quite other shape is "one of those"? Differing individuative schemes are possible here. Davidson merely invokes an unexplicated relation of "samesaying." Sellars (1963b) offers a more elaborate scheme: For him, an item will count as a •Broccoli causes erysipelas• just in case that item plays approximately the same inferential role within its own surrounding conceptual framework that the sentence "Broccoli causes erysipelas" plays within ours. Other possibilities are available. We might count a thing as a •Broccoli causes erysipelas• if the thing has the same truth-condition as does our sentence "Broccoli causes erysipelas," or if the thing has the same truth-condition, computed according to the same recursive procedure. Later on I shall make special use of this availability of alternative methods of individuation.

It would be strange if the ontology of belief and the logical form of belief-ascriptions had nothing to do with each other. Yet, until recently, semanticists investigating belief sentences, particularly those semanticists working within the possible-worlds format, have paid no attention to the question of what psychological reality it is that makes such sentences true. (But see Kraut [1979], Partee [1979a, 1979b] and Stalnaker [1984].) Likewise, philosophers of psychology have paid little attention to the semantics of belief sentences – an exception here is Fodor (1978) – and in some cases have offered psychological accounts of belief that seem to render semantical

8

matters totally obscure.[3] The representational account is the only current one that brings semantics and psychology together. Moreover, if we choose an individuative scheme for linguistic types that can be formulated without reference to language-independent propositions Platonistically construed, we can rid our theory of such objects. This is desirable, not primarily because propositions are "creatures of darkness" or whatever, but because it is hard to see how entities that have no causal powers can play any indispensable role in a theory whose job is to explain actual physical motion.

2. *The representational account enables us to understand the intentionality of beliefs to be of a piece with the reference or aboutness of language.* One of Sellars's most important contributions to the philosophy of mind has been to show that if whatever accounts for the referential character of lingusitic tokens is something that also can correctly be predicated of brain events, then a unified theory of intentionality can be obtained that will apply equally to speech and thought. The importance of this conditional has been heightened considerably by recent elaboration of Kripkean causal-historical theories and other naturalistic theories of reference and aboutness (see Devitt [1974, 1981], Fodor [1987]). Field (1978) made the related point that the representational account provides what is for now the only very attractive answer to the question of how it is possible for a mere aggregate of insensate, purely physical particles to be in an intentional state. (N.B., I do not mean to claim that the aboutness of sentences is *logically or ontologically prior* to the intentionality of thoughts or beliefs; see Section IV of this chapter.)

3. *The representational account explains why beliefs have the same standard sorts of semantical properties that sentences have.* Beliefs have truth-values, bear entailment relations to each other, and so forth. Moreover, there are indefinitely many possible beliefs, which seem intuitively to be put together out of a finite stock of basic conceptual building blocks; the representational account can explain this neatly by exploiting the Tarskian recursions that we suppose effect the truth-valuations of formal and (with luck) natural languages.

4. *The representational account predicts the many grammatical parallels that have been found to hold between propositional-attitude verbs and verbs of saying.* Vendler (1972) exhibits striking similarities between the

---

3 In the original version of this chapter I cited Dennett (1978) as a prime example, but this was overhasty; see Section V of Chapter 3.

grammatical behavior of belief-sentence complements and that of assertion-sentence complements. Fodor (1978) points out that a theory of propositional attitudes should explain the highly suggestive fact, noted by Sellars, that the complement clauses incorporated within our canonical names for beliefs are, literally, sentences being used in a special way.

5. *The representational account is empirically motivated by the "computational paradigm" that dominates current work in cognitive psychology.* Fodor (1975, 1981b) argues persuasively that the computational processes carried out by any interesting department of the brain, being computational, must be couched in some system of notation, and that this system of notation needs to share enough of the characteristic features of natural languages to count as an internal language itself. I have no crisp answer of my own to the question of what warrants counting a particular notational system as a *language*, but I should think that the following conditions may be jointly necessary and sufficient: that the system's well-formed formulas have truth-conditions, corresponding to sets of possible worlds in the familiar way, and hence that their tokens have truth-values; that the elements of the formulas are capable of denotation and similar semantical relations; and that the truth-conditions of the formulas be determined recursively by the elements' semantical values.

Some philosophers are appalled, for a number of disparate reasons, at the idea that each person has a private, personal, "language of thought." I shall say more about this subsequently, but for now let me note that I do not suppose there to be any single, unified language of thought in which all of a person's cognitive activity is carried out; I shall point out in the next section that just the opposite is suggested by the homuncular model: Distinct subpersonal and sub–. . . subpersonal agencies that bear very different responsibilities probably differ according to their respective office jargons.

6. *The representational account is virtually required in order to answer the question of where the speech center gets its inputs.* In working on a homuncular map of the human speech center (1984a, Chapter 11), I stumbled on an argument to show that syntactic/semantical structures are not created within the speech center itself. But because the job of the speech center is precisely to produce sententially structured items as outputs, in the form of instructions to motor subroutines, it must therefore have accepted sententially structured

items as inputs. But what it accepts as inputs are presumably thoughts and occurrent beliefs.

7. *The representational account affords us a good start toward solving the "problems of the inputs and the outputs" that N. J. Block has raised as an objection to functionalist theories of the mental.* Block (1978) has challenged the functionalist to find a characterization of inputs, functional states, and outputs that would be useful in psychology and that is neither so physiologically detailed as to engender species chauvinism nor so abstract and general as to encourage bleeding hearts to award mental states to entities that plainly do not have them (such as complex economic systems that happen to "instantiate" abstract machine programs). I have argued in reply (1981a, 1987) that syntactic/semantical characterization of the type provided by the representational account will do the trick

8. *The representational account has strong potential for solving certain puzzles about the attribution of belief.* I shall take this up at length in Chapter 4; I have in mind problems of substitutivity in belief contexts, Kripke's related puzzle (1979) about translation and disquotation, and the notorious intractability of ascriptions *"de se."* Moreover:

9. *The representational account provides compelling solutions to ontological problems of belief identity and individuation, and in particular dispels the vexing illusion that self-regarding beliefs have special, scientifically inaccessible facts or propositions as their objects.* This matter too will be disposed of in Chapter 4.

I shall now briefly note a few ways in which the appeal of the representational account is enhanced once the account has been embedded in the homuncular model.

IV   REPRESENTATIONS AND HOMUNCTIONALISM

Information storing is a relatively simple and ubiquitous activity. We should expect to find that some quite simple devices engage in it. Not every case of storing a sentence-like entity counts as a propositional attitude; otherwise the very page you are now reading would properly be said to have beliefs or thoughts. As I have said, the storing must be a matter of bearing certain complex functional relations to other jobs performed by our various homuncular agen-

11

cies. This page has no subagencies, or at least none that makes use of the sentences physically stored on it.

Nevertheless, anything that is functionally complex enough to behave in certain characteristics goal-directed ways is a likely proprietor of beliefs. This leaves it open – indeed positively suggests – that not only we ourselves but our component homunculi may have beliefs, or at least crude belieflike information-bearing states. No doubt beliefs or quasi beliefs would differ from agency to agency; many presumably, would be beliefs about other homunculi at the same level of institutional abstraction. For example, homuncular employees of the perceptual system would have beliefs or "beliefs" about the orientation of the eyeballs or about texture gradients.

In making this suggestion I am differing with Dennett (1978) in a way he would consider crucial. He insists (p. 105 and elsewhere) that the concept of "belief" applies – if at all – only to full-fledged (host) persons and cannot be extended even one institutional step downward to the immediately subpersonal level. I see no convincing reason for this prohibition, although I agree that the "beliefs" of smaller and less talented homunculi will get less and less interesting, and less and less paradigmatic, as they lose complexity. Notice, by the way, that a belief held by one of my homunculi need not be, and almost certainly will not be, a belief that he is storing for me. From perceptual analyst Fred's believing that boss Lycan's eyeball is oriented 45 degrees to the left, it does not follow that Lycan believes that his eyeball is oriented in that direction. Nor does it follow from the fact that I believe that Frege was a mathematician that the storage facility that harbors my •Frege was a mathematician• has the belief.

In fact, I think, dropping Dennett's restrictions would gain us a number of advantages. To mention a few:

1. We already can be sure that a person contains not one storage device, but many of the appropriate sort at various different levels of abstraction. By allowing that some of the person's immediate subordinates may themselves have beliefs, we can increase the power of our homuncular theory to sort out psychological and conceptual anomalies involved in the positing of "subconscious" beliefs and perhaps in describing cases of multiple personality and other peculiar disorders.

2. By allowing subpersonal perceptual analyzers or decision mak-

ers to have beliefs, we can block what many philosophers will consider to be an objectionable repercussion of Fodor's original argument (1975, p. 27). Fodor maintains that cognitive processes are computational processes, that computation presupposes a medium of computation, and that a computational medium must be a representational system of some kind. On the basis of linguistic and psychological evidence, he says, we can make fairly reliable inferences as to what this representational system or language of thought must be like; in fact, the evidence shows that the system is very like a natural language. Now, the troublesome repercussion is that this language of thought belongs to the person whose cognitive processes are being explicated in terms of it; so it seems to follow from Fodor's view that the computations performed on sentences of the language of thought are being performed by the person in question. In particular, if I am that person, I myself must be said to form and test hypotheses concerning physical objects on the basis of information about the values of "physical parameters of environmental events" (pp. 44–47); in order to learn a natural language, I must learn, and hence believe, instances of Tarski's Convention T, couched in the language of thought (pp. 80–81); and if a syntax of the sort posited by linguists is indeed operating within me, I must represent abstract syntactic structures to myself and perform syntactic operations on them (pp. 114–116). All this mental activity on my part is of course tacit, or subconscious.

Philosophers have always been suspicious of appeals to tacit mental activity, and many will respond with outrage to the claims I have just listed – rightly, in my opinion. The third claim (alleging tacit knowledge of syntactic rules) has come in for particularly rigorous and telling criticism, in philosophical comments on its defense by Chomsky (see Harman [1967], Stich [1971], and Devitt [1981]). I think the most conclusive criticism is that the tacit-knowledge hypothesis is, or should be, superfluous. A syntactic theory is as genuinely explanatory as anyone could wish when it is regarded merely as a functional diagram of the workings of a mechanism functioning within a speaker or hearer; the further hypothesis that the speaker somehow tacitly knows or has epistemic access to the mechanism adds nothing useful and just raises awkward questions. Fully recognizing this, Fodor acknowledges the nastiness of his conclusions, but replies (pp. 52–53) only that the distinction between what a person does and what merely happens within that

13

person, though real and important, is not a *psychological* distinction and need not be accommodated within cognitive psychology.

I daresay Fodor agrees that this reply is a weak one. If we allow homuncular subordinates to have beliefs, we can explicate the desired distinction psychologically after all and see why Fodor's main argument need not be taken so far as to commit us to the tacit-knowledge view: From the fact that computational processes occur within me, it does not follow that I am doing the computations. In fact, it seems obvious that in the case of syntax, my homuncular speech center is doing them. Fodor's inference is similarly blocked in each of the other two cases. From the fact that I employ a perceptual analyst (Fred) who receives messages about the values of certain physical parameters and forms hypotheses concerning macroscopic physical objects, it does not follow that I form any such hypotheses, and from the fact that my speech center knows some T-sentences written in a "language of thought" it does not follow that I know them or that that "language of thought" is the language of *my* thought (Lycan [1981a], n. 20).

3. By allowing subordinate homunculi to have beliefs, we can explicate Stephen Stich's intuitively real distinction (1987b) between beliefs and "subdoxastic states." (A "subdoxastic state" is a contentful state that figures prominently in the "proximate causal history" of a belief but does not itself count as a belief in the ordinary sense, such as a state that carries information about degrees of binocular disparity and contributes thereby to the business of depth perception.) My having a belief is a matter of a representation's being stored by some subagency of mine; my being in a subdoxastic state is a matter of a belief's being held by some subagency of mine. I have already argued that these are distinct states of affairs.

It is worth repeating that there may be a different computational language for every different kind of subagency operating within me. Very probably there is no single "language of thought," though it may turn out that a few computational languages may valuably be described as being languages in which I think, as opposed to languages used only by various subordinates of mine. It seems obviously true to say that (sometimes) I think in English, as Harman (1973) maintains, but it also seems fairly clear that at a deeper level I think in logical structures of some sort (the formulas that serve as input to syntactic transformations, if one thinks that sentences of natural languages are generated in that way); there may be other

14

languages in which I think as well. At least one may be species-universal, though there certainly is no a priori reason to think so. I regard the further question of which of these languages is the "real" language of thought as a pseudoquestion.

In what little space remains, let us turn to a few prominent doxastophobic criticisms.[4]

V   OBJECTIONS

Objection 1. Dennett (1978) offers a number of apparent counter-examples to sentence-storage theories of believing. The examples include beliefs that come in large groups, such as the mathematical belief that 10,057 > 10,056; beliefs one has always held but never brought up explicitly before, such as the belief that zebras do not wear overcoats in the wild; and what we might call matters of standing policy, such as a chess-playing computer's "belief" that it should get its queen out early. Certainly it is implausible to suppose that the corresponding sentences are stored as such in the heads of people who hold these beliefs. It follows that the stored-sentence model cannot be the whole story.

But it does not follow that anything I have said so far in this chapter is false. I have distinguished occurrent beliefs, which are actual episodic (though not necessarily conscious) states of persons, from "tacit" beliefs, which are not occurrent states but are merely (something like) dispositions to form occurrent beliefs. Tacit beliefs may, for now, be thought of as dispositional design features (i.e., as counterfactual properties of persons, whose categorical bases lie in the nature of the persons' homunctional architecture). Ascriptions of tacit belief might merely be left as abbreviated counterfactuals or (better) cashed in general terms of what the subject is designed to infer from what (given certain sorts of stimuli) or the like. We shall see in Chapter 3 that the notion of tacit belief presents unanticipated and nasty difficulties, but they are not difficulties for the present conception of thinking or occurrent belief.

4 In the interest of justice we should distinguish between doxastophobic objections and objections that are merely criticisms of the representational account, because one might hold that beliefs are psychologically real, genuine inner states of individuals without holding that they are storings of representations. This distinction is ignored by doxastophobes and doxastophiles alike; but we should note that the latter category includes opponents of representationalism, including Chisholm (1958), Vendler (1972), and Collins (1979).

15

It should be clear that each of Dennett's alleged counterexamples is a tacit belief in the foregoing sense, if it is a belief at all. Before I read Dennett's book, my belief that $10,057 > 10,056$ and my belief that zebras do not wear overcoats (or homburgs, or leisure suits) in the wild were never occurrent; insofar as I held them at all, they were dispositional. Most people never believe either of those things occurrently, but it is likely that most people are conditioned and/or soft-wired to store and employ the corresponding mental tokens when the occasion arises.[5] The case of the chess-playing computer is not as clear, since it is underdescribed; but I would say that either the computer is soft-wired to play back the instruction "Get your queen out early," or it is soft-wired to play back the instruction "Get your queen out" early, or it merely is soft-wired in such a way to be disposed to get its queen out early without having a belief of any sort.

Dennett considers a move something like mine in Chapter 3 of *Brainstorms* (1978): The representationalist might restrict his representationalism to a small class of "core" beliefs or posit an "extrapolator-deducer mechanism" that generates new explicit beliefs "when the situation demands it" (p. 45). I shall discuss this move, and Dennett's skeptical questions about it, in Chapter 3.

Objection 2. There is a tendency in the recent literature to overstate the commitments of this representationalist theory, and indeed to caricature it unmercifully, as if the representationalist were suggesting that inside each believer's head is a tiny blackboard with all the believer's stored representations written in chalk, or that evil, politically motivated scientists might be able to spy inside our heads with their cerebroscopes and report our innermost convictions to the Thought Police. It should already be clear why no such absurd straw-man consequences in fact flow from the representationalist view, but let me say another word or two about the matter, borrowing an example from Stephen Stich (1979). Many people balk at representationalism because they hold that higher animals and prelinguistic children have beliefs. If dogs, say, have beliefs

5 Some philosophers might balk at calling tacit belief a genuine case of belief, unless the categorical bases of the relevant dispositions were spelled out so explicitly as to make the tacit beliefs specific structural states of an organism (in which case we would charge the theorist with species chauvinism). I take this up in Chapter 3.

but have no language, how can belief be a matter of bearing a functional relation, or any other relation, to a quasi-linguistic item? Is that idea not just silly, in the case of dogs?

One possible answer to this would be to suppose that the relation is counterfactual. That answer has possibilities, but I think there is a much more straightforward one: Suppose Lassie is digging at a particular spot because she believes she buried a bone there earlier in the day. Are we really to suppose that no inner state of Lassie keys on the spot in question and guides her to it (and would have guided here to it even if various obstacles have been placed in her path)? Are we to suppose that no inner state of Lassie is a specialized "bone" (or whatever)[6] response and is causally connected in this instance, to the state that keys on the spot? That seems to me very unlikely. And all that the representationalist is saying is that some such states of Lassie's central nervous system are performing functions and related ones; that is all it takes for Lassie to accept a •Bone here•.

The "sentences in the head" view of cognition has taken a gleeful bashing in recent years, but only in its strongest and most presumptuous forms – rather silly parody versions that have really been intended by few of its proponents, if any. Let us briefly pause to distinguish a few types and grades of "sententialism" or representationalism, in order to identify the actual commitments of what I am defending under that term.

Minimally: One might speak of "sentences" or "formulas" in the head if either (A) brain states or episodes have sentencelike syntactic structures and bear causal relations to each other in virtue or rulelike regularities holding between elements of their syntactic structures, on the model of an uninterpreted formal calculus, or (B) individual brain states or episodes have *truth-conditions*. These two alternative requirements are mutually independent. *A* certainly does not entail *B*; perhaps less obviously, *B* does not entail *A*, since there could be syntactically primitive, fused symbols that were somehow assigned truth-conditions by God or Mother Nature. But the satisfaction of *A* alone would be uninteresting, since almost anything in the brain might count, for some explanatory purposes, as a "syntactically" structured item manipulated according to for-

---

6 I must concede to Stich that there can be no straightforward identification of Lassie's inner predicate with *our* concept "bone." My present use of the word "bone" in describing Lassie's belief is less than fully accurate (but it is fast).

17

mal "rules," if the brain exhibits intricate and articulated enough causal regularities. Articulate structure is truly *sentence*like, at least to a representationally minded philosopher, only if it somehow ties into semantic properties. Thus our minimal grade of representationlism should be *B*, the possession of a truth-condition.[7] A theorist will count as a Minimal Representationalist just in case that theorist posits brain states that have truth-conditions.

I call this particular form of representationlism "Minimal" because a theory that identified cognitions with anything less would not be comparing its posited inner states to linguistic entities in any even faintly interesting way. (Moreover, if a theory does not conceive thoughts as inner states at all, it falls into some not very plausible form of instrumentalism about them, whereas if it does not assign them truth-conditions, it loses its ability to account for the intentionality of beliefs.)

Actually there are any number of ways in which the Minimal idea might be implemented, depending on the type of quasilinguistic item one associates with the subject by way of the belief relation.[8] All the distinctions here matter, because each particular approach is subject to objections that the others avoid.[9] But let us

7 I here pass over purely syntactic or "conceptual role" views of cognition that self-consciously abstain from "wide" notions such as truth and truth-conditions. This is for much the same reason I gave against leaving *A* to stand alone as a requirement for mental sentencehood; see also my discussion of "Conceptual Role" semantics in Chapter 10 of *Logical Form in Natural Language* (Lycan [1984a]).
8 For example, Sellars counts me as believing that *P* iff I bear the right functional relation (call it Big B) to a "dot-*P*," by which he means a token of the *"P"* type, and something is "dot-*P*" iff it plays the same inferential or truth-conditional (etc.) role as the English sentence that replaces *"P"* does in our common public language. (Different versions are available here, depending on how the "etc." is filled out.) Or the subject is held to bear some presumably subjunctive relation to a public linguistic tokening. E.g., I believe that *P* iff I am disposed to assent to some sentence having the same semantical structure as the English sentence that replaces *"P"*; or, according to Stich (1983), I believe that *P* iff I am in "the state" I *would* be in if I were to utter this: *P*. Or, third, a different Sellarsian view counts something as a dot-*P* iff the thing plays the same inferential or truth-conditional (etc.) role as the item between the dot-quotes plays in the belief-ascriber's own internal representational system. This third schema, close to Brian Loar's (1981), falls midway between the first two.
9 For example, if the third option mentioned in note 8 is correct, then indeterminacy sets in heavily: What you believe – i.e., what I ascribe to you when I make you the subject of a belief-sentence – depends on my own beliefs and inferential habits. If my beliefs are screwy enough (think of Burgean and Stichian examples), I will have trouble ascribing specific beliefs to you at all. But if the preceding, second option is correct instead (as I myself am inclined to say), then the relevant theory

18

pass over these particular intramural troubles. *Higher grades* of representationalism result from adding further, strengthening conditions to *B*. The next condition to be added is an obvious implementation of *A*: that the relevant inner state have syntactic structure and have its truth-condition in virtue of referential relations between its syntactic elements and things in the world, these primitive semantic values being compounded *through* the operative syntax. (We might call this new definition *B/A*.)

There would be little point in imposing our syntactic requirement if we were not interested in *inference*. We may therefore naturally specify *C* that our doxastic inner states also stand in causal relations to each other of the sort that constitutes inferences, at least inference of the nonoptional sort. Let us call the view that results from addition of the latter requirement *"Forthright Representationalism,"* since it is stronger and significantly farther out of the closet than is Minimal Representationalism. Forthright Representationalism's more robust notion of a mental sentence has an obvoius motivation: that only on the assumptions of articulate intrasentential structure and inferential relations between sentences could we have a flexible *system of* representation or *language* of thought. (A plant might have a small repertoire of states, each of which had a very specific truth-condition, without giving us reason to attribute to it a general representational capacity in any interesting sense.)

What further requirements might someone want to place on "mental sentences"? Any number have been suggested in the literature, with varying degrees of seriousness: (D) that the human representational system features syntactic and semantic categories like those of a natural language; (E) that the relevant representations involve concepts consciously familiar to us humans; (F) that formulas logically related to a given representation be *mereo*logically related to that representation; (G) that one's language of thought be at least distinctively analogous to a *particular* natural language such as English or Japanese; or perhaps (H) that the language of thought or the concepts that figure therein be *innate* in one lunatic sense or another. These various requirements could be imposed in various combinations (even all at once), yielding such possible positions as Granite-Jawed Representationalism, Wild-Eyed

of names in belief contexts goes haywire, because proper names do not have fixed, standard inferential (etc.) roles in English *qua English* (well, perhaps "Clark Kent" and "Superman" do, but "Cicero" and "Tully" do not).

19

Representationalism, Rabid Representationalism, Rape-and-Loot Representationalism, Homicidal Representationalism, and Nuclear Holocaust Representationalism.

I think most theorists disclaim any stronger thesis than the Forthright form of representationalism, but then it is not clear either that anyone has ever needed to accept any stonger form or that anyone else does.[10] Forthright Representationalism seems to me to be *representationalism properly understood*. Any number of professed "antisententialists" in fact accept it;[11] I claim we should all accept it too, even if we reject any stronger representationalist thesis.

Objection 3. Another reason people balk at representationalism is that they think the representationalist is making the obviously false claim that the intentionality of public linguistic items is logically or ontologically prior to that of beliefs and thoughts. This impression is encouraged by talk – engaged in even by representationalists – of "sentences in the head," "brain writing," "inscriptionalism," and the like. In fact, this talk is misleading in exactly the way we would mislead if we were to speak of public linguistic tokens as being "thoughts out in the open air." Thoughts are representers in the brain, made of brain stuff; bits of language are representers out

10 Perhaps barring some early impetuous ventures of Harman's (1973) and Fodor's (1975).
11 One example, I would claim, is Stalnaker (1984). Stalnaker contrasts the Sellarsian inner-speech paradigm with an opposing picture that shows the intentionality of thought as being in every way prior to that of speech, and he announces his intention to defend a version of the latter at the expense of the former. Ironically, though, the account that eventually emerges is as clear a specimen as one could wish of the naturalistic sort of representationalism that I advocate here. Another example is Paul Churchland (1985, 1986; cf. Churchland and Churchland [1981] and P. S. Churchland [1986]), who argues persuasively for a "phase-space sandwich" model of sensorimotor coordination and other psychological capacities, as opposed to any sort of linear, natural-deduction model of mentation. Churchland seems to admit that his vaunted "simultaneous stimulation at the appropriate coordinate intersection" on a topographic map of the sort he champions has a truth-condition; otherwise the topographic map would not be a *map*. Moreover, on Churchland's model, simultaneous stimulation in the upper grid of a sandwich directly triggers coordinate stimulation of the lower grid, which is effectively a motor instruction (motor instructions are similarly truth-valued, according to whether the relevant bodily movements are in fact carried out). Thus we find a rudimentary sort of practical inference. Along these lines it is easy to show that Churchland is not only a Minimal but a Forthright Representationalist, or so I have argued at length in an unpublished comment on Churchland (1985).

in the open air, made of sound waves or ink marks; tape recordings are representers made of patterns of magnetism; and so on. We seek a general theory of representation that covers all types of representers.

Objection 4. The recent literature on "methodological solipsism," chiefly Putnam (1975a), Fodor (1980), Stich (1978a), and Burge (1979), has enforced the distinction between what is "in the head" and what is not. Two people can be exactly alike "inside their heads," molecule for molecule, and so be in the same causal, functional, or psychological condition – the same belief state, to borrow Perry's (1979) terminology – but differ in belief object, or proposition, believed; thus their beliefs may differ in truth-value. Or they may believe the same object or proposition in two different ways (*via* two different belief states) and so behave differently. What is in the head is what causes behavior; what is not is causally impotent, since it is past and gone, or at least could work only through what is in the head or supervenes on head contents. Therefore, argues the methodological solipsist, psychology should treat only of what is "autonomously," or at least superveniently, in the head; it should describe belief states but not belief objects. And so belief states (and perhaps their physiological substrata) are the proper objects of psychology. Yet belief objects are what invest beliefs with their characteristic semantical properties, including aboutness, truth-value, and entailment relations, and it is in terms of belief objects that common sense individuates and identifies beliefs per se. So methodological solipsism entails that such properties contribute nothing to the causal roles of beliefs and hence have no claims on the attention of psychologists; accordingly beliefs per se have no claim on the attention of psychologists.[12] Stich (1978a) concludes:

> The autonomous psychological properties [what is in the head] do not determine a truth-value, an appropriate reference or a represented state of affairs. So the state of exhibiting one (or more) of these autonomous properties itself has no truth-value, is not referential, and does not represent anything. And this, I would urge, is more than enough reason to say that is is not a belief at all. (p.586)

12 Fodor does not go quite so far as to draw this consequence in so many words: indeed he rejects it. It is pointed out by Stich (1980) and by Rey (1980); I presume Fodor would accept the version of methodological solipsism I have limned here.

Michael Stack (1980) has put forward a similar argument: Beliefs, if there are any, have both causal roles and truth-value. Belief states have causal roles and belief objects have truth-value, but no one kind of thing has both a causal role and a truth-value; therefore there are no beliefs.

These arguments are simply fallacious. The moral of solipsism is that belief states function independently of belief objects – that a belief's semantical properties per se contribute nothing to the belief's causal role. This is an important and rather surprising result, but it does not entail that beliefs have no semantical properties. To believe that P is to bear the appropriate functional relation to a representation that has both a certain computational surface and a truth-condition. The representation's computational properties fully determine the belief's causal role; its truth-condition fully determines the belief's semantical features. That the two are independent fails to show that both aspects of the belief are not completely real. And there is "one kind of thing" that has both a causal role and a truth-value: a belief-state–belief-object pair. I shall say more of these matters in Chapter 4, particularly in response to the question why psychologists or epistemologists should care about the semantical or other "wide" properties of beliefs.

Objection 5. Surely not all mental representation is discursive. Some representations take the form of maps, pictures, or at any rate, pictorial images. And, perhaps contra Pylyshyn (1973) and chapters 9 and 10 of Dennett (1978), their iconic character cannot be explained away in sentential terms. Is the representational account not then crucially incomplete, in that it takes just interpreted logical formulas as its paradigm for mental representation?

It is important to recognize that my proposal concerning beliefs is not meant to be extended to all forms of mental representation. I do not claim to reduce all perceptual experience, or dreams, or mental images, to sentential structures. So it is misguided to try to refute my thesis by pointing to forms of representation (such as these) to which no particular sentences uniquely correspond. In fact, there is a direct argument to show that every belief does have a corresponding sentential structure (barring problems concerning denumerability, impredicativity, and so forth): Every belief I know of is a belief *that* – a belief that such and such is the case. The verb "believe" can take as its grammatical object only a "that" clause or some pronoun that anaphorically stands in for one. Therefore any actual or hypothetical report of a belief would be a tokening of a compound sentence containing a sentential complement that expressed the content of the belief. Thus, to each belief that is even hypothetically reportable there corresponds an actual or potential sentential structure. To put essentially the same point in a different way: No doubt there are many sorts of mental processing that trade in structures that are nonsentential. But why would we have any inclination to call any of the relevant processing states *beliefs*, in particular?

What about beliefs that seem to have pictorial or otherwise non-discursive items as elements or constituents of their own? (This point derives from Grandy [1979].) For example, there is my belief that a poison symbol looks like [Picture a poison symbol here]. Or take my belief that the opening phrase of Handel's Hallelujah Chorus goes: [You know how it goes]. In the face of examples like these, must I not back off and admit that some beliefs are not merely storings of sentences?

In reply I remind the reader of the preceding argument. To the two beliefs I have mentioned there correspond the English sentences "A poison symbol looks like *this*" and "Handel's Hallelujah Chorus goes like *this*." The demonstratives in these two sentences *refer* in their respective contexts to things that are probably nondiscoursive, picturelike entities, and so Grandy's observation may prove that psychology must posit mental pictures of some kind, but the fact that our two sentences refer in passing to mental pictures does not count against the claim that beliefs per se are storings of sentences, any more than does the fact that the sentence "Richard Nixon wolfed down the egg roll" refers to an egg roll. Sentences simply do contain singular terms (including demonstratives) that refer to things. Alternatively, if one wants to insist that mental icons are themselves constituents of some representations and are not merely the referents of mental demonstratives, it is open to us to hold that the icons themselves act as self-referring singular terms in the language of thought, and thus that semantically they are names as well as pictures. If so, my Sellarsian version of representationalism is not threatened.

23

There are any number of other objections to be faced. Some I shall take up in the rest of Part One and I hope to deal with the rest in later works. For now, I claim to have shown only that the case for belief is exceedingly strong.

2

Psychological laws

What is a psychological law? Narrowly and familiarly understood, I suppose, a psychological law would be a lawlike, universal statement that correlates some psychological state or event in an organism with things that can happen to the organism, with behavior on the organism's part, or with other psychological states or events. But on a broader and probably more useful understanding of the term, a psychological law may be taken to be a law of psychology, considered as a technical discipline and a self-conscious science. Thus, such a law may be expected to incorporate unfamiliar jargon of any of various kinds, either in alluding to theoretical entities newly introduced or in its description of the otherwise ordinary mental and physical phenomena that are its topic.

I THE QUESTION OF PSYCHOLOGICAL LAWS

What would a psychological law, in this sense of the term, look like? Obviously that would depend on one's psychological theory or theories – particularly on their vocabularies and on their projected, potential, or fancied axiomatizations. Somewhat less obviously, it would depend on one's philosophical theory of mind, so far as this can be distinguished from one's psychological theory. Brentano's or Meinong's purported psychological laws would be written in a language quite different (both lexically and syntactically) from Hobbes's – or from W. V. Quine's. For some years the accepted philosophical theory of mind was the Identity Theory, as defended by U. T. Place and J. J. C. Smart. As Smart developed it, the Identity Theory identified psychological or mental state- and event-types with neurophysiological state- and event-types, a key motivation for this identification being to explain supposed type–type correlations between the mental and the neurophysiological.[1]

1 Other materialists, who have been called Identity Theorists, have not shared this

25

It was said that such correlations had already been noted in laboratory experiments on humans, and it seemed reasonable to expect that other tests would establish beyond scientific doubt that the correlations were lawlike and not merely accidental. Since the Identity Theory, if true, is itself lawlike (on the assumption that any true metaphysical theory is at least lawlike so far as it applies to physical affairs at all), and since it entails or predicts the existence of our lawlike type–type correlations, it explains them, and, moreover, explains them in the neatest possible manner. (What better way to explain a lawlike correlation between As and Bs than by supposing, in the absence of significant evidence to the contrary, that in fact As are just Bs?)[2] Thus, some of the Identity Theorist's psychological laws would correlate events described in mental terms with events described neurophysiologically; others presumably would detail neurophysiological interchanges that involved those physical states and events that are also mental. Psychophysical laws, codifying lawlike correlations between mental events and neurophysiological events, are therefore bound up with the Identity Theory in two ways: Their existence is entailed by the theory, and their existence, allegedly established on independent empirical grounds, is strong evidence for the theory.

In a series of papers (1970, 1973, 1974), Donald Davidson attacked the Type–Type Identity Theory at just this point, on the basis of what he called "the Principle of the Anomalism of the Mental" (PAM): "There are no strict deterministic laws on the basis of which mental events can be predicted and explained" (1970, p. 81). I quote some related passages:

1. The mental is nomologically irreducible; there may be true general statements relating the mental and the physical, statements that have the logical form of a law; but they are not lawlike (in a strong sense yet to be described). (1970, p. 81)

motivation and have not necessarily believed that any such correlations existed; David Lewis (1972) is an obvious example. In this chapter I reserve the term "Identity Theory" to refer to Smart's type–type view. (Smart, however, has protested to me in correspondence that he never intended to posit as broad a type–type identification as I and others have attributed to him.)

2 Jaegwon Kim (1966) has attacked this reasoning. (For an excellent discussion of issues concerning psychophysical laws and psychophysical causation, see also Kim (1979).) David Armstrong has also objected (in correspondence) that there cannot be explanations of this kind if laws are taken as relations between distinct universals (cf. Armstrong [1978a; 1983]).

26

2. The generalizations that embody such practical wisdom [concerning actual de facto mental–physical correlations] are assumed to be only roughly true, or they are explicitly stated in probabilistic terms, or they are insulated from counterexample by generous escape clauses. (1970, p. 93)

3. Mental events *as a class* cannot be explained by physical science. (1970, p.100; italics mine)

4. What emerge are not the strict quantitative laws embedded in sophisticated theory that we confidently expect in physics, but irreducibly statistical correlations that resist, and resist in principle, improvement without limit. This does not mean there are any events that are in themselves undetermined or unpredictable; it is only events as described in [mental] vocabulary . . . that resist incorporation into a closed deterministic system. These same events, described in appropriate physical terms, may be as amenable to prediction and explanations as any. (1974, pp. 42-43)

Davidson's skepticism concerning psychological laws spreads, naturally enough, to psychological explanation, and by that route to psychology itself, considered as a scientific discipline. In some (not too exact) sense, Davidson holds that because psychology cannot yield genuine laws and does not treat of genuine natural kinds, psychological "explanation" is not genuine explanation in the sense of revealing underlying realities in nature, but is, rather, a kind of interpretative – and in part evaluative – scheme that we impose on certain beings for our own purposes of dealing with those things. Hence his title, "Psychology as Philosophy."

My purpose in this chapter is to sketch a format for psychological theory that I believe resists Davidsonian skepticism, illuminates the notion of a psychological law, and supports my homunctionalist ontology of the mental; in the process I shall set out Davidson's view, pinpointing what I think is his key skeptical argument, and rebut it. After applying my format very briefly to the notion of believing, in particular, I shall try further to exhibit the way in which belief states are real entities to be found in nature, while accounting backhandedly for the lure of skeptical Davidsonian intuitions.

A few more introductory words about the passages I have quoted: First, notice that the claim Davidson makes in passage *1*, which is what he attempts to defend in Section II of "Mental Events" (1970), is not precisely the same as PAM. The claim that there are no psychophysical laws does not entail that mental events (qua mental) cannot be explained or predicted at all, since such events might be

27

explained or predicted (qua mental) on the basis of purely psychological laws (laws involving only mental predicates), which might themselves be strict and deterministic. Davidson says (1970, p. 81) that the denial of the existence of psychophysical laws, together with some "reasonable assumptions," yields PAM, but he does not say what reasonable assumptions he has in mind. Possibly he believes that (owing to his "Principle of Causal Interaction") some of the things we shall have to explain about mental events are their causal interactions with physical events; a set of purely psychological laws could not accomplish this. In any case, Davidson thinks there cannot be any purely psychological laws either; hence PAM.

Passage 2 gives us some idea of what he requires of a genuinely lawlike statement. A law must be precise, must admit no exceptions, must have no escape clauses or ceteris paribus provisos, must not be probabilistic, and (he adds in "The Material Mind" [1973, p. 713]) must be supported by its instances.[3] Passages 3 and 4 remind us that, since for Davidson laws and explanations are linguistic items – namely, sentences – an event is explained only under some description, and what explains it under one description may not explain it under another. When Davidson speaks for "mental events as a class," he means mental events qua mental – that is, under a mental description.

II DAVIDSON'S ANOMALISM

Davidson goes on to defend the Token Identity thesis, that is, the claim that every mental event-token is identical to some physical event-token. This claim is entailed by the Type–Type Identity Theory but does not entail it and Davidson denies the Type–Type Theory on the basis of PAM. Thus, Davidson's theory of mind, which he calls "anomalous monism" (AM), asserts token–token identity between mental events and physical events but at the same time denies type–type identity between mental events and physical

3 There are, of course, laws of physics that are explicitly probabilistic. But these laws are still "strict" and "deterministic" in Davidson's sense, because the probabilities themselves are absolutely precise and determined without exception or escape clause by the containing physical theory. Notice that these strong constraints on what is to count as a genuine law entail that whenever an actual case of psychophysical causation occurs, that case falls under some genuine law in the mathematically strict sense. This claim is essential to Davidson's later defense of his own monism.

events or any other particular sort of events; this is what is distinctive about the view.

There are several grounds for initial dissatisfaction with AM. First, as a metaphysical theory, AM is exasperatingly coy. It amounts to monism simpliciter; it denies that a person has two different sorts of event-properties, one of which is spiritual or immaterial, but refuses to say anything more about the nature of mental entities, except perhaps that there is no more to say. If AM is true, then whatever we do eventually find out about the physiological basis of human desire, say (if there is anything even statistically approaching a single sort of physiological basis), will plainly not be generalizable to desire in other species. It has been argued by many that this in itself is all to the good; but AM also implies that there are no laws, even purely psychological ones, on the basis of which we might extrapolate facts about our own and our experimental subjects' desires to the desires of others. AM thus frustrates psychology by blocking significant generalization at every turn. It would also forestall some obvious shortcuts in research programs.

Davidson could reply to this in either or both of two ways. First, he could say that if AM is metaphysically laconic, at least that makes it more likely to be true. To be precise, what is cautious is the specifically metaphysical part of AM (the Token Identity thesis), and that, Davidson might point out, is a virtue, not a flaw. PAM, of course, is not cautious at all, since normally we are inclined to suppose that there are lawlike psychophysical correlations (even Descartes granted this, at least to a limited extent). As for my whining about lack of generalizability and the frustration of research programs, Davidson could respond that that is just too bad. If there are no correlations, there are no correlations, and if PAM has been sufficiently well defended on independent grounds, then we should just conclude that psychology is a much more elusive and less rigorous discipline than, in our youthful optimism, we had hoped it was.

I do not think we can let it go at that. A second objection to AM will bring out the reason why. As I have observed elsewhere (1974), philosophers who have offered noneliminative theories of mind have generally been taken to be offering theories of the *nature* of mental entities, or programs for obtaining such theories. We expect such philosophers to tell us, to the best of their technical abilities,

29

what it is to have a belief, what it is to have a desire, what it is to be afraid, and so forth – In short, we expect the philosophers to show us the metaphysical/scientific essences of the various mental events, states, and processes. My objection to AM is that it cannot do this.

Of course, Davidson's claim seems to be precisely that there is no scientific essence of belief, of desire, or of fear, assuming that it takes genuine laws to make a scientific essence. Belief and the rest simply do not have (single) scientific natures. So Davidson need not be impressed with my second objection either. On this desolate understanding of AM, what Davidson seems to be saying amounts to the thesis that there is no single such state as belief (desire, fear, etc.) – that things we happen to group together under a well-worn common term do not in fact have anything nonaccidentally in common and do not form a natural class or kind.

Nice as scientific natures and essences are, we must remind ourselves (following Wittgenstein) that ordinary physical objects sometimes do not have them either. Tables and chairs do not figure in strict deterministic laws qua furniture; and since tables are very likely related to one another only by family resemblance, there is probably no metaphysical or scientific essence of tablehood. Now, Davidson might reasonably ask, why should we blanch at the thought that "desire" and "thought" and "belief" might be family-resemblance notions as well? It is possible that our use of the word "desire" or "want," for example, is governed only by loosely overlapping criteria involving distal stimuli, verbal utterances, apparently goal-directed behavior, phenomenal urges of certain sorts, related emotional reactions, and perhaps even more scientific considerations such as physiochemical reactions to drugs and the like. We have been troubled by the thought that desire as a type might disappear entirely if AM is true; but AM evidently need not be taken to have such a serious consequence; for ordinary family-resemblance concepts, it seems, are also anomalous in Davidson's sense, and they do not "disappear entirely" as types. Mental categories are no worse off than many of the gross physical-object types that even philosophers take for granted.

I believe that this final response sounds as plausible as it does only because of a common confusion concerning the notion of a mental state-type. The important thing to notice is that the type "desire" is a genus, an umbrella category that serves only to subsume all the many and richly varied specific types of desires that there are. (This point is often overlooked in discussions of mind–body gerrymandering.) We may agree that it is presumptuous to suppose that "desire" and "belief" are crisp natural kinds; in fact, it seems overwhelmingly probable that these generic categories are merely loosely bound family-resemblance collections (though I would insist that only a well-developed future psychology could establish that claim decisively). But it is far less plausible to contend that specific types, such as "having an urgent desire (of such and such a phenomenological description) for a cool, frosty beer" or "believing strongly that it is sunny outside Caldwell Hall this afternoon," are loosely bound family-resemblance notions rather than natural kinds.

Remember, too, that psychological laws concerning desires and beliefs will probably not be statable entirely in layman's language. We can expect that no commonsense psychological generalization stated in ordinary English will be strict and lawlike. Genuine psychological laws, as I said in beginning this chapter, would incorporate futuristic technical jargon, as well as mention of familiar mental items. So our inability to think of any plausible examples of psychological laws off the top of our heads (or off the top of current psychological theories) is no evidence against the existence of such laws.

Finally, we have at least one powerful motive for hoping that the mental is not anomalous, which distinguishes its case from that of tables and chairs: Although no one has ever formulated a scientific theory of furniture qua furniture (so far as I know), psychologists have thought and worked under the assumption that a genuinely scientific psychology is possible, occasionally with encouraging results. More to the point, we have considerable use for as scientific a psychology as we can get our hands on, since as intelligent human beings, we set great store by the understanding and prediction of behavior. This dims the appeal of AM somewhat, even in AM's family-resemblance version, and encourages us to keep looking for something better, bearing in mind that some of our mental concepts may have to be cleared up and regimented, in bracing but harmless ways.

On this last point – cleaning up and regimentation – I am at pains to advocate a very liberal view. Unlike David Lewis (1972), and unlike Dennett (1978) and Stich (1982, 1983), I am entirely willing to give up fairly large chunks of our commonsensical or platitudinous theory of belief or of desire (or of almost anything else) and decide that we were just wrong about a lot of things, without drawing the inference that we are no longer talking about belief or desire. To put the matter crudely, I incline away from Lewis's Carnapian and/or Rylean cluster theory of the reference of theoretical terms, and toward Putnam's (1975a) causal-historical theory. As in Putnam's examples of "water," "tiger," and so on, I think the ordinary word "belief" (qua theoretical term of folk psychology) points dimly toward a natural kind that we have not fully grasped and that only mature psychology will reveal. I expect that "belief" will turn out to refer to some kind of information-bearing inner state of a sentient being (more on this in Chapter 4), but the kind of state it refers to may have only a few of the properties usually attributed to beliefs by common sense. Thus, I think our ordinary way of picking out beliefs and desires succeeds in picking out real entities in nature, but it may not succeed in picking out the entities that common sense suggests that it does.

III   DAVIDSON'S MAIN ARGUMENT

Perhaps, it might be thought, Davidson does not really mean to insist that desire has no scientific nature or essence. In "Mental Events" (1970) he concentrates on defending claim *1* and obtains PAM primarily by inferring it from *1*; so possibly the main point is just that desire has no physical (and, in particular, no neurophysiological) nature or essence. This less startling claim, though still incompatible with the Identity Theory, is nowadays almost universally granted; Putnam (1967) and others, years ago, exposed the chauvinistic presumptuousness of extrapolating observed human psychophysiological correlations outside the human species. (See Lycan [1974].) And even within the class of human beings, Smart's vaunted type–type correlations have not materialized on any large scale. (See e.g., Mucciolo [1974].) Rather, it is generally thought that to be a mental entity of some particular kind (say, to be a belief or a thought or an intention or a desire) is to play a certain functional role in mediating between the stimuli that impinge on one's owner and the owner's resulting behavior; mental state- and event-types are correlated or identified with roles of this sort, rather than with whatever various physiological states or events happen to play these roles in various human beings and other sentient creatures on this occasion or that. Thus, according to such a view, mental entities have no physical essences, but they do have functional essences. And distinctive sorts of psychological laws would fall out of such a view – not psychophysical laws but psychofunctional laws.

Let us again consider what I have argued (1981a) is the most promising current theory of this kind: Homunctionalism.[4] As in Chapter 1, let us see a human being or other sentient creature as an integrated collection of component subsystems or agencies that communicate with one another and cooperate to produce their host creature's overall behavioral responses to stimuli. A psychologist who adopts the homuncular format and applies it to human beings will describe an individual by means of a flowchart that portrays the person's immediately subpersonal agencies and their various routes of communicative access to one another.[5] Each of these agencies, represented by a "black box" on the original flowchart, will in turn be described by a flowchart that breaks it down into other, more specialized subsystems that corporately produce its behavior, and so on; and each of the subsystems, sub–subsystems and sub– . . . subsystems will be characterized in terms of its job or function, within the corporate hierarchy.

Thus, as before, the psychologist will posit an Executive Unit, a Speech Center, a Buffer Memory, a Perceptual Analyzer, and so forth, at the immediately subpersonal level and will employ more specialized systems-theoretic jargon characterizing the components of those agencies in turn; eventually, if the psychologist intrepidly continues this exploratory descent through the subject's institutional architecture, he or she will ultimately be using neuroanatomical terms, which at their own level, are job-descriptive too.[6] In

---

4 The philosophical theory or picture of the psychological to which I am attaching this term derives from Jerry Fodor (1968a) and Dennett (1978), although it is suggested by certain research programs in cognitive psychology and in artificial intelligence (it goes back at least to Herbert Simon and to the psychologist Fred Attneave). See also Cummins (1975, 1983) and Haugeland (1978) for useful discussion. In "Form, Function and Feel" (1981) and *Consciousness* (1987a) I have tried to bring out the considerable virtues of the view and to apply it to the task of accounting for "feels" or qualia within a materialist framework.
5 For more detailed illustration and commentary, see Dennett (1978, particularly Chaps. 9 and 11), and again my *Consciousness* (1987a).
6 In "Form, Function and Feel" (1981) and *Consciousness* (1987a), I argue that job-descriptive or teleological characterization reaches farther down toward fundamental physical reality than is usually recognized and that even the Identity Theor-

33

the end, the psychologist will be able to explain the subject's behavioral capacities by reference to the joint capacities of the subsystems that mediate them; and if a deeper account is desired, the psychologist will explain the capacities of the subsystems in terms of the joint capacities of their own respective components, and so on down – although at some point the psychologist would have to turn biologist, then chemist, and finally physicist in order to bring this explanatory process to completion.

As I have said, the homuncular model has great advantages to offer both psychology and metaphysics, but in this chapter I want merely to use the model to rehabilitate the notion of a psychological law, in response to skeptical Davidsonian arguments concerning the propositional attitudes. As always, I propose to identify the attitudes (and all other mental states) with occurrences of institutionally characterized states in their owners' various subpersonal and sub– . . . subpersonal agencies at various levels of corporate abstraction. I mean this proposal as a reductive type-identification of mental states with functionally characterized states. Thus, a typical homunctionalist explication would take the form: "To be in mental state S is for one's ϕ-er to be in functional state $S(\phi)$."

As is well known, functional or job-descriptive types are irreducible to more concrete types such as physical types; a valve-lifter or an adding machine or even a typewriter can be made of any of a number of different kinds of material. Notice that this irreducibility affords Homunctionalism an important advantage as a philosophical theory of mind. As Davidson says, our mental concepts as a family do seem to comprise a "seamless whole," quite disjointed from the family of physiological concepts and from that of physical concepts; and despite the naturalistic temper of the past two decades, the actual prospects for reducing the mental directly to the physical have never really seemed very bright. This is what we would expect if Homunctionalism is correct. I maintain that the apparent seamlessness of the mental realm is the genuine irreducibility of homuncular types to any more concrete types, and the difficulty of detailing a reduction of the mental even to the

---

ist is a functionalist – one who locates mental types at a very low level of institutional abstraction. Ned Block has urged against this that at least when one descends from the neuroanatomical level to the level of chemistry, no teleological element remains, but consider the etymologies of such chemical terms as "hydrogen" and "oxygen."

homuncular results from our ignorance of the organizational plan of the human corporation itself at a sufficiently low level of abstraction. Thus, Homunctionalism has the virtue of helping to explain (in part) why there is a mind–body problem in the first place.

What kinds of psychological laws fall out of a homunctionalist theory of the mental? Presumably those laws (perhaps involving determinate and precise transition probabilities) that can be read off a flowchart of the homuncular type, along with (of course) the metaphysical laws that would follow from the identification itself of mental states with homuncular states. And so the Homunctionalist can consistently agree with Davidson that mental entities have functional essences and that there are true psychological laws, namely, psychofunctional ones of our homuncular sort. But before going on to assess this suggestion and to see whether it successfully blocks Davidson's skepticism, let us advert again to the particular propositional attitude – belief – and to the information-storage paradigm defended in Chapter 1. Besides being intrinsically plausible (or so I claimed), it is a good position from which to start as regards the matter of psychological laws, in order to see what can be accommodated within it and what modifications or departures might later be forced by encounters with less tractable phenomena. Even at the onset we would have to draw careful distinctions between many kinds, modes, and levels of information and many kinds, modes, and levels of storage. (We would arrive at these distinctions by drawing on our ordinary commonsensical concepts and refinements of them, by careful attention to people's introspective reports under usual and unusual circumstances, and by following the implications of technical findings in cognitive psychology and neuropsychology.) For example, beliefs of some kinds must be distinguished from memory traces, and the relation between belief and memory charted in detail. (The same goes for beliefs and perceptual states.)

A different kind of complexity will have to be introduced into an information-storage model if we are to account for the relative degrees of firmness of belief (from "tentative" to "rock-bottom"). Each of our posited information-bearing entities[7] will have to be

---

7 I do not mean anything particularly technical by "information" here, and I am certainly not presupposing any one mathematical representation of informational content. However, I mean "information" less in the Shannon-Weaver or Bell

35

assigned some quantitative measure of strength. Obviously, a simple numerical tag will not suffice, so long as it is unconnected to any of the believer's conative apparatus, because the strength of a belief surely is a relational property: a matter of the belief's use in inference, the way in which it is produced and sustained by its source of evidence, and its de facto authority in determining action. Some combinations of factors of this kind must be marshaled by an account of belief-strength.

What kind of homunctional state might a belief state be? Again, I take it to be obvious that beliefs have structures of some kind, both on intuitive and on theoretical grounds. Intuitively, because the belief that Donald is intelligent and the belief that Donald is a vegetarian share an element of some kind, presumably a mental representation of Donald, as do the belief that Donald is intelligent and the belief that Dan is intelligent; theoretically, because (it appears) we must suppose Dan's belief that the liquid in front of him is beer and his desire to drink beer share a component if we are to explain their joint function in causing Dan to reach for the liquid in front of him. This leaves us with the question of what kind of structure to attribute to beliefs in our homuncular model.

As I have said, I predict that our theory will want to characterize occurrent beliefs in semantical terms, construing them as being playbacks of internal representations patterned either after the sentences of the believer's native (natural) language or after the well-formed formulas of some logical theory. More accurately: To judge or believe occurrently that P is to harbor some internal representation that has semantical properties analogous to those of the sentence that replaces P. What makes such a state of affairs constitute a belief that P is the representation's distinctive semantical properties; what makes it a belief that P is the nature of the harboring, storage, or playback – the representation's contribution to the believer's inner bureaucratic order of business. Of course, insofar as a "representation" of the sort I am invoking approximates a little sentence in the head, I am as before positing the apparatus of "language of thought," since any sentence is a sentence only relative to some language. I take, however, no outlandish view of that apparatus, – no stronger view than that I have called "Forthright

Telephone sense than in Carnap's and Bar-Hillel's sense of "semantic" information.

36

Representationalism." In particular (again), I would not suppose that there is any single, unified language in which all cognitive activity is carried out: Just the opposite is suggested by the homuncular model, since distinct homuncular agencies that perform very different tasks will probably differ accordingly in their respective office jargons. But let us now return to the anomalism issue.

IV ANOMALISM AND FUNCTIONALISM

The Homunctionalist agrees with Davidson that mental entities have no physiological or other physical essences and that there are no (true) psychophysical laws, but it is consistent with this to maintain that mental entities (our specific state- and event-types) have functional essences and that there are true psychological laws, namely, psychofunctional ones. Is this, as I have suggested compatible with Davidson's preferred view of the psychological? And do beliefs or desires, after all, have something in common that makes them beliefs or desires, consistently with Davidson's strictures?

It seems that Davidson would not want to give in so easily, contrary to what I mendaciously proposed at the beginning of the preceding section. If, in the very abstract sort of psychology we are considering, beliefs and other mental entities are to be defined in terms of their functional roles and/or their relations to each other, then these roles and relations must be presumed lawlike. This is tantamount to supposing that there are purely psychological laws, or psychofunctional laws, or both. On the basis of such laws, the occurrences of mental events could be predicted and explained, but this is exactly what PAM rules out. Therefore, if PAM is correct and if the belief that P has a distinctive essence, this essence cannot be a functional role any more than it can be a physical character.

This leaves Davidson with three options: (1) to capitulate and concedes that claim 1 is all he really meant, repudiating his inference from 1 to the full-fledged PAM; (2) to concede that psychological states and events have scientific essences, even though those essences are neither physiological nor functional; or (3) to continue to insist on PAM in its uncompromising form and to deny that psychological states and events form any natural kinds whatever. Option 1 is unattractive, since it renders Davidson's view almost entirely

37

uncontroversial, thus robbing it of interest. It also would not serve Davidson's purpose of spearheading a positve argument in favor of the Token Identity thesis. Option *2* would commit Davidson to seeking some new, so far unenvisioned sort of metaphysical nature for mental entities, presumably one that somehow failed to yield psychological laws concerning these entities, and his text betrays no inclination at all toward taking such a line. Therefore, if we are to understand Davidson as holding an interesting view that is anything like his text taken fairly literally, we must understand him as choosing option *3*. And, as we have seen, *3* entails repudiating Homunctionalism and almost any other current theory of the mental;[8] so Davidson's arguments for PAM are carrying a heavy load and demand close scrutiny.

His reasons for adhering to PAM are obscure; they are the most elusive element in "Mental Events" (1970), although they are clarified a bit in "The Material Mind" (1973) and in "Psychology as Philosophy" (1974). Davidson seems to be resting his case on a number of different general theses about language and translation, about the grammatical properties of propositional-attitude expressions, about scientific theories tout court, about psychological methodology, and about the Belief-Desire-Perception Cycle. But he takes no pains to distinguish these theses, and at some points seems to assume that they are all equivalent, or at least come to much the same thing. I shall catalog them and then focus on the few that seem to bear the most weight.

1. The Belief-Desire-Perception Cycle[9] *and related points.* This is the first consideration that Davidson appeals to (1970, p. 91), though he says only that turning our attention to the Cycle will "sharpen our appreciation of" the alleged anomalism of the mental. He picks up this theme again in later papers (1973, p. 721; 1974, p. 43). He concludes, "Beliefs and desires issue in behavior only as modified by further beliefs and desires, attitudes and attendings, without limit. Clearly this holism of the mental realm is a clue both to the autonomy and to the anomalous character of the mental" (1970, p. 92).

2. The assumption of rationality in psychological explanation. David-

---

8 David Lewis's view (1972) is perhaps an exception, since Lewis defines mental expressions in terms of the platitudes and folk wisdom in which they figure.
9 See, e.g., Chapters 2 and 3 of Harman (1973).

son gives at least four different arguments in support of this (1970, pp. 96–98; 1974, pp. 45–51).

3. A rather subtle point about lawlikeness and confirmation, and the distinction between "homonomic" and "heteronomic" generalizations. Heteronomic generalizations are portrayed as a kind of hybrid, standing between genuinely lawlike generalizations, on the one hand, and totally unlawlike generalizations, such as "All emeralds are grue," on the other (1970, pp. 92–94; see also 1973, p. 713).

4. The claim that the required precision and correctibility are obtainable only within a "comprehensive closed system" (1970, p. 94).

5. The need for synthetic a priori "constitutive elements" in a theory able to give rise to genuine laws. Davidson advances an analogy (1970, p. 96) having to do with the measurement of length, which he intends as an illustration of his general point (a similar analogy is put forward in "Psychology as Philosophy" [1974, p.49], and he then argues that rationality (cf. item *2*) is a constitutive element in psychological explanation and prediction (p. 98; see also p. 47). Thus, this kind of consideration is intended to explain item *2*, and probably item *1* as well. It seems to me that it may also explain *3*.

6. The indeterminacy of translation, and its use against the possibility of alternative conceptual schemes. Davidson appeals to considerations concerning translation in "Mental Events" (1970, p. 97), in "The Material Mind" (1973, p. 714), and on pp. 51–2 of "Psychology as Philosophy" (1974, pp. 51–2).[10] Indeterminacy is tied to the "holism" of the mental in "The Material Mind" (p. 721); it also seems to be part of the explanation of item *2*.

7. The intentionality of the mental and the intensionality of mental expressions. Davidson follows Quine in taking this consideration to be "of a piece with" item *6*. And, although Davidson does not mention the fact, Quine thinks that intentionality and intensionality by themselves make the mental anomalous, even if they are not simply the same thing as the indeterminacy of translation.

Davidson does not clearly distinguish *1* from *2*, evidently thinking that *2* is either just the same as *1* or else merely an explanation of it. This is not quite right. Although it may be true that *2* explains

10 To grasp his point fully, one must be familiar with Quine's presentation of the indeterminacy doctrine (1960, Chap. 2) and perhaps with several more recent papers by others such as Wallace (1972), Rorty (1972), and Davidson (1973–4). Davidson applies all this to the present issue in several of his papers (1970, p. 97; 1973, p. 714; 1974, pp. 51–2).

1 in some sense, the point about the Belief-Desire-Perception Cycle can be made without any reference to rationality; Davidson introduced it simply in terms of the failure of Analytical Behaviorism. Nor, so far as I can see, does item *1* require *2*; superficially, at least, it seems that the Cycle would obtain whether or not psychologists were methodologically constrained in favor of ascribing rationality to their subjects. But I do not think that the distinction between *1* and *2* is crucial to a successful evaluation of Davidson's defense of PAM. Item *1* is widely considered congenial, and Davidson defends *2* at some length; we can take him as offering both together in support of PAM.

Four separate arguments are used to establish *2*, though (again) Davidson himself does not clearly distinguish them (1970, pp. 96–7; 1970, p. 97 and especially 1974, pp. 50–1; 1970, pp. 95–6, 98; and 1974, pp. 45–51). I shall not go through these arguments, since I think that at least two of them are convincing and give us excellent reason to accept *2*; so let us grant Davidson *2* and go on to ask whether *1* and *2* do militate strongly in favor of PAM. Davidson writes:

Any effort at increasing the accuracy and power of a theory of behavior forces us to bring more and more of the whole system of the agent's beliefs and motives directly into account. But in inferring this system from the evidence, we necessarily impose conditions of coherence, rationality, and consistency. These conditions have no echo in physical theory, which is why we look for no more than rough correlations between psychological and physical phenomena. (1974, p. 43; see also 1970, p. 98)

This passage contains the most direct and explicit argument that Davidson gives for PAM, or rather for the weaker claim (*1*) that suggests the principle to him. Three obvious questions arise: (1) What exactly does Davidson mean by saying that the cycle and the rationality assumption "have no echo in physical theory"? (2) Why does it follow that there cannot be strict, lawlike psychophysical generalizations? (3) Even if the latter does follow, does the argument also prove that there cannot be laws of psychology at all? Let us take up claim *1* first.

One thing that Davidson does not mean is that the seamlessness of psychological theory is not a feature of physical theory. Just as psychology has its rationality assumption (accompanied by the Cycle) as a "constitutive element" or ideal, so physical theory (as Davidson's measurement examples are designed to indicate) has constitutive ideals of its own, and the holism that comes with them. Where psychology assumes rationality, physics assumes the transitivity of length and other magnitudes. Davidson seems to mean, rather, that rationality in particular is not a constitutive ideal in physics and in fact does not figure in physical explanations of human movements at all. When we explain an action in everyday terms of beliefs, perceptions, motives, desires, and reasons, we (must) assume rationality and a general stock of shared background beliefs. When we explain that same action physically, we refer only to chemical, electrical, and mechanical goings-on. (Notice that the two explanations, both sentences, will refer to the action in question under respectively different descriptions, one in terms of something a person did and the other in terms of a more or less specific motion that occurred in an object. Davidson holds that if we are speaking properly, the former description will be a term of psychological theory, whereas the latter will be part of the vernacular of physics or biophysics.)

If this were all that Davidson meant in saying that his first two considerations "have no echo in physical theory," no one would quarrel with him. But now we must ask why this relatively unexciting fact should matter. In particular, why does it entail or suggest that there cannot be strict psychophysical laws? Davidson maintains that the trouble with psychophysical generalizations of this sort is that they involve some sort of linguistic incongruity, brought on by mixing terms that are not "made for each other." Elsewhere he hints that the point is instead epistemological: "There cannot be tight connections between the realms if each is to retain allegiance to its proper source of evidence" (1970, p. 98). But more to the point (turning now to my third question) Davidson's considerations certainly do not show that psychofunctional vocabulary would not be "tightly closed," since according to Homunctionalism, black boxes of a sufficiently high level of institutional abstraction are described in virtually psychological terms, as things are now; so Davidson's argument fails against Homunctionalism even if it succeeds against the Type–Type Identity Theory, and so fails to prove PAM, even if it proves claim 1.

Possibly Davidson's point is, rather, the epistemological one: Given a neural process that in fact caused a certain bodily motion, we cannot show under a mental description of that process that it caused that motion (even when the latter is mentioned under an

41

action-theoretic description) without the addition of a host of other assumptions about the agent's psychological capacities and states of mind. That observation by itself does not entail that we cannot show the mental causation to have occurred at all, but perhaps Davidson holds that the number of needed background assumptions is indefinitely large. (Note the phrase "without limit" in quoted passage 4.) This is an extremely interesting hypothesis, and if true it would be strong evidence for thinking that we could not formulate strict psychophysical laws unless we were able to find some axiom schemata to bring indefinitely many assumptions under one rule, which is unlikely. It would also impugn Homunctionalism, as well as the Identity Theory, in the same way. If this is what Davidson intends, we would have to add to his argument the premise that the Cycle is indefinitely large, and we would have to spell out the rationality assumption by saying that the number of different shared beliefs and inference rules that we must posit in psychological explanation is without limit.

How could Davidson motivate these strengthened theses? Perhaps by looking at some cases of mental ascription and some cases of motivational explanation and by showing that we always have to keep adding psychological assumptions in order to approach, on the one hand, a sufficiency relation between mental ascription and behavioral-evidence-plus-other-mental-assumptions and, on the other, a complete and lawlike explanation of the subject's behavior. If Davidson could show that more and more assumptions had to be added successively in each case and that no end was in sight, this would be good evidence for thinking that the process would continue indefinitely – that there would always be counterexamples to any generalization connecting mental events and behavioral or other mental or physical events. (That he might support PAM in this way is suggested by his remarks on pages 44–5 of "Psychology as Philosophy.") But, pending his offering at least a rough algorithm for generating such counterexamples, I think we must regard his case based on the Belief-Desire-Perception Cycle as unproved.

David Sanford has reminded[11] me of Davidson's remark:

It is an error to compare a truism like "If a man wants to eat an acorn omelette, then he generally will if the opportunity exists and no other

---

11 In his characteristically acute comments on a version of this material that I presented at Oberlin College at the Twentieth Oberlin Colloquium in Philosophy, April 1979, personal communication.

desire overrides" with a law that says how fast a body will fall in a vacuum. It is an error, because in the latter case, but not the former, we can tell in advance whether the condition holds, and we know what allowance to make if it doesn't. What is needed in the case of action, if we are to predict on the basis of desires and beliefs, is a quantitative calculus that brings all relevant beliefs and desires into the picture. (1974, p. 45)

Sanford adds:

Before we can show that the desire, *qua* desire, caused the behavior, we must determine that no other desire overrides; yet this sort of condition is not appropriately mentioned in the formulation of a proper law because there is no independent way of telling when it obtains. (personal communication)

I grant that this difference between Davidson's truism and the law of falling bodies poses an epistemological problem for the homunctional psychologist. It seems that in order to be justified in attributing a desire to a subject, we must antecedently know something about that subject's desires, or lack of them; the rationality assumption (or perhaps some other assumption that makes certain desires a priori likely or unlikely) is needed to block the regress. But there are two points to be made in mitigation of this:

1. Davidson's truism may be a "law" or folk psychology, but it is not the sort of lawlike statement that one would find in a homunctionalist psychology. As I have said, homunctionalist laws will be highly technical and detailed generalizations that could be read off an immensely complex flowchart of the sort I have described, and they will be couched in our characteristically job-descriptive subpersonal jargon. Granted, they will contain ceteris paribus clauses of a sort that I shall discuss in Section VI of this chapter, but those clauses will be of quite a different sort from those that interest folk-psychological truisms of the sort that Davidson illustrates. So Davidson's illustration is not a counterexample to anything that I maintain here.

2. It is not clear why an epistemic defect in a putative law should make the law less of a law. I take it that a generalization might in fact be both true and lawlike, this being a metaphysical matter, and still pose nasty epistemological problems. Suppose Homunctionalism is correct, or rather (not to beg the question), suppose that every human being is at least in part a homunctional system of the sort I have described. Then, for all Davidson's arguments have shown, there will be homunctionalist laws governing the behavior

43

of human beings, whether or not we can ever devise a methodology sophisticated enough to enable us to discover those laws.

In his own anomalist writings (1978, pp. xvi–xvii, 28, and 105; also 1981a, 1981b), D. C. Dennett has given the rationality assumption an argumentative twist that is somewhat different from Davidson's: When we ascribe beliefs or desires to people, we do so against the backdrop of a general assumption that the people's other mental states and conditions are rational to at least a minimal degree. But the concept of rationality is a *normative* concept; when we call a person's beliefs rational, we are evaluating both the person and the beliefs. If psychology essentially involves evaluation and (as Davidson agrees) cannot proceed a step without it, then is it not after all quite different from chemistry or physics?

It is hard to discern exactly what is being claimed. Let us distinguish three possible theses that are suggested by Dennett's recent writings (although more may be lurking in the neighborhood):

1. We are entitled to regard behavioral facts as evidence in favor of propositional-attitude ascriptions only by virtue of our making an assumption that is in part a normative assumption.
2. When we ascribe a propositional attitude – say, a belief – to an organism, we commit ourselves, through doxastic logic or the probability calculus or some other description of an ideal believer, to a normative claim about what else the organism ought to believe.
3. A belief-ascription is itself a normative remark concerning the organism to which the belief is ascribed.

I shall not go into these claims in any detail (for an excellent discussion, see Van Gulick [1980]), but we should have to be shown an argument that derives the anomalism of the mental from any of them. Thesis *1* is an epistemological thesis and so is not likely to entail a metaphysical one. (Recall our discussion of the case of the acorn omelet.) Thesis *2* is so obvious that it would be surprising to find out that it entailed so substantive a doctrine as PAM. When I ascribe a pain to an organism, I commit myself, through the hedonic calculus or the Categorical Imperative or some other description of an ideal agent, to a normative claim about what we ought to do for that organism, but that fact does nothing to show that the pain is not a real, straightforward, factual inner state of the organism. Thesis *3*, I suppose, has the best chance.

But *3* is the least plausible of the three claims. Belief-ascriptions do not at all seem to be normative remarks. When we impute a

44

belief to someone, we do not thereby praise the belief as being a reasonable one. On countless occasions an amateur or professional psychologist has explained someone's behavior by ascribing to that person a belief or a desire or both that is or are admitted by everyone to be stupid, silly, irrational, perverse, sick or the like (cf. Fodor [1981b]). Besides, even if psychologists did routinely characterize the beliefs and desires they posit as being "reasonable" ones, I should think that reasonableness of this sort could easily be naturalized in crypto-evolutionary terms; "reasonableness" would be cashed in terms of promoting fitness of one kind or another. Thus, propositional-attitude ascriptions would not be irreducibly normative. Finally, if the beliefs posited by psychologists are ideal beliefs, in the sense of being the beliefs that the psychologist thinks the subject ought to have, how could they help us predict the subject's actual behavior, given that the subject in fact does not live up to the ideal in question? It seems these normative "beliefs" would generate the wrong predictions.[12]

In a longer (unpublished) manuscript from which the present chapter is drawn, I argue that Davidson's next three considerations – 3, 4, and 5 – are parasitic, in that they simply stand or fall with the first two. I shall omit discussion of them here, and move directly to Davidson's appeal to the indeterminacy of translation.

V QUINE

As Quine understands it, the underdetermination of translators' "analytical" hypotheses by their observational evidence supports

12 In naturalistic psychology of the kind I am envisaging, it is difficult to leave room for the genuinely normative notions that are the subject matter of logic and of the theory of epistemic justification generally. How does a naturalistic theorist, who holds that a complete causal description of the natural order is all there is for science or philosophy to offer, reconstruct the distinction between rational and irrational beliefs? Alternatively: What would a naturalist's philosophy of logic look like? This question has received little attention in the recent literature on philosophy of psychology, despite the gathering momentum of the "naturalization" of epistemology spearheaded by Armstrong (1973) and Goldman (1975, 1980, and elsewhere). Naturalistic epistemologists typically concentrate all their efforts on relatively immediate perceptual knowledge, where it *is* plausible to explicate justification and epistemic "obligation" in terms of causal sufficiencies obtaining within mechanisms. But as soon as we move any distance away from this epistemologically idiosyncratic kind of belief, the inferences that people ought to draw and the inferences that people do draw are going to diverge quite a bit, and no naturalistic causal-functional account of the latter will have much to say about the former. (See, however, Sober [1981] and Chapter 7 in this volume.)

PAM in a direct way that makes no mention of the Belief-Desire-Perception Cycle or the rationality assumption. Quine takes the underdetermination of analytical hypotheses, together with some other assumptions about scientific method and about the linguist's enterprise, to show that analytical hypotheses are indeterminate. Quine holds that analytical hypotheses are not true or false reports of any objective fact but are "correct" or "incorrect" only relative to prechosen translation manuals that have been originally selected more or less arbitrarily, on the basis of sheer convenience.

I cannot here go into Quine's reasons for holding this extremely strong position. (See Chapter 10 of my *Logical Form in Natural Language* [1984a]; also Martin and Smith [1974].) I want only to show its relevance to PAM and the force it would have if true. The first important point to see is that the indeterminacy of translation would infect ascriptions of propositional attitudes to other persons (and ultimately to ourselves): When we impute to a speaker of German the belief that it is snowing, we are in effect translating that speaker's words or other expressive behavior into words of our own.[13] If translation is indeterminate, then our ascription of the belief that it is snowing to the German is indeterminate. The same would go for desires, fears, hopes, and so forth. And to say that the ascription of beliefs and desires to the German is indeterminate is to say (on Quine's usage) that there is no fact of the matter concerning what particular mental states the German is in. So if there were strict laws correlating neural states with mental states, then there would be a fact of the matter concerning the German's beliefs and desires; it would be deductively determined by his actual neural states and the psychophysical laws. Therefore, if translation is indeterminate, as Quine and others believe, there are no psychophysical laws, and claim *1* is vindicated. And this time a similar argument could be wielded against psycho-functional laws and in favor of the full-fledged PAM as well, for there is presumably also a fact of the matter concerning what homunctional states the German is in.

I believe, then, that one who denies PAM ought also to deny the indeterminacy doctrine in its Quinean form. The doctrine is unlikely to trouble the Identity Theorist, in particular, since Quine's discussion of the mind–body problem in *Word and Object* (1960)

13 This connection is nicely brought out by Harman (1969).

's) attempt to split off psychology from the "hard" sciences
a quite different sort of enterprise, a poor relation or black
some kind.

here is a final concessive word to be said concerning the
ness of psychological laws, and to a small extent it vindicates
n's skepticism on this score. I said in Section III of this
that the laws of a homunctionalist psychology would be
t can be read off a flowchart of the type I described. Thus,
ctionalist law would take the form: "If an organism of
eceives an input of type Y while its ϕ-er is in state A and
in state B (etc), then (it is probable to degree n that) the
will spit out an output of type Z."

er, a "law" of this form would seem to be subject to
n by hardware malfunction. And, given the prevalence
re malfunction, at least among those of us living in dan-
es like these, we can be sure that such falsification will
ous. Does this not confirm Davidson's thesis that there
uine and true psychological laws?

ous reply is available: The notions of a thing's "having
ch is in a state A" or "having a ψ-er which is in state
ctional notions, defined in terms of their satisfactory
d foreign relations. A hardware breakdown does not
aws that we read off our flowcharts; rather, it causes
formerly described by the flowchart to cease to be
scribed by that flowchart – that is, to cease to realize
program(s). This would mean that the organism no
ϕ-er and a ψ-er, and so the organism is no longer of
annot be a counterexample to our law.

s reply is so obvious as to raise the suspicion that the
fiable. And this suspicion is easily confirmed. For the
now understanding it may be rewritten as follows:
sm receives an input of type Y, and if the organism
if the ϕ-er is in state A, and if the organism has a
ψ-er is in state B (etc.), then (it is probable to degree
anism will spit out an input of type Z." Now, the
ns "ϕ-er" and "ψ-er" are defined by the set of condi-
in the relevant flowchart; so any law of the foregoing
utologous.19 (Simplest example: "If an organism re-

ches on what I think may be the same point (1975, p. 28).

50

appears to show that no reductive materialist of the standard sort
can hold Quine's views on translation and reference anyway (or so
George Pappas and I have argued [1976]). More importantly, on
our Quinean interpretation, the argument from genuine indeterminacy of translation proves too much: The genuine indeterminacy
of propositional-attitude ascriptions warrants the claim that there
are no beliefs or desires in nature; to ascribe "beliefs" or "desires"
to the German is to engage in a bit of useful but entirely subjective
interpretation of his behavior pattern. Therefore, a proponent of
anomalous monism (AM) who is committed to the claim that there
are belief- and desire-tokens in nature, seemingly must deny the
full-scale indeterminacy of propositional-attitude ascriptions anyway. A champion of indeterminacy who is also a materialist must
be an eliminative materialist of some sort.[14]

Finally, what about intentionality and intensionality? Davidson
has run together several distinct points here. First, there is that at
which he hints on page 97 of "Mental Events" (1970), particularly
in note 15: Quine has claimed that intensional sentences are irreducible, in that they have no nonintensional equivalents. Quine also
maintains, somewhat surprisingly, that the irreducibility of intensional sentences necessitates, and is necessitated by, the indeterminacy of translation.[15] If so, and if indeterminacy implies PAM,
as I have argued it does, then the undisputed intensionality of our
central mental ascriptions itself implies PAM. Further, Quine holds
independently that intensional expressions cannot be incorporated
into serious science. (See Sections 41 through 45 of *Word and Object*.)
PAM follows directly, if we assume that we need intensional
expressions in order to give mental descriptions of events.[16] But
the first of these points has the same flaw as does the Quinean
argument that I based on indeterminacy – that of proving too much;
the second depends on Quine's weighty complex of views on re-

14 Or so Pappas and I contend in "Quine's Materialsm" (1976). Quine himself
questions the tenability of the reductive–eliminative distinction in the first place,
and he explains his view of the mind–body problem somewhat differently in
more recent works (1975, 1978).

15 Quine (1960, p. 221). I try to explain the connection further in my *Logical Form
in Natural Language* (1984a).

16 Roderick Chisholm, who has defended this claim in a number of works, agrees
that intensional expressions cannot be incorporated into physical science; but he
argues, following Brentano, that this simply calls for a separate science of the
mental. The possibility of such a science is ruled out by PAM; Quine accordingly
rejects that part of Chisholm's view.

47

ferential opacity, physics, metaphysics, and "serious" science, and, pending a final evaluation of that complex, there is no immediate reason for scrapping Homunctionalism.

A second point subsumed under our final consideration is Brentano's, which Davidson follows Chisholm in conflating with the thesis of the intensionality of our paradigmatic mental verbs. According to Brentano, the distinguishing feature of mental states, events, and processes is their "aboutness." This feature too has been taken to preclude the possibility of integrating psychology into physical science, or indeed into serious science at all; if it does preclude these possibilities, then presumably it also rules out the existence of psychological laws. It has never been clear, though, that "content" or "aboutness" cannot be ascribed to entities that are in fact neural items, particularly when those neural entities are referred to under psychological descriptions. The vindication of such ascriptions has been a major motivation of Dennett's own work for years (see, in particular, *Content and Consciousness* [1969]), and I have already touted the ability of a Sellarsian brain-writing theory of belief and other propositional attitudes to ride the coattails of the aboutness of sentences, especially when we modify Sellars's own account by telling a causal and/or teleological story about denotation.[17] Even if there cannot be laws correlating mental entities, their contents, and neural entities, it is still quite plausible to think that the contents or intentional objects of mental entities can be characterized in psychofunctional terms.

VI   ADJUDICATION

The upshot of this discussion of Davidson's arguments is that the most convincing support for PAM comes from the Belief-Desire-Perception Cycle, but that support is very weak, in view of the intervention of Homunctionalism as an attractive program for an ontology of the psychological. So we have been given no particularly convincing reason to accept PAM (and hence no convincing reason to accept AM as a theory of mind). But neither have we any very concrete reason, not counting hope, for supposing that PAM is false. What is really at issue is the question of what phil-

17 Admittedly, the causal account will run into trouble in the case of beliefs "about" fictional entities, but there are encouraging signs that this trouble can be overcome; see Devitt's *Designation* (1981).

osophical reality lies behind the adm
ceptual interrelations between our v:
and the concomitant holism of the m
considerations such as those that I l
tionalist welcomes the complexity
directions for a homuncular model c
modates the holism in insisting (as
inescapably relational character of
Further, as we have seen, the H
explanation of the apparent seaml
lack of congruence between the f:
family of physicalistic concepts th
lem in the first place. So the Hoi
on a great deal, including the n
otherwise) relating the mental qu
the Homunctionalist is not a spe
they disagree?

There seems to be only on
The Homunctionalist, as I ha
existence of psycho-functiona
But now it is the time to inqu
the "genuineness" or "strictn

Functionalists in general l
whether they intend the law
be "genuine," "strict," and c
ambitiously Davidson unde
more plausible his view will
among functionalists, it w
interest. There may well tu
laws in biology, or in cher
there are any absolutely de
ter.[18] (More about this sh
larger issue of determinis
science; my main concern

18 Elliott Sober has suggeste
contains tacit ceteris parib
as "closed systems," "per
– that such laws usually e:
it makes their antecedent
munctionalist psychology
way.

Putnam
as being
sheep o

But t
genuine
Davidsc
chapter
those tha
a homur
type X r
its ψ-er i
organism

Howev
falsificatic
of hardwa
gerous tim
be ubiquit
are no gen

An obvi
a ϕ-er whi
B" are fun
domestic a
falsify the
the organis
correctly de
the relevant
longer has a
type X and
Indeed, th
law is unfals
law as we ar
"If an organi
has a ϕ-er an
ψ-er and if th
n that) the or
functional ter
tionals codifie
form will be ta

19 H. P. Grice to

ceives an input of type *Y*, and if the organism has a component such that if the organism receives an input of type *Y* it will spit out an output of type *Z*, then the organism will spit out an output of type *Z*.") But a tautology is a law of logic, not a "law" of psychology.

In his comments on an earlier version of this chapter (cf. n. 11), David Sanford pointed out:

Although no malfunction can falsify a tautologous conditional, a malfunction does present the problem of locating which parts of the antecedent of the conditional are false. . . . Something can malfunction without everything malfunctioning. The organism can still have a ɸ-er, indeed still have a ɸ-er in state *A*, if the malfunction is elsewhere. Flowcharts invite us to locate malfunctions when they occur.

This is true, important, and crucial in particular to the sort of psychophysical research that inspires Homunctionalism in the first place. But to take account of it would require giving up the simple method proposed by David Lewis (1972) for defining mental and homuncular terms explicitly by way of Ramsey sentences, and I am not sure what to adopt in place of that method. Presumably what we need is some way of exploiting and making precise the notion of something's approximately realizing a particular homuncular flowchart. No doubt there are various formal ways of trying to spell this out, but at present I see no chance of discovering strict, deterministic, exceptionless, and nontautological psychological laws; after all this effort and verbiage, we may have to concede to Davidson that every psychological generalization must be qualified by ceteris paribus or other escape clauses. Indeed, we would have to be careful to see that such qualifications did not themselves render the generalizations tautologous; it seems to me that we could do this only by appealing to "normal functioning" or to some other background condition that smacks of norms, and what Davidson suspects is precisely that we must choose between the tautologous and the normative. This might even be why he (and Putnam) contend that psychology is not really a science.

Ausonio Marras (1980) has remarked that to put the problem in this way is to ratify the unwarranted assumption that all genuine explanation is explanation in terms of strictly exceptionless laws. The type of explanation favored by the Homunctionalist, vividly and compellingly described in the works of Fodor and Dennett, is not deductive-nomological explanation of that sort but is functional explanation of the sort we give every day in biology, in experi-

51

mental chemistry, in automotive mechanics, and in engineering generally. It is explanation of the behavior of a single organized system in terms of the joint workings of the system's components. Such explanation does not presuppose the existence of strictly exceptionless mechanical laws, precisely because of the nonnegligible likelihood of hardware breakdowns. Its rational structure is still unclear and controversial. Yet there is no doubt of its value, of its epistemic genuineness, or of its status as scientific in any but a plainly neologistic sense of that word. (On this, see also Cummins [1983].)

The following observation will reinforce the present point: Our difficulty is occasioned by the possibility of hardware breakdown. Now, hardware breaks down, not only in computers and in human bodies; it breaks down in other biological systems as well. Chemistry too is subject to hardware malfunction: Laws of chemistry (pure chemistry, not physical chemistry) are falsified by disruptive subatomic events produced by radiation and could be protected against such falsification only by the assumption (parallel to our "obvious" reply a few paragraphs back) that an "atom" that has been split by radiation no longer counts (functions!) as an atom. This is intuitively right, though it raises the specter of tautologousness, just as the "obvious" reply did.[20] Further, quite commonly, satisfactory explanation of phenomena in one science requires descent to a more fundamental science one level or even two levels down (hence "physical chemistry," "biophysics"), without damage to the status of the higher-level science as a science.

In short: If my "hardware malfunction" objection shows that the mental is anomalous in the sense Davidson intends, then it also shows that the biological and the chemical are anomalous too. And so Davidson should have entitled his article "Psychology, *Biology, and Chemistry* as Philosophy"; he fails to show that psychology is a nonscience in a way that makes it unlike a truly factual, decent, hard-nosed discipline.

The final disposition or disposal of the issue of psychofunctional laws, it seems to me, rests with the future success of the homunctionalist (or some other functionalist) program. If functionalist phi-

20 Elliott Sober observes (in correspondence) that although a chemist always has the opportunity of treating a chemical law as unfalsifiable, "a *good* chemist will not choose to do so." This brings us back to the problem of "locating the malfunctions when they occur."

losophers and psychologists together manage to put forward a fairly detailed psychology that explains and predicts not only behavior but also every esoteric and finely articulated phenomenon that philosophers, psychologists, and neuroscientists can describe, then we will have excellent reason for thinking (1) that the Belief-Desire-Perception Cycle, though large, is finite and completable, (2) that intensionality and intentionality are compatible with a functionalist materialism, and (3) that translation is not indeterminate after all. Should it turn out that Homunctionalism and other functional programs end in disappointment for more sweeping reasons, we will have to consider explaining this by concluding that AM is correct after all. As for present research, however, the homunctionalist ontology permits and contributes to an already ongoing program for psychology, whereas the defender of AM has no program, but only the conviction that no truly scientific psychology is possible; and so, it seems to me, we have no choice but to pursue Homunctionalism or some other functionalist ideal wherever it may lead us.[21]

21 Versions of this chapter were presented (under various titles) at the Fourteenth Annual University of Cincinnati Philosophy Colloquium, February 1978, the University of Auckland, Victoria University of Wellington, the University of Adelaide, the University of Melbourne, and the Twentieth Annual Oberlin Colloquium in Philosophy at Oberlin College, April 1978 (with David Sanford's acute comments mentioned earlier).

3

Tacit belief

At this moment (even as I write) my wife, Mary, believes that my necktie looks like a prize from the state-fair coconut shy. This harsh observation occurred to her a few seconds ago, and she has just voiced it. "That tie looks like a prize from the state-fair coconut shy," she said. I have remonstrated, but she remains unshakable in her conviction. She holds her belief candidly, militantly, and in so many words.

My wife also believes a number of other things, or so we might routinely suppose: that she is less than 18 feet tall; that $10,329 > 10,328$; and that snow in Stockholm does not turn bright orange just as it hits the ground. In fact, it seems she believes an *uncountable* number of other things – for example, that she is less than $6 + n$ feet tall, for any positive real number n. But all these other beliefs differ crucially from her regrettable belief about my tie (and not just in truth-value), for they have never occurred to her; she has never said any such things to herself, and she is unaware that she has these beliefs, unless in a very rarefied sense of awareness. In Chapter 1 (in response to an objection of Dennett's) I distinguished two kinds of belief: "explicit" and "implicit," or "tacit," belief. The distinction is fairly familiar; and theorists almost irresistibly suppose that tacit belief may itself be defined in terms of explicit belief or judgment, typically as the *disposition* to judge,[1] but that is about as far as discussion has gone to date.

My purpose in this chapter is to argue (against my own interest) that the distinction aimed at here is a vexed one at best, even granting that there is just one such distinction, and that serious work needs to be done if we are to carve doxastic reality at whatever joint(s) it may actually have. I shall begin by observing that the notion of "explicit belief" suggested by the preceding two chapters

---

1 E.g., Sellars (1958, p. 521) and de Sousa (1971); more recently, Powers (1978) and Richardson (1981).

is crude and neologistic and shall then argue for its replacement by a more accurate notion of occurrent *judgment*. Then I shall ask exactly what contrasting notion we really have of "merely tacit" belief and whether anything in fact answers to this label.

I assume, as always, that we all talk silently to ourselves. From time to time we make mental judgments, and judgings in this sense are inner episodes that play certain roles in our behavioral economies. What makes the judgment that P a *judgment* that P is its characteristic type of functional role; what makes it a judgment *that* P is its having a certain internal structure, its consisting of proper parts arranged in a certain way, and, in virtue of this, its bearing certain inferential relations to other possible or actual judgments and certain causal and/or teleological relations to things in the world. Crudely, to judge is to host and manipulate a representation, an inner formula of some sort that has both a distinctive causal surface and a semantical content.

This sort of thing is going on in Mary. She represents my tie to herself, or at least she harbors what is in fact a representation of my tie, and this representation hooks up in a causally potent way with her concept of prizehood, a representation of the state fair (or perhaps just of the coconut shy itself), and so forth – the result being her tactless overt speech act; there may be other, nonverbal results as well, if I am not careful to make my own visits to the dry cleaner. A specific state of her is correlated in a referential way with my tie, another state of her with prizehood, another with the state fair, and so forth, and these in turn are correlated causally with some other concepts having ominous normative and even visceral features.

However the details may go, it is not this sort of thing that is going on in Mary with regard to the concept of being less than 18 feet tall or with regard to the number 10,329 or snow in Stockholm. There is no plausible sense in which these things are represented explicitly within her at this very moment, much less hooked up with the other relevant concepts in even a quiescent way. (For one thing, since the human brain is a finite device, it is unlikely to be able to represent each of indenumerably many propositions.) In particular, she never episodically *judges* that she is less than 18 feet tall, or the like. So, in the article on which Chapter 1 is based, I identified "explicit" belief with judging and "tacit" belief with the disposition to judge.

To frame the difference in that way, however, is to make it a distinction between a kind of episode or *event* and a dispositional *state*, and I now think that is wrong, or at least pointlessly neologistic. For as several philosophers have pointed out (see particularly Hunter [1980] and Vendler [1972]), "believe" is not an action- or event-verb but a state-verb. Beliefs are not happenings; there are no datable events of "believing that *P*," though there are datable events of judging or of *coming* to believe. So although our distinction between judging and being disposed to judge is itself perfectly sound, it seems that only the latter is properly called belief.

Yet it is still natural to distinguish between explicit and tacit beliefs, even within the class of dispositional belief states. At least, it is plausible to think that some belief states involve explicit representation in a way that other belief states do not; explicit representation may constitute part of the categorical bases of the relevant dispositions. A paradigm case of this would be one in which a previously tokened representation is now stored quiescently in long-term memory. (Actually, this use of "stored" is misleading. The original token was an event that is now past; *it* is not "stored" anywhere. Rather, as one of its causal consequences, some sort of characteristic trace or formula having its same computational shape is stored.) The stored formula is accessible to various executive agencies and can be hauled out on cue, resulting in a new judgment or tokening bearing the same computational shape.

Notice that this state of affairs is an *occurrent* one, despite its also having dispositional features. The subject actually and occurrently stores the representation over a certain period of time. Even though no judging need be taking place and this actual storage is not an episode, it hardly merits the deprecatory label "tacit." Given that we have abandoned the older use of the term "occurrent belief" as meaning "judgment,"[2] it seems entirely proper to reintroduce it as applying to such cases. In this sense, for example, people have

---

2 This older usage can be found in Sellars (1969, p. 514), De Sousa (1971), and Foley (1978, p. 312). A variant terminology is that of Harman (1978), who uses "occurrent" to mean "conscious"; this seems misleading (see the concluding paragraph of this section of my chapter).

occurrent beliefs even when they are asleep and hosting no mental events: Sleeping people still have representations stored in long-term memory.[3]

Of course, there are still cases of what people ordinarily call "believing" that do not fit this new model of occurrent belief either. Indeed, my wife's beliefs about snow in Stockholm, and the like, do not fit it, because the relevant representations never have previously been tokened and surely do not inhabit her long-term memory or any other department of her internal bureaucracy. So we must still try to posit a contrasting notion of "tacit" belief. No drastic departure from our first attempt is required, however; we may still identify tacitly believing that P with being disposed to judge that P and to store the appropriate formula as a result.

Notice carefully that neither our original distinction between judging and being disposed to judge nor our new distinction between actual storage and being disposed to judge-and-store coincides with the difference between conscious and unconscious belief (cf. Armstrong [1973, pp. 7–9] and de Sousa [1971, p. 76]). A person need not be conscious in order to have an occurrent belief in our new sense of actual storage; for that matter, a person need not be conscious of every judgment he or she makes. The occurrent–tacit distinction applies within the class of unconscious beliefs.[4]

---

3 Thus, beliefs can be occurrent without being occurrences. It should be noted, though, that the existence of occurrent beliefs in our new sense is an empirical matter (and not just because the existence of sentient beings at all is an empirical matter); the representation-storage theory of cognition might turn out to be false, or, as Dennett (1981b) points out, the representations that human beings actually store might not correspond in any way to the beliefs attributed to subjects by common sense.

4 Unless there is such a thing as a *conscious but tacit* belief, which I doubt. It is an interesting question whether we ever introspect beliefs. On both phenomenological and theoretical grounds, I doubt that, too; what we introspect, in the way of cognitive items, are judgments, and we infer our knowledge of our beliefs from those. (But cf. Vickers [1969].) N.B., I do not mean to deny that there are unconscious mental occurrences.

Note that if there are tacit beliefs, there are presumably also tacit desires, intentions, and other propositional attitudes. Lynne Rudder Baker has pointed out to me that a good theory of *tacit intentions* would help resolve the problem bruited in Kripke (1982) regarding the difference between computing *plus* and computing "*quus*" (though personally I do not feel the force of that problem,

I wish we could leave the matter at that, but in fact we cannot, for there are counterexamples to the sufficiency of our new analysis of "tacit belief," showing it to be too liberal. Here are two:

1. *The opinionated people.* They are Peirceans, in that they abhor being agnostic on any subject, but not Peircean enough, in that in them the "irritation of doubt" triggers not inquiry but snap judgments. On many occasions, at least, when they entertain a proposition for the first time, they immediately affirm the proposition or deny it, depending on what else is going on in their global psychology at the time. (Let us take "global psychology" broadly here, to include any mental or neurophysiological condition that has psychological influence.) Thus, at a time *t* our subjects have countless dispositions to judge – determined by their global psychology – but we would not count these as antecedently existing beliefs, however tacit.

2. *The randomized opinionated people.* These are like the first opinionated people, except that whether they affirm or deny the proposition they newly entertain at *t* is determined by an internal coin-flipper whose physical constitution and overall occurrent state at *t* grounds counterfactuals regarding what judgment they would make concerning whatever proposition is next entertained.[5]

These examples show that not every disposition to judge, or even every disposition to judge-and-store, counts intuitively as a belief of any sort.[6] We need to find an additional necessary condition

since for the very reasons Kripke offers I doubt that human beings ever do literally compute *plus*).

5 Counterexample *2* is really a special case of *1*, since the coin-flipper is part of the randomized opinionated man's global psychology. These counterexamples work, more generally, against almost any simple dispositional account of belief, such as Ramsey's analysis in terms of dispositions to bet (our opinionated people may be betting people as well).

6 Bas van Fraassen has asked me (in conversation) why we should not allow that the opinionated men *are* tacit believers in virtue of their readiness (after all) to judge, to bet, and so on. But the opinionated men themselves would disavow any standing tacit beliefs and acknowledge (perhaps with pride) that they had made up their minds on the spot. ("Wasn't that a little bigoted of you?" – "Ah, stick it in your ear.") Other counterexamples are available as well: Foley (1978, p. 312n) points out that, being a good introspector, I am disposed to assent to the proposition "I am entertaining a proposition" whenever I entertain it, but surely I do not constantly tacitly believe it. Audi (1982) also suggests by implication that being disposed to judge is not necessary for tacit belief; intuitively, I

of believing tacitly that *P*, presumably some restriction on the kind
of categorical basis the relevant disposition to judge may have.[7]

III EXTRAPOLATOR-DEDUCERS

An obvious move is to posit what Dennett (1975) calls an "extrapolator-deducer," that is, a device that operates on occurrently
stored formulas or "core beliefs" and generates relatively obvious
consequences of those occurrent beliefs when the occasion arises.
Thus we might suggest that to believe tacitly that *P* is to be disposed
to judge that *P*, in virtue of the operation of one's extrapolator-
deducer in drawing inferences from preexisting core beliefs. This
specification of the disposition's categorical basis rules out our opinionated people. It also has the virtue of revealing how appeal to
tacit belief figures in the explanation of action: Public statements
are results of inner judgments, and judgments are (sometimes) man-
ifestations of dispositions to judge, produced by the activity of the
extrapolator-deducer that is the disposition's categorical basis. Public statements get made on newly bruited topics because their utterers have tacit beliefs – that is, because the appropriate judgments
are triggered by the utterers' extrapolator-deducers' operating on
core beliefs.

This account faces two problems, and both are serious.[8]

First, we must find some way of restricting our analysans still more
as regards the range of the extrapolator-deducer, for if we were to

> believe every instance of "*n* < 2," where *n* is replaced by any member of the
> series 1, 1 1/2, 1 3/4, 1 7/8, ..., but since some of the later members of that
> series can be expressed in no less than millions of numerals, it is unlikely that I
> would assent to them if queried. (I suppose one might reply to this by insisting
> that owing to the complexity of such expressions, I cannot really entertain them
> in the first place, and so they are not counterexamples to the claim that if I were
> to entertain them I would give my assent.)

7 My problem here is not unrelated to that raised by Levi and Morgenbesser (1964),
and again compare Audi (1982). I am grateful to D. M. Armstrong, Stephen
Stich, and Alvin Goldman for the protracted discussion and criticism that for
some reason were needed to make me see it at last.

8 A third is raised by Dennett (1975): that the extrapolator-deducer will have to
have tacit beliefs of its own and hence will require the services of a second
extrapolator-deducer, which will in turn, etc. But I am not sure that I see why
the first extrapolator-deducer need have tacit beliefs. Dennett alludes to Lewis
Carroll's problem of Achilles and the tortoise, but that problem in itself does not
afflict any extrapolator-deducer that is simply hard-wired to draw inferences of
certain standard forms.

count just anything potentially deducible by the device as being tacitly believed, then we would have to suppose that every normal person tacitly believes all the provable theorems of arithmetic, all tautologies, and all the other consequences of his set of core beliefs. But surely the pretheoretic concept of tacit belief does not stretch that far; not even tacit belief is closed under deduction. Intuitively, what we count as being tacitly believed at t is just those propositions that the extrapolator-deducer would infer *more or less immediately* if appropriately triggered at t.

The problem is to specify a type of "immediacy" that sustains this intuition. Temporal immediacy suggests itself; we might try to count a proposition as tacitly believed just in case the extrapolator-deducer would spit it out within, say, one second of being queried. But this interpretation would introduce an unwanted parameter into our analysans. The temporal immediacy of an inference is relative to the intelligence or quick-wittedness of the subject who makes the inference; David Lewis's extrapolator-deducer spits out a good many more propositions in one second than mine does. Yet just in virtue of that difference in deducing speed (let us drolly assume that Lewis and I are otherwise alike), we should not want to credit Lewis with holding tacit beliefs at t that I do not hold. What one believes, even tacitly, is not relative to one's intelligence.

A more natural and psychologistic interpretation of "immediacy" of inference would be a proof-theoretic one, couched in terms of the number of steps required for the derivation of a newly entertained proposition from core beliefs. A proposition would count as tacitly believed just in case the extrapolator-deducer would derive it in fewer than n steps. But the difficulty here is parallel and just as obvious: Length of derivation depends entirely (and pretty dramatically) on one's choice of a system of rules of inference; formula A may be S_1-derivable in two steps but S_2-derivable in no fewer than sixteen. Yet as before, what one believes, even tacitly, is not relative to a choice of axiomatizations. Nor will it help to pursue the proof-theoretic strategy by specifying the logical system *that the subject* (or the subject's brain) *actually uses*, for we do not and perhaps cannot ever know which system that is in fact; on the latter analysis, we would never know what any subject tacitly believed.[9]

9 Nor is ease of linear derivation all that is relevant to our judgments of tacit belief. Consider Powers's (1978) well-known trick question: "Is there a four-letter English word ending in the letters EE, ENN, WHY?" (The students search the

No other interpretation of "immediacy" occurs to me; so I shall give up for now and conclude this section by raising a closely related general point: Immediacy, on any analysis, is going to be a matter of degree, like speed and length of derivation, and the degree of immediacy required by a given extrapolator-deducer theory of tacit belief will be chosen just in virtue of its correspondence to our intuitive ascriptions of tacit belief. That correspondence aside, however, the choice of such a cutoff point seems ontologically arbitrary. A subject whose judgment that P is produced with sufficient immediacy (in whatever sense) would count as antecedently having held the tacit belief that P, whereas a subject whose judgment that P is produced only slightly less immediately by an otherwise similar process would not, but would be described by the extrapolator-deducer theorist as having newly come to believe that P on the basis of having deduced it on the spot. But it seems wrong to suppose that what distinguishes a genuine (though tacit) believer at t from a nonbeliever at t is nothing but a slight variation in the value of a single magnitude – at least of any magnitude of the sort likely to figure in a suggestion made by the extrapolator-deducer theorist, so long as we are supposing, for the sake of discussion, that tacit belief is a real, albeit dispositional, state of a subject and has causal powers. Of course, we may later want to question the latter assumption.

An interesting variation on the extrapolator-deducer strategy is proposed by Field (1978), one that I think does eschew treating tacit belief as a real state of subjects. Though he cites Dennett (1975), Field does not himself explicitly invoke a deducing *device*; rather, he sees tacit beliefs as being simply the "obvious consequences" of explicitly represented beliefs, letting this phrase stand on its own and evidently leaving ascribers of tacit belief to judge for themselves which consequences are "obvious." (Field notes that the vagueness of the notion of obviousness explains the vagueness of some of our intuitions about ascriptions of tacit belief.) Now again, it seems to me that if this proposal is right, then no tacit belief is a genuinely

alphabet for a few moments and reply, "No" or "I don't think so.") "Is 'deny' a four-letter English word ending in EE, ENN, WHY?" – "Oh, sure." It seems that the students tacitly believed that "deny" is a four-letter, etc., but did not even tacitly believe that *there is* a four-letter, etc., even though the latter follows, in one forehead-smackingly simple step of existential generalization, from the former. (For brief discussions of Powers's example, see Castañeda [1980] and Boër and Lycan [1986a].)

inner behavior-causal state of a subject, and in particular, a subject's tacit beliefs will be in the eye of the beholder in that they will depend on what the beholder finds obvious. We should like to say that when Smedley first hears the question "Was Chillicothe, Ohio, vaporized by a 75-megaton hydrogen bomb in August of 1979?" and answers "No," this is *because* he has tacitly believed all along that no such tragedy occurred. If we are to continue in this vein, we cannot just observe that the answer "No" is an obvious consequence of other things Smedley believes, for that alone would be no explanation, until supplemented by an account of Smedley's ability to *compute* obvious consequences of his explicit beliefs, which would bring us back to extrapolator-deducers again. On Field's proposal, for me to say of Smedley that he tacitly believes that no hydrogen bomb vaporized Chillicothe is for me to say no more than that Smedley has some explicit belief or other of which "No hydrogen bomb vaporized Chillicothe" is *by my lights* an obvious consequence; I specify no inner state of Smedley. Further, the indexicality of the phrase "by my lights" ensures that ascriptions of tacit belief will be true only relative to ascribers, since what is obvious to you may not be obvious to me. (Note that intelligence and quick-wittedness are not the only variables here. Even among people of generally equal deductive ability, there are disparities in what they find obvious: vel-Introduction, for example.) We might strive for some more objective, non–person-relative notion of obviousness, but that would lead us back toward our proof-theoretic interpretation again. Or we might understand "obvious" as meaning obvious *to the subject* rather than to the ascriber, but that would lead us back to the sad gap in quick-wittedness between David Lewis and me.

For these reasons I do not think Field's option will help us, though we should keep it in mind as a *deflationary* analysis of tacit belief, should we come to desire one. More on this will follow.

The second major difficulty facing the extrapolator-deducer strategy, which applies to Field's analysis as well, is this: If tacit beliefs are the counterfactual output of an extrapolator-deducer, what is the deducer's input? When Smedley instantly replies "No" to our question about the nuclear obliteration of Chillicothe, we are to suppose this to be a result of the deducer's generating a judgment to that effect by inference from some set of explicitly represented premises – explicitly represented, that is, prior to Smedley's being asked. But it is hard to think of any specific premises that the average person *would carry around in his or her head* that entail Chillicothe's nonobliteration. "Chillicothe exists today," or perhaps "A relative of mine was living in Chillicothe in 1980" might serve, but these do not themselves entail that Chillicothe was not vaporized in 1979; we need the further premise that no one rebuilt Chillicothe between August 1979 and January 1980, which though reasonable, is surely not explicitly stored. "No one has ever detonated a hydrogen bomb in the eastern half of the United States" is a possibility, I suppose, but I doubt that many people have ever explicitly represented that to themselves either. It is easy to come up with obvious truths that everyone (seemingly) believes and that entail that no hydrogen bomb vaporized Chillicothe, but (again) there is no evidence that ordinary people have ever represented any of them explicitly.[10]

I think it is this difficulty that makes some people skeptical about representationalism generally, or at least about the linear-deduction or theorem-proving model of information accessing that comes naturally to formal logicians but has been seen for at least a decade to be a nonstarter qua realistic recipe for knowledge representation by machines. In light of what is sometimes called the "frame problem,"[11] one is tempted to junk the notion of explicit storage tout court and to move toward a more thoroughly dispositional or holistic account of belief. But (1) as I said in Chapter 1, I think there are fairly compelling reasons why we cannot throw away "core beliefs" entirely, and (2) toward *what* more "thoroughly dispositional" account could we move? If we are not behaviorists, our complete analysis of belief must specify some fairly characteristic etiology for behavior that is distinctive of belief or face the usual

---

10 Several people have pointed out to me that the extrapolator might perform inductions as well as deductions. That would make the problem of the premises easier in principle, but I am still hard put to think of premises, even for an induction-regarding Chillicothe, *that are stored explicitly*. It is easy to reconstruct Smedley's reasoning in any of several ways, but all the ways that occur to me appeal to unrepresented premises.

11 See, e.g., Moore and Newell (1974), Minsky (1975), Winograd (1975, 1976), Winograd and Bobrow (1977), Lehnert (1979), Pylyshyn (1979), Dreyfus (1979), Fahlman (1979), and Dennett (1983). N.B., I am not suggesting that the frame problem is specific to tacit belief; it would arise even for a suitable large mass of explicitly stored belief.

counterexamples and charges of circularity and Turing-Test-ism (cf. Block [1981]).

In effect, the extrapolator-deducer strategy has run smack into the frame problem itself. To solve the problem, one must delimit some initial body of preset context-free background information and some ingenious mode of organization to be imposed on it, and then construct both a set of procedures for revising the background information under various conditions and a set of search and accessing processes, in such a way as to maximize the facility and accuracy of one's machine in performing relatively novel tasks (or, more properly, to strike the optimal balance of facility against accuracy). Artificial Intelligence researchers (notably Minsky [1975], Schank and Abelson [1977]) have abandoned the list-of-stored-premises-plus-set-of-deductive-inference-rules model in favor of various nonlinear modes of storage and styles of search involving "frames," "plans," templates, schemata, or the like, and various heuristics that operate on them; so, too, we may want for psychological purposes to replace our linear extrapolator-deducer with some other kind of extrapolator. If not frames, in Minsky's sense, perhaps we store stereotypes or even fuzzy global images of some sort. Smedley may extrapolate his newly explicit belief about Chillicothe not by deducing it stepwise from any set of premises but by reading it off an image of an undisturbed Middle America, green with lawn and white with picket fence, populated by pleasant, ordinary-looking (or, more likely, faceless) people going contentedly about their daily business. (There is plenty of psychological evidence for the claim that we think in stereotypes of some sort, typically inaccurate ones; see, e.g., Rosch [1977] and Nisbett and Ross [1980].) Thus, we might be able to save the extrapolator idea without running into our second difficulty, at least. On the other hand (cf. Chap. 1, Section V), some argument would have to be provided to show that Smedley's Reaganesque image did not itself constitute or contain a sentential representation – say, of the that-Middle-America-is-undisturbed kind – or something of that nature. There is such a thing as ideogrammatic writing, after all; some iconic representations are verbal as well.

Pending a breathtaking solution to the frame problem, however, I am pessimistic about the extrapolator strategy for the analysis of tacit belief. Alternative realistic accounts do not leap vibrantly to mind. But let us have one more try.

64

In effect, our task is to explain why our opinionated people do not have tacit beliefs prior to making those snap judgments, given that all along they were *disposed* to make those judgments. What, intuitively, is wrong with the opinionated people? One salient feature that they share is that they are not rational: Snap judgments are not considered or reasonable judgments, and as seekers of reliable informants you and I would put no stock in the opinionated people's opinions. Perhaps this is why we do not perceive their judgments as manifesting antecedently held tacit belief.

We must be careful here. That a judgment is irrational or unreasonable does not (alas) entail that it is not a genuine belief-manifestation. People say stupid things usually because they believe stupid things. So it is not the irrationality, in the normative sense, of the opinionated people's judgment that shows them not to be true tacit believers. It is more that their judgments are not based on reasons at all, either good reasons or bad reasons. Evidence plays no role in their formation. So perhaps we can define belief as: the disposition to judge *on the basis of reasons (good or bad)*.

This would require an analysis, in turn, of the notion of "basing." Such analysis has been provided most notably by Swain (1981a, 1981b) and Tolliver (1980); see also Harman (1970), Armstrong (1973, Chap. 6), Lehrer (1974), and Pappas (1981a). I cannot review the details here, but it is generally agreed that the notion of basing is a counterfactual or causal one: A belief B is based on a reason R if the subject would not have held B but for having R, or if R figures appropriately in the causal ancestry of the subject's holding B, or some complex elaboration of one or both of these.

Notice that in order to understand such definitions we must have an antecedent understanding of what sorts of things "reasons" are; otherwise the analysans may be far too easily satisfied. Paradigmatically, reasons are other beliefs, and the causal ancestry in question is a process of inference, but Swain (1981b, Chap. 3) argues compellingly for a broader notion of "reason-states" that includes perceptual states, memory states, inner states such as pain that kick off introspectings, and so forth. We must simply agree on a list of such things – the *kinds* of things that can be reasons – before we ask and answer the question of what the basing relations consist in. So let us fall in with Swain's idea and accept his sort of list.

65

Having done so, let us now plug this notion of "basing" back into our newly proposed definition of belief. If we take *inference from a prior belief* as our paradigm of what it is for something to be based on a reason, we run immediately into trouble: If to believe is to be disposed to judge on the basis of reasons, and if the paradigm of "judging on the basis of reasons" is inferring from prior belief, then our account collapses back into the extrapolator theory and is subject to the same objections (the immediacy-specifying problem and the difficulty of finding premises). And it seems to me that similar objections could be raised for the sorts of reason-states I have mentioned: If a subject, appropriately stimulated, makes a judgment that is based on a perceptual state, on a memory state, or (through introspection) on a mental state of any other sort, how "immediate" must the basing mechanism be if we are to count the resulting judgment as manifesting a prior tacit belief? And what, again, are the candidate reason-states for some of our recondite cases? Some plausible examples do come to mind, as in the case of my present belief that my office door is open behind me. I did just judge that my door is open, owing to my having recently and accessibly stored that perceptual information, and that makes it natural to say that since entering my office I have "tacitly believed" the door to be open, even though there may have been no explicit representation to that effect actually stored anywhere within me. (What is stored is just a perceptual memory trace, the *reason* for my subsequent judgment.)

In addition, there are more counterexamples to the sufficiency of our present analysans:

3. The rationalizing opinionated people. It seems there could be opinionated people in our earlier sense who not only jump to conclusions on being queried but manage to do so on the basis of simultaneously trumped-up reasons.

One might try to block this by requiring that the reasons themselves have been occurrently or tacitly stored all along, but such a condition either (respectively) collapses the present account into the extrapolator theory again or launches a regress of tacit beliefs that seems to me vicious.

4. The excited raconteur. He is regaling his dinner companions with a voluble account of some startling incident, waving his arms and talking much too loudly. If he were simply to entertain the proposition that he was talking too loudly, he would instantly

realize (and judge) that it is true. But not having entertained that proposition, he does not already know or believe it in any sense. (I owe this case to Audi [1982].)

No other proposals, or at least no very plausible ones, occur to me; so I think it is time that we considered giving up on a realistic notion of tacit belief. That leaves us with two options: to give up on tacit belief, period, and maintain, contrary to common sense, that there is no such thing,[12] or to adopt some instrumentalistic or otherwise deflationary account of the truth of ascriptions of tacit belief. Which is preferable?

V INSTRUMENTALISM VERSUS ELIMINATION

There is a good deal to be said in favor of going instrumentalist. Other things being equal, we prefer not to trample common sense if a plausible instrumentalist interpretation of tacit-belief ascription can be found. And contenders are available: Field's option, as discussed in Section III, for one, and, for another, Dennett's theory (1971, 1981a, 1981b, 1981c), according to which (crudely summarized) a creature believes that P just in case the creature *ought* to believe that P, given the way the creature is situated in its environment, and one can achieve predictive success by attributing that belief accordingly.[13] (The apparent circularity here is to be removed, Dennett says, by specifying the interpretative strategy we are to use in making our attributions and the system of epistemic norms that it ineliminably involves (1981b, p. 59; cf. 1981c, pp. 57–60].) Of the two, I incline toward Dennett's proposal, since it shows some promise of avoiding the relativity incurred by Field, as re-

---

12 D. M. Armstrong has advocated this option in conversation. It has made its way into print just once that I know of: "It is . . . clearly necessary that any proposition which someone is to believe should be, at least at some time and in some guise, present to his consciousness: it must, as the jargon had it, be entertained" (Mayo [1967, p. 147]).

13 E.g., any creature ought to form correct perceptual beliefs concerning the objects immediately confronting it, and ought to believe all the logical consequences of those beliefs, and ought to draw all the inductive inferences warranted probabilistically by them, and so on. Insofar as real organisms fall short of this ideal of rationality, they fall short of being true believers, according to Dennett. The reason that belief-ascription works as well as it does, and the reason that organisms live up to the norms of rationality as well as they do and hence count to some degree as believers, is that they are the products of *good design* on Mother Nature's part, as a result of natural selection.

marked on earlier; even if common sense really treats tacit belief instrumentalistically, I do not see that it allows for the particular kind of relativity induced by Field's notion of obviousness.

A second reason for preferring instrumentalism to elimination is that it is still officially an open question whether there are any occurrent beliefs in the sense carved out in Section I.[14] If so, and if (we suppose) there simply are no tacit beliefs, then it is a fortiori an open question whether or not there are any beliefs at all – whether anyone has ever in fact believed anything – and this openness is an even more crass affront to common sense than is the elimination of tacit belief in and of itself. Nor is common sense all that is at stake. It seems to me that anything that is *judged* is believed, even though beliefs differ in categorial status from judgments – and it would take a lot to convince me that no one has ever judged.[15]

Finally, instrumentalism leaves open the possibility of an explanatory role for beliefs to play. As I noted in the preceding section, we think that people make the judgments they do in many cases because hitherto tacit beliefs have been brought to their minds. Moreover, ascriptions of tacit belief warrant behavioral predictions just as securely as do ascriptions of occurrent belief: If you ask Mary whether she is 18 feet tall, you will receive (in addition to a very peculiar look) a clear, crisp "No" in reply.[16]

---

14 Harman (1978) emphasizes this and waxes pessimistic. Dennett (1975, 1981b) also expresses the gravest doubts and makes (1981b, p. 49) the worthwhile point that even if there is explicit representation in the human brain, "there is no reason to suppose the core *elements*, the concrete, salient, separately stored representation-tokens (and there must be some such elements in any complex information processing system), will explicitly represent (or *be*) a subset of our *beliefs* at all. That is, if you were to sit down and write out a list of a thousand or so of your paradigmatic beliefs, *all* of them could turn out to be virtual, only implicitly stored or represented, and what was explicitly stored would be information (e.g. about memory addresses, procedures for problem-solving, or recognition, etc.) that was entirely unfamiliar." However, as against this, it would be very surprising if judgments, inner tokenings, were *never* the results of accessing stored representations having the same semantical features.

15 Perhaps there is a notion intermediate between judgment and occurrent belief, in my storage-in-long-term-memory sense, that would serve. For example, let a "superoccurrent" belief be the holding of a judgment in short-term memory. Being in a state of belief might be like sitting and hearing the reverberation of your judgment just before it fades from the specious present. If something like this can be made plausible in the face of (e.g.) Wittgensteinian criticism, then I would be happy to eliminate the tacit beliefs.

16 These points have been emphasized to me by Robert Matthews, Bas van Fraassen, and Mike Meyer.

It should be noted that the actual explanatory role of tacit belief is not so clear as the foregoing remarks suggest, particularly if we have self-consciously eschewed a realistic treatment of such beliefs. The proximate cause of a judgment is either the accessing of an occurrent belief (in the actual-storage sense) or the searching of some other kind of information-store, perhaps unknown to common sense, at the instigation of the relevant stimulus. If any such type of storage were taken as the categorical basis of a dispositional tacit belief, realistically understood, then it would be natural to cite such a tacit belief as a cause of the judgment, but we are *not* now understanding tacit belief realistically. If we understand our ascriptions of tacit beliefs, rather, as just expressing subjective measures of obviousness, à la Field, or our normative opinions in regard to rationality, à la Dennett, they do not seem to be causal hypotheses at all. Indeed, the idea that tacit beliefs figure in the "executive order of nature" is an obstacle to instrumentalism, not an advantage that instrumentalism has over elimination. It pushes, rather, against both, back in the direction of a realistic account, if only a plausible one could be found.

One might cite tacit beliefs as causes of nonverbal behavior, bypassing occurrent belief and judgment entirely. For example, it is not unnatural to suggest that among the causes of my having sat down in this chair was my tacit belief that it would hold me. Not unnatural, perhaps, but not obvious either, particularly (again) on an instrumentalistic understanding of tacit belief. The underlying intuition seems to be that I would not have sat down if I had not believed that the chair would hold me. But the antecedent of this counterfactual is ambiguous; it can be read in either of two ways: "If I had not held the (tacit) belief that the chair would hold me" and "If I had held the belief that the chair would not hold me." On the former reading, the counterfactual seems to me no more obvious than the causal thesis itself, whereas on the latter reading, it simply does not support the causal thesis at all. As before, the causal thesis pushes toward realism rather than toward instrumentalism, as against elimination, and in the case of nonverbal as opposed to verbal behavior it is not so obvious that common sense ascribes a causal role to tacit belief in any case.

But it may still be true that tacit beliefs play an explanatory role, since not all explanation is causal explanation. Sometimes we explain (albeit shallowly) by merely putting the explanandum in context, by subsuming it under a particularly illuminating generalization or by classifying it in an unforeseen way. (Humeans and positivists tend to think that all explanation is of this nature.) Sometimes to explain is to rationalize or to vindicate, to show that the explanandum is a good thing in some sense. If Dennett's instrumentalism is a correct account of belief-ascription, then explanation of behavior by reference to beliefs and desires is of this rationalizing sort. Thus, the instrumentalist can at least explain away the intuition that beliefs are causes and still has the advantage over the eliminativist of preserving their weaker explanatory role.[17]

A few sources of dissatisfaction remain. First, there is as yet no *well–worked-out* and successfully defended instrumentalist contender in the field; Dennett's view in particular, has been criticized vigorously and with effect (Stich [1981], Fodor [1981b], Richardson [1981], and Bechtel [1982]). Second, the bifurcation of belief into kinds, one treated realistically and the other instrumentalistically, is regrettable. The occurrent–tacit distinction is drawn by common sense, to be sure, but if, as in Chapter 1, we take our Sellarsian representationalist theory of occurrent belief seriously, not just as metaphysics but as a semantical theory of belief-sentences (cf. also Lycan [1984a], we shall probably have to concede that the belief predicate is at best paronymous as between occurrent- and tacit-belief ascriptions. For surely neither the presumably functional relation that an occurrent believer bears to his or her stored representation nor the derived relation that the believer bears to the complement of our belief-sentence is the same relation as that which a tacit believer (instrumentalistically construed) bears to the latter, if any.[18] This lexical ambiguity is unpalatable.

17 See, however, Paul Churchland's (1970) criticism of William Dray's (1963) version of this view. Churchland points out, in particular, that attitude ascriptions figure as the antecedents of subjunctive conditionals concerning behavior, which is hard to explain on the present version of instrumentalism.
18 What relation this is taken to be depends on the specific version of instrumentalism at hand. Most versions seem to me to make a mystery of the semantics of belief-sentences and to make it puzzling why belief-sentence complements are, in Sellars's phrase, "sentences used in a special way." In the paper on which Chapter 1 is based, I accused Dennett, in particular, of this fault, but falsely, for I now see the germ of a Dennettian explanation of Sellars's datum: Beliefs are identified by sentential complements because it is sentences over which the epistemic norms of logic and probability theory are defined, and it is these normative sciences that (according to Dennett) make beliefs beliefs. Sentential complements mark points in epistemic-normative space.

Third, it seems to me that even tacit belief requires some real executive goings-on in nature. Conceptual preparation, for one; just as a subject cannot occurrently believe that the X is F without having the concepts of X-hood and F-ness, it seems wrong to ascribe tacit belief to such a person either. My wife, Mary, could not even tacitly believe that our daughter's Sunday dress has not been zipprodted if she did not know what zipprodting is.[19] An instrumentalist might get around this point by providing an instrumentalist account of concept possession – concepts are only abilities, after all. But it seems that the *intentionality* of tacit beliefs also requires the usual apparatus of causal chains. If no inner state of Mary is causally grounded in the city of Stockholm, she cannot correctly be said to have even a tacit belief *about* Stockholm. Any instrumentalist theory will have to take account of this, and any theory that does will be beginning, at least, to edge toward realism.[20] (Here again, there is no comfort for the eliminativist unless realism has been utterly written off.)

The situation is unsatisfactory. Realism, instrumentalism, and eliminativism concerning tacit belief are all unpromising, yet they seem to be the only choices. Only the devising of a new realist analysis or the working out of an instrumentalist line will settle the matter. Until then, Mary will have to keep her thoughts about my tie freshly occurrent, if she wants me to do anything about them. I will never give in, anyway.[21]

19 No, sorry, my lips are sealed.
20 Dennett can probably handle this difficulty by invoking (1) the causal ancestries of the "core elements" he mentions in the passage quoted in note 14 and (2) the environmental source of the perceptual beliefs that initiate for him the whole business of belief-ascription.
21 I must thank, in addition to the friends and colleagues mentioned in preceding footnotes, Pat Manfredi, Lisa Kearns, and Mike Meyer for their very helpful discussion of this chapter.

4

Representation and the semantics of belief-ascription

This chapter digresses a bit. I have been claiming that to think is to harbor an internal representation. A representation is a real, physical, psychological entity, and when we ascribe thoughts and beliefs, what we are ultimately talking about is real, physical, psychological entities, even if we are not aware that that is what we are doing. If this is right, we should expect representationalism to illuminate semantical puzzles about belief-ascription, as well as about the ontological nature of belief itself – and so it does, as I prophesied in Chapter 1 and as I shall briefly exhibit here. (For fuller details, see my "Paradox of Naming" [1985].) As I said, I count this a significant virtue of the representational account.

I   KRIPKE'S PUZZLE

For example: Saul Kripke (1979) raises the following problem (for brevity I put it here in terms of Kripke's standard "Cicero"/"Tully" case, instead of setting out the more elaborate "Londres"/"London" case that Kripke himself[1] emphasizes): Suppose Jones sincerely says, "Cicero was bald and Tully was not," unaware that Cicero and Tully are one and the same person. It is plausible to think that (1) any competent speaker of English who sincerely says, "Cicero was bald and Tully was not" believes (the proposition) *that* Cicero was bald and Tully was not. But there is considerable reason to think that proper names are rigid and connotationless designators (Kripke, 1972),[2] and if names are rigid and connotationless, then

---

1 Kripke contends that his own puzzle is not the usual sort of Fregean puzzle about substitution of coreferring singular terms but is deeper and more general. Moreover Devitt (1984) has argued that my version of representationalism cannot handle Kripke's more advanced puzzle cases. I think both these claims are false and am preparing a paper to that effect.

2 The evidence comes largely from Kripke (1971, 1972), who has defended the opposing Millian tradition by pointing out that if names abbreviated definite descriptions or otherwise expressed contingent properties of their referents, (1)

(2) the sentence Jones has uttered is false in any possible world, and to believe what it expresses is to believe an explicitly contradictory proposition; yet (3) Jones, we may suppose, is fully rational and is not so confused as to accept any explicit contradictions; he is guilty of ignorance, but not of crass logical error. The puzzle is that theses *1*, *2*, and *3* comprise an inconsistent triad. Also, we are faced with a hard factual question: *Does Jones believe that Cicero was bald, or does he not?*

In some earlier works – chiefly "Knowing Who" and "Who, Me?" (Boër and Lycan [1975, 1980]) – I leaned toward denying thesis *3*, uncharitable toward the luckless Jones as that may seem, and toward answering Kripke's hard factual question by saying that Jones does believe that Cicero was bald *and* does believe that Cicero (= Tully) was not bald. But even if one grants that sometimes even fully rational people can believe contradictions when they are mistaken as to the references of the names they use, one still feels that there should be no *unequivocal* answer to Kripke's hard question. The question has a strong "yes and no" feel to it.

The representational account accommodates, and I think explains, this air of equivocality. I mentioned that the representationalist has a choice among several different individuative schemes by which to tell which tokens count as •[so-and-so]•s and which do not. But representationalists have always tended to presume that one such scheme is correct, or at least standard, to the exclusion of others. Now, suppose we abandon that presumption and hypothesize instead that *two* alternating schemes are in play: Sometimes we group our tokens into types, à la Sellars, according to the inferential roles they play within their authors' conceptual schemes – or, we might say in Fodor's terms, according to their *computational* roles. At other times we individuate them according to sameness of truth-condition, regardless of inferential or computational role. The context and the conversational point of one's belief-ascription

---

certain sentences would be tautologous or contradictory that are not, in fact, tautologous or contradictory; (2) certain names that denote distinct individuals would denote the same individual; (3) serious problems would flow from the then presumed *equivocity* of names; and (4) a name would denote different individuals in different possible worlds. Rather, Kripke maintains, a name denotes an individual quite independently of any contingent property the individual might have and hence denotes that same individual in any world in which it exists. Mill seems to have been right in contending that the semantical function of a name is simply to pick out its bearer, and it follows that names are rigid in the sense defined.

determine which of the two schemes is to be used in evaluating the ascription. Typically, we shall use the computational scheme when what concerns us is explanations and predictions of behavior, since it is a belief's computational role and not its truth-condition that determines its causal contribution. We shall use the truth-conditional scheme when we are more interested in truth-related aspects of belief, such as the believer's reliability as an informant or success rate in achieving his or her goals.

With our two-scheme hypothesis in mind, let us address Kripke's questions. First: Does Jones believe a contradiction? Let us grant that when Jones says, "Cicero was bald and Tully was not," he does so partly as a result of having inwardly affirmed a mental analogue of that sentence. Thus, Jones believes a •Cicero was bald and Tully was not•. The problem is that according to thesis 2, this amounts to believing a •Cicero was bald and Cicero was not•, because this thesis entails that the names "Cicero" and "Tully" have exactly the same semantical function; the two tokens displayed within the dot-quotes express exactly the same belief. Now, *is* Jones's mental analogue of "Cicero was bald and Tully was not" really a •Cicero was bald and Cicero was not•? That depends on which of our two individuative schemes we choose to employ. If we use the truth-conditional scheme, Jones's mental utterance does count as a •Cicero was bald and Cicero was not•. *In one sense*, then, Jones does believe a contradiction. But it is not a sense in which "believing a contradiction" inpugns one's rationality. For Jones has no way of deducing from his mental token anything that he could recognize as a contradiction; nothing that he carries with him in his head enables him to tell that his mental token of "Cicero" and his mental token of "Tully" represent the same person. Alternatively put, Jones has no *syntactic* way of detecting his semantical anomaly. The relevant contents of his head are analogous to an uninterpreted formal calculus, equipped with rules of natural deduction. In the absence of "$a = b$" as an axiom, it would be positively irrational to infer, by substitution of 'b' for 'a,' even if on some preferred interpretation that could be supplied by an external observer, that 'a' and 'b' are assigned the same referent.

And this brings us to the sense in which Jones does *not* believe a contradiction: the sense that results when we employ the computational rather than the truth-conditional scheme. According to the computational criterion, Jones's mental token of "Cicero was

74

bald and Tully was not" does not count as a •Cicero was bald and Cicero was not•, since the representations associated with the names "Cicero" and "Tully" play obviously distinct computational roles for Jones (and, accordingly, distinct causal roles in determining his behavior). From "Cicero was bald and Tully was not," for example, Jones would infer that Cicero had a property that Tully lacked, and would not infer "Tully was bald" or "Tully lacked hair." But from "Cicero was bald and Cicero was not," Jones would either start madly inferring every sentence he could think of, à la C. I. Lewis, or he would go into cognitive spasm of some sort. (Given a generous helping of downward causation, Jones's circuitry might turn black and give off smoke.) Thus, in this sense (according to this individuative scheme), Jones does *not* believe that Cicero was bald and Cicero was not, even though he believes that Cicero was bald and Tully was not. It is probably psychologically impossible to believe an explicit contradiction *computationally individuated*.

Thus, in this sense – on this individuative scheme – Jones does not believe that Cicero was bald and Cicero was not, even though he believes that Cicero was bald and Tully was not.

What about Kripke's hard question? Does Jones in fact believe that Cicero was bald? For the representationalist that means, Does Jones believe a •Cicero was bald•? Yes; Jones affirms a mental analogue of "Cicero was bald." But to the proponent of thesis 2, the latter judgment suggests that Jones also believes that Tully was bald, despite Jones's protests to the contrary. Does Jones in fact believe that Tully was bald? For the representationalist that means, Does Jones believe a •Tully was bald•? On the hypothesis that our two diverging individuation schemes are both on call, the answer is, quite properly, "Yes and no." On the truth-conditional scheme, Jones's inner analogue of "Cicero is bald" does count as a •Tully is bald•; that is the sense in which Jones does believe that Tully is bald. But on the Sellarsian scheme, Jones's inner token does not count as a •Tully was bald•; since it plays quite a different inferential role for him from the one that would be played by an inner analogue of "Tully was bald." Although the inner representation that Jones associates with the name "Cicero" and the one he associates with the name "Tully" are in fact representations of the same person, Jones puts them to different computational uses.

The representational account offers a resolution of Kripke's puzzle, then, by affording us the means of revealing a pragmatic ambiguity in belief-ascriptions – an ambiguity in the reference of the plural demonstrative underlying the complementizer "that," as determined in context – that predicts the felt "yes and no" quality of Kripke's questions. I have sketched this resolution crudely and hurriedly, because to make it precise and provide it with further motivation would require a long separate discussion (some of which I undertook in "The Paradox of Naming" [1985] and in Chapters 3 and 4 of *Knowing Who* (Boër and Lycan [1986]). Nonetheless, it seems to me as promising as any proposed solution I have heard.

II SEMANTICAL CONTENT

But in virtue of what would a brain episode or its parts be a *representation* of X or of *F*-ness or of anything else? How is it possible for purely physical events to have "aboutness" or intentionality? That depends on what we think it takes for *anything* to have aboutness, for anything to refer or be intentional, and on whether our answer to that question is extrapolable from paradigm cases in public language – say, to the more recondite case of brain activity. This is an old, old story, first told in modern times by Sellars and subsequently amplified and sophisticated by Hartry Field (1978), Jerry Fodor (1975, 1987), Robert Stalnaker (1984), and others. (See also Harman [1973] and Rosenberg [1974].) A lesson of the past fifteen years' work in the theory of reference is that what mediates linguistic aboutness is causality – causal chains of certain roughly specifiable types and/or reliable functional links consisting in the specific sensitivity of linguistic expressions to their referents, owing to conditioning and/or to teleological considerations.[3] However the details of these connections might go, the important points to note are (1) that the connections are *naturalistic* (they are real relations to be found in nature) and (2) that other physical items besides public linguistic tokens can bear them to objects: Brain events, in particular, can have the appropriate sorts of etiologies and can be conditioned responses showing specific sensitivity to particular objects and types of object. Thus, we have every reason to think, or at least to hope, that brain events can be intentional in almost the same way that bits of language are.

3 Cf. Wimsatt (1968), Dennett (1969), Harman (1973), Bennett (1976), Stalnaker (1980), Fodor (1987), and others.

So: To judge or "occurrently believe" that *P* is to bear what I shall still call the "belief" relation to an inner representation whose syntactic/semantic structure is analogous to that of the sentence that replaces "*P.*" (More on this analogousness will follow shortly.) The belief relation itself is a distinctive *functional* relation, consisting in the representation's playing a certain type of functional role – that is, doing a certain type of administrative job within the functional hierarchy that is the believer itself. Obviously the role that is characteristic of judgments, as opposed to desires, intentions, and so forth, has to do with storage, with mapping, and otherwise with serving as a guide to action.

Several authors have, I think, glanced off the distinction between our two individuative schemes without entirely realizing that that was what they were doing. Hartry Field, Jerry Fodor, David Lewis, Stephen Stich, and most recently John Perry have hinted at it.[4] But, interestingly, they have in effect taken sides (different sides) on which of the two schemes is correct, or at least on which is vital to the concept of belief and which negligible. Fodor and Lewis assume that beliefs are essentially causal entities invoked to explain behavior and that their semantical properties are by the way, whereas Stich and Perry insist that the truth-values of beliefs (and the reliability of informants) are what matter and that explaining behavior is not very important after all. Now, this seems to me a funny sort of thing to quarrel about. Sometimes we are interested in explaining and predicting behavior; at other times we are interested in truth and reliability. Which of these interests is objectively paramount seems to me an idle question. And if my Sellarsian semantics is right, our language affords us a pragmatic choice in belief-ascription that matches our pair of alternative interests nicely.

If it is our computational individuative scheme that pertains directly to the explanation of behavior, then this is the scheme that would officially be mobilized by cognitive psychologists, at least

4 These schemes are similar but distinct. For Sellars, linguistic roles (as marked by rules of assertibility, rules of inference, and the like) are essentially normative, whereas for Fodor computational roles are (I take it) more purely causal. My own preference is for a cautious fusion of the normative and the causal in the form of the teleological.

Incidentally, the two-scheme approach preserves Kripke's "disquotation" principle (1979), to the effect that *S* will sincerely and competently assert *P* only if *S* believes that *P*. For what that is worth; I have some independent doubts about the principle.

77

insofar as their official concern is the explanation of *individual* behavior. Thus the psychologists would forswear the semantical individuative scheme and would not characterize beliefs according to their semantical properties. (The *propositional* content of a belief – identifiable, let us say heuristically, with the set of worlds in which the belief is true – is irrelevant to the belief's psychological role; surprising, but obvious enough when you think about it.) Now, Stephen Stich has taken these facts to prove that the psychologists would no longer be talking about beliefs at all and in that sense would no longer be *cognitive* psychologists. I have tried to show that in view of the availability and the probity of the computational individuative scheme, Stich's conclusion does not follow; but it does leave us with the problem of saying how the psychologists *are* to talk. In the paper on which Chapter 1 is based, I suggested (n. 11) that cognitive scientists would have to describe beliefs using "some appropriately neutral syntactic code," by which I intended, adhering to our usual computer analogy, some kind of machine language. This is a perfectly tenable theoretical suggestion, so far as I can see, but considered as practical advice, it does not help much. For not even computer scientists or computer operators adhere to machine-code description in dealing with their machines from day to day; and we have no machine language for the brain, in any case.

A better suggestion would be simply to fix the parameters that effect the valuations for the subjects' inner representations. That is, allowing that the semantical values of the constituents of the representations are determined in part by causal, historical, and social antecedents outside their owners' heads, there still exists a valuation function, V, from contexts and representations to propositional objects, which both determines the representations' propositional objects given the relevant sets of intra- and extracalvarian factors and serves as our interpretative manual for the subjects' speech and behavior. V is complicated and subtle, but plainly we have at least an effective working grasp of V (however incomplete) as part of our linguistic competence; we are usually able to tell what other people are talking and thinking about. Now, given that our psychologists grasp V and are also fairly well in command of the contextual factors that are among V's arguments, they can simply describe their subjects' inner states modulo that set of factors, which set is part of their shared background information in any ordinary research context. (In just the same way, a computer operator describes his or her machine as just having "computed Robin Roberts's batting average" or whatever, not because reference to Robin Roberts occurs completely inside the skin of the machine, which it obviously does not, but because the operator is filling in contextual information about the etiology and social background of the relevant computational states of the machine.) The only caveat is that the psychologists must not forget that that is what they are doing and lapse into supposing that reference to Robin Roberts or to anything else is somehow determined by what is inside their subjects' heads. There is no harm so long as they and we remember that genuineness of reference makes no difference to the homunculi in the driver's seat.

All this presupposes that the psychologists have epistemic access of some sort, however indirect, to the subjects' representations, and that is highly problematic. But it was problematic anyway. I see no special difficulty, of the sort suggested by Stich's argument.[5]

Nonetheless, a question remains: Why should psychologists, or for that matter even philosophers, concern themselves with "wide," nonautonomous properties of beliefs? What theoretical benefit do these properties supply? In particular, of what use is the common-sense conception of *de re* belief (cf. Lycan [1987])?

III   THE USES OF BELIEF, "WIDELY" CONSTRUED

The actual content and, a fortiori, the *de re* status of a belief matter nothing to the believer's internal organization but are only historical, etiological properties. Mode of presentation is what matters to behavior; the worldly objects of the belief do not. In the case of indexical beliefs, sameness of behavior goes with sameness of inner indexical and its computational role, not with sameness of truth-condition. Moreover, as Dennett has noted (1982, pp. 86–7), the truth of a *de re* ascription affords no brute-behavioral predictions: Knowing that I believe *of* the hatchet murderer of my mother, wife, and daughter that I am now shaking hands with him, what can you predict that I shall do (even given trite, normal desires and emotions, and so forth)? Our question, then, is, Since neither *de re*

5 Field (1978, pp. 48, 51); Stich (1978a); Fodor (1980, p. 67); Lewis (1981, pp. 288–9); Perry (1982). Loar (1981, p. 117) makes a point very similar to that which I am pushing here.

nor any other notion of wide belief per se plays any role in the explanation of bodily motions, of what value is it to psychology?

A number of possible answers are suggested by the recent literature on methodological solipsism and the explanatory utility of semantical concepts. Some do not work. Here I shall offer four that I think do work, or will when suitably fleshed out. Each takes the predictable form of arguing that a purely solipsistic or "narrow" psychology would miss some useful generalizations about behavior or about something closely related.

Lest anyone think this odd – that a *complete* narrow psychology could miss important generalizations, even though it could predict the smallest nods and twitches (Are the generalizations upheld by something extraneous to the physical levers and pulleys? Are the predictions made by magic?) – let us recall that the same phenomenon is rife even in (for present purposes) noncontroversial sciences such as biology. Useful, important, and lawlike generalizations hold at higher levels of nature without being stable in terms of quarks and leptons before the heat-death of the universe, and the higher-level theories that capture these generalizations afford predictions that could not be made in "real time" even by a superhuman Laplacean intelligence, if it knew only the microphysical laws that govern the motions of quarks and leptons through the void. (A Laplacean demon would be frustrated and out of place in the macroscopic world in which we live.[6] So we should not be surprised if the same thing holds of psychology that holds of biology, automotive engineering, computer science, and economics.) On to the answers:[7]

1. Without question, nonsolipsistic mental concepts are expendable in the explanation of behavior described as brute physical motion. But most of the behavior we want explained is not described in terms of brute physical motion (and if it were so described, our desire to explain it would vanish). Zenon Pylyshyn (1980) has noted[8] that much of it is described rather in semantical or, at least, intentional terms, as in "said that *P*," "tried to do *A*," "reached for the *X*." In order to explain behavior under these descriptions,

---

6 For graphic illustrations of the demon's plight, see Dennett (1981c) and Sober (1984, Chap. 4).

7 For related arguments, see also Fodor (1986).

8 I too have stressed the point, though for a quite different reason, in "Form, Function, and Feel" (1981a, pp. 44–5).

we have to "carry the intentional interpretation inward" and attribute contentful states to the subject; a person would not say that
P if the person did not believe that P (unless he or she had inter-
vening desires), nor would the person try to do A if he or she did
not want to do A.[9]

Even so, one might say, as Stich (1983) does, that even if ordinary
people have need of attributing content, reference, and truth-value
to the inner states of others, it does not follow that psychologists
also have that need, where "psychologist" is spelled with a capital
ψ. Psychologists in Stich's sense may have refined and gerryman-
dered their data base, moving it entirely away from the taxonomy
that common sense and ordinary language impose on behavior.
Indeed, since the language of brute physical motion is far less theory-laden than is everyday action-language, that is methodologically a good thing. On the other hand, it is not in fact, or not
commonly, done. I know of no experiments actually performed
on human beings in psychology laboratories that have restricted
themselves to the explanation of brute physical motion couched in
syntactic machine language. If we like, we can make it true by
stipulation that *de re* belief is useless to the Psychologist, but only
by also making it true that there have been very few actual Psychologists in the real world to date.

In appealing to behavior intentionally described rather than brute-
physically described, I have begged the question against the fiercest
sort of methodological solipsist, who is skeptical about *the whole
intentional/semantical package deal* and about intentional description
of anything whatever. Such a skeptic would never grant that bits
of behavior intentionally described could stand as data to be taken
for granted by philosophers, even if they are taken for granted (and
unavoidably so) by ordinary people. The intentional description of
behavior is laden with precisely the suspect folk psychology that
the skeptic finds (so far) groundless. Thus, argument *1* has no force
at all.

This reply raises a puzzle. That intentional description is folk-

9 Psychological behaviorists used to make their view plausible by restricting their
experimental subjects' environments in such a way that a desire, purpose, or
intention could be manifested in only one brute-physically described way (such
as by pressing a bar), thus masking the intentionality of action. It seems to me
that Stich (1983) is indulging in a similar ploy when he relies on his paradigm of
deductive reason in Chapter 8 and when he votes for a retaxonomizing of behavior.

81

theoretical explanation of behavior is a commonplace of current philosphy of mind. As we have seen, however, what intentional description explains is behavior intentionally rather than brute-physically described, and so the skeptic concludes that its claim to fame is fraudulent, since the intentional description of behavior is as theoretical as is propositional-attitude ascription itself, and in the same way. Yet this is not quite right, for as Sellars originally saw, public (particularly linguistic) behavior still precedes intentional psychology in the order of explanation; the notion of public speech is prior to that of private speech or thought and is only later explained by it. In real life, public speech episodes serve as data, in their semantical *rather than* their brute-behavioral guises; people learn semantical descriptions of verbal episodes long before they learn brute-behavioral descriptions, if they *ever* learn brute-behavioral descriptions of oral speech. The point is parallel to one that is commonly urged against sense-datum theories in epistemology, the argument that sense-datum vocabulary is arcane and highly sophisticated in comparison to ordinary talk of public middle-sized objects, and indeed derivative from it. I do not make the corresponding derivativeness claim for the case of brute-behavioral description, but it does seem that speech episodes and other behavior action-theoretically described count as *data* in any ordinary sense of "data" and in at least one excellent technical epistemological sense,[10] despite the fact that in some way or other they presuppose the availability of propositional-attitude explanations. The exact structure of the cycle or circularity here is unclear to me, but I am loath to think it vicious. The matter needs much more investigation. Fortunately there are other reasons why the semantical properties of beliefs are not expendable.

2. Learning and informing seem to require semantics. Chantal says to me, "Il pleut," a sentence I know to be true in her language if and only if it is raining. My best explanation of her saying this is that she believes it is raining and wants me to believe that too. From the additional premises that she is unlikely to be mistaken about the weather (she is looking out the window as she speaks) and that she is unlikely to want to deceive me, I infer that it is raining, and thereby learn that it is.[11] I could not have made this

10 I have in mind a pragmatist rather than a positivist notion of a datum. I shall formulate and defend this notion in Chapter 8.
11 Note that someone who did not know the truth-condition of Chantal's utterance

inference without relying on the lemma that Chantal's belief is *true*. And in general, if the beliefs people express in speech had no common referents out in the world, we would be forever doomed to talk past each other.

Here too it may be urged that *learning* and *informing* are intentional acts, indeed most naturally defined precisely in terms of *beliefs* "widely" construed: so the argument is almost explicitly circular. But subjects' ability to use other subjects as authorities, however described, is a highly distinctive and robust phenomenon, an appearance that surely must be saved somehow, even if one eschews semantical description. The question then becomes, is there an adequate solipsist account of this phenomenon, that makes no appeal to semantical properties of subjects' inner states? Since (as we have seen) solipsist explanations of behavior explain only *brute* behavior, and since instances of what we would ordinarily call learning from authority per se have nothing brute-behavioral in common, it is hard to think of any solipsist explanation that has any chance of generalizing across all cases of learning from authority. Such cases seem to form a natural kind in psychology, but intentional characterization also seems needed to frame the generalizations whose nexus constitute this kind.

3. As Putnam (1978) and Boyd (1981, 1985) have maintained, the truth of beliefs is needed to explain why subjects are so successful in achieving their goals: They are generally successful because their beliefs are usually true and so guide them reliably in action. Note that truth is not needed to explain *any one* instance of success; any one instance could as well be explained by a narrow, solipsistic functional diagram put together with facts about the subject's immediate environment.[12] But such divide-and-conquer explanations do not generalize across an open-ended history of successful actions. (I owe this point to Kim Sterelny [1983].) Moreover, we want to

would not gain this information intuitively because he or she would not know what the utterance meant. This sort of case has been emphasized by Ernest LePore and Barry Loewer (1981; see also LePore [1982, 1983] and Loewer [1982]). Sterelny (1983), however, has observed that their account does not readily extrapolate to propositional attitudes other than belief; hope, gladness, and fear do not afford inference by authority in LePore and Loewer's way, even though they are expressed by utterances of the appropriate sorts. Their semantic contents and other "wide" properties presumably derive (by way of an explanatory network) from those of beliefs.

12 See Devitt (1984, Sec. 6.7). Stich (1983, p. 168) also exploits the strategy in question against an anticipated objection to methodological solipsism.

generalize over *groups* of people as well. Groups are successful in part because of their propensities for true beliefs and in part because of their intercommunicative abilities (cf. answer *2* and my *Logical Form in Natural Language* [Lycan (1984a) Chap. 10, Sec. 1]), for which semantical notions are also needed.

4. We do not know, and probably never will know, the "syntactic code" or uninterpreted machine language of any human brain. Thus, the assignment of referents (and consequently truth-values) to subjects' thoughts is needed as a way of indexing their internal states. Without cutting them open – and in my case, even after cutting him open – we know nothing of their insides; we can describe them only by reference to the outside. The same is true of computers: As I have said, we speak of some one computer as "computing Robin Roberts's batting average," even though internally the computer is running exactly in parallel with a physically identical machine next door whose operator quite correctly describes it as "computing the GNP of Pitcairn," because we do not know what the computer is doing as described in machine code. And *both descriptions are correct*, even though nothing strictly inside either machine suffices for their correctness.

Obviously, none of these four arguments is fully convincing as it stands, but I think that together they point in the right direction. At any rate, I hope to have shed some light in this section on the uses of doxastic aboutness.

IV SELF-REGARDING BELIEF

As I have said, the representational account provides a very compelling solution to the ostensible problem of self-regarding beliefs. The problem (see Castañeda [1966, 1967]) is roughly this: A person, say Smith, apparently may believe that *he himself* is *F* without believing anything that we could express in nonreflexive terms. (E.g., Smith may believe that he himself is in danger without believing that *Smith* is in danger, since he may have amnesia or otherwise fail to be aware that he himself is Smith.) Likewise, he may believe that he himself is in danger without believing that *that* man he is ostending is in danger, even though the man he is ostending is himself reflected in a mirror. There seems to be no way for us to express the content of Smith's belief without resorting to what

84

Perry (1979) calls the "essential indexical" and hence no way to express it outside a belief operator at all:

(1) *He himself is in danger

is ungrammatical out of context. The problem is exacerbated when we state it in terms of *change* of belief: Suppose Smith believes that that man he is ostending is about to be pounced on by a crazed, homicidal puma, but unbeknownst to Smith the man he is ostending is again himself reflected in a mirror. He will proceed on his way, unconcerned about his own safety, until he turns and sees the puma in the flesh and thereby suddenly acquires the belief that *he himself* is about to be pounced on, which change of belief will prompt an immediate and striking change in behavior. Yet how is this apparent change in belief content to be expressed? Smith already believed that *that* man he was ostending was about to be pounced on; he already believed what Kaplan (1975) calls the "singular proposition" $<$Smith, $\hat{x}(x$ is about to be pounced on)$>$. So what he comes to believe upon seeing the puma in the flesh is not that proposition. Yet what he does come to believe, that he himself is about to be pounced on, has exactly the same truth-condition as that singular proposition and is true in just the same possible worlds. Thus, although we must agree that Smith has acquired a new belief, there is no clear sense in which the new belief differs in content from what Smith believed all along.

Perry (1979) argues that our pretheoretic notion of belief "content" is confused, and he proposes to split that notion into two, distinguishing Smith's "belief *object*," or proposition believed, from his "belief *state*," which is what is going on in Smith's head. It is the former that determines the truth-value of Smith's belief, the latter that causally determines Smith's behavior. In this case Smith's belief object remains the same throughout the story, but his belief state changes; we might say, he believed the proposition $<$Smith, $\hat{x}(x$ is about to be pounced on)$>$ all along but suddenly came to believe it first-personishly as well as third-personishly.[13] I find this

13 This bifurcation of the notion of a belief's "content" predicts an ambiguity in the notion of two people's having "the same belief," and this ambiguity is readily discerned. Suppose Jones believes that he (himself) is underpaid, Smith believes that *he* (himself) is underpaid, and Brown agrees with Smith that Smith is underpaid. Which two of the three have *the same belief*? Surely in one sense Jones and Smith have the same belief, and in another sense Smith and Brown do. Which is the correct sense? That depends on whether one is more interested in

very plausible (Steven Boër and I have defended an elaborate semantical view that is nicely consonant with it [1980, 1986]), but it
is only a schema for a solution, not a solution itself, so long as
"belief state" and "first-personishly" remain unexplicated.

The representational account yields an explication. Before seeing
the puma, Smith believed a •That man is about to be pounced on•
but did not believe any •I am about to be pounced on•. But what
about the choice between our two individuative schemes? Is there
not a sense (generated by the truth-conditional scheme) in which
Smith has believed all along that he himself is in danger? I think
there is, though Smith would not have expressed that belief in the
first-person way; what he was believing was in fact that he himself
was about to be pounced on. Admittedly this sense is hard to hear,
and there are two clear reasons why it is: First, as I have said, the
truth-conditional individuative scheme is typically imposed when
what concern us are the truth-values or other semantical aspects of
beliefs; the computational scheme is imposed when what we care
about is causal effects. And the case of Smith is clearly of the latter
type: What interests us about it is the question of exactly what made
Smith take sudden evasive action. Thus, imposition of the truth-
conditional scheme here is felt to be inappropriate. The second
reason is that reflexive pronouns such as "he himself" may well
serve as *conventional signals* to the effect that the computational rather
than the truth-conditional scheme is to be imposed. Drawing on
the theory of "lexical presumption" developed in Chapter 5 of our
Myth of Semantic Presupposition (1976), Boër and I have argued (1980,
1986) that something like this is so.

If these two reasons are sound, then it is no surprise that Smith's
original mental analogue of "That man is about to be pounced on"
is not normally counted as an •I am about to be pounced on•; plainly,

causes or in semantics; there is no fact of the matter, contrary to what is evidently
presupposed by Stich (1978a) and by Stack (1980). (Compare: Smith pats himself
on the back. Brown walks over and pats Smith on the back. Did Smith and
Brown perform *the same action*? Let us not start choosing up sides; it is hardly a
factual question.)

Perry's bifurcation also explains the evident absurdity, derided by Dennett
(1978, Chap. 3), of the idea that politically motivated neurosurgeons might
succeed in "cracking the cerebral code" and examining one's beliefs through a
cerebroscope. A cerebroscope can scan only what is in the head, so it cannot
scan one's belief *objects* and hence cannot reveal the propositions one believes.

the representation that Smith associates with "That man" and the one he associates with "I" play very different computational roles and accordingly produce very different behavior, which is exactly what our theory should predict.[14]

14 The material presented in this chapter began life as a memorandum written in 1979 to the Task Force on the Propositional Attitudes at the University of Massachusetts, Amherst. I am grateful to the late Herbert Heidelberger and to his cofounder Murray Kiteley for allowing me to join the Task Force during 1979–80.

PART TWO

Justification

5

Reliabilism

It is past time to turn to theories of epistemic justification. Reliabilist theories dominate the current epistemological scene. This is due in large part to Armstrong's *Belief, Truth, and Knowledge* (1973). After briefly sketching Armstrong's view, I shall compare it to some of its siblings and descendants, exploring alternatives and suggesting improvements as I go; but in the end I shall reject reliabilism entirely.

I THE THEORY

Armstrong's particular version of reliabilism begins with his now celebrated thermometer analogy. Just as a thermometer in perfect working order is a reliable indicator of its environmental temperature, in that by physical necessity it reads "$T°$" only if the temperature is in fact $T°$, a knower is a reliable indicator of states of affairs in his or her environment in that by physical necessity the knower believes that P only if it is the case that P. A law of nature must be at work that ensures this conditional in virtue of some subset H of the knower's attributes. More precisely (p. 170), subject A knows noninferentially that c is a J iff: A believes noninferentially that c is a J, and

1. Jc
2. $(\exists H)$ (Ha & there is a lawlike connection in nature [such that] (x) (y) (if Hx, then [if $Bx\,Jy$, then Jy]).

Of course, "H" must be restricted, on pain of trivial satisfaction of 2; in response to a counterexample of Max Deutscher's, Armstrong insists that "H must not be so specified that the situation becomes unique, or for all practical purposes unique. H must be such that the situation has some real probability or at least possibility of being repeated" (pp. 171–3). Other counterexamples require two more qualifications: The members of H must be "nomically relevant" to the lawlike connection, in the sense that "if H together with any belief whatsoever ensures a situation of the sort J, then the actual belief held must ensure H" (p. 180), and A's belief must be a natural *sign* rather than a cause of what it represents (pp. 181–2).

This analysis demands *absolute* reliability of the knower. It does not permit even the least "empirical" (= nomological) possibility of error. Thus, it has the virtue of accommodating the common intuition that "If I know, I can't be wrong," without dismissing that slogan as a mere scope-confusion of a tautology with an obvious falsehood. Armstrong appeals almost directly to this absolutist intuition: "If there is an empirical, as opposed to a logical, possibility of error, surely we are not justified in attributing knowledge?" (p. 184). And like Dretske (1971), he cites the Lottery Paradox: Assuming the principle that if I know that P and that Q and . . . , then it must at least be reasonable for me to believe their conjunction, he argues that since I cannot reasonably believe the conjunction of the standard lottery propositions, I cannot claim to know any of them, no matter how high their probabilities run.

Armstrong extends his account to general and then to inferential beliefs. Knowledge of a general fact is (roughly) a disposition to enlarge one's set of particular beliefs "in such a way that not merely belief, but reliability of belief, is transmitted according to general rules" (p. 220; for details see p. 204). Likewise, a belief that is based on inference counts as knowledge if the inferential process preserves or transmits nomic reliability in such a way as to maintain satisfaction of point *2* (pp. 206–7).

I have already mentioned two virtues of Armstrong's analysis: its capturing of the absolutist intuition and its elucidation of the Lottery Paradox. There are others: (1) It rules out Gettier cases. In any standard Gettier case (cf. Gettier [1963]) the subject's belief is based on an antecedently justified false belief, but this could not happen if Armstrong's nomic requirement were satisfied. By the same token, the analysis affords a clear sense in which, as we all like to say, "it's just an accident" that the Gettier victim is right. (2) I think it can be shown that the vagueness of Armstrong's characterization of the set H is an advantage rather than a drawback of the analysis, in that the characterization correctly predicts some resulting vagueness in our intuitions about cases. It also predicts the split in people's judgments about certain contested examples, such as Harman's (1973) cases involving "evidence one does not possess" and Goldman's (1975) "barn" case.[1] (3) The analysis falsifies the "KK" thesis (the claim that if I know, then I must know that I know) and thereby spikes facile skeptical arguments that make essential if tacit use of the contrapositive of that thesis. To be a reliable sign, a knower's belief need not be known by the knower; on Armstrong's view, it need only *be* reliable. This observation, made by externalists generally, has a way of clearing the air, although, as we shall see in Section V of this chapter, it is not entirely unobjectionable. (4) The analysis is pleasingly naturalistic.[2]

1 The split can be construed as a disagreement over what properties may reasonably be included in *H*; see my "Reliability, Laws and Counterfactuals" (1979a), from which the present section is drawn. My "Evidence One Does Not Possess" (1977) offers some resistance to Harman and Goldman.

2 Indeed, Armstrong's own reliabilism grew directly out of Chapter 9 of his naturalist classic *A Materalist Theory of the Mind* (1968).

   The naturalistic motive has come through so strongly in the writings of such leading reliabilists as Armstrong, Dretske, and Goldman that subsequent authors have tended to *identify* the "naturalization" of epistemology with reliabilism, as if one had to be a reliabilist or else believe in ghosts. Of course this is a mistake; there are at least three quite different and competing programs that are no less naturalistic. One is the causal theory that reliabilism has pretty well replaced; for two others, see, respectively, Sober (1978) and the view that I defend in Chapters 7 and 8. Sober motivates a psychobiological competence–performance distinction, in order to deal with the discrepancy in nature between what ought to be believed and what gets believed. In Chapters 7 and 8 I take an explanationist line and construe our basic canons of hypothesis preference as topic-neutral cognitive strategies that would be favored by the evolutionary process.

   Moreover, reliabilism per se does not even very strongly suggest naturalism. I wonder why Armstrong does not list *Descartes* among his reliabilist predecessors on p. 159 but has washed his hands of him three pages earlier. Surely Descartes is a titan among reliabilists. The "absolutist intuition" is the mainspring of his epistemology, and he goes on and on about it; see, e.g., Rule II of the *Regulae*, and the discussion following. Descartes's chief epistemological concern is to *eliminate any possibility of error*. According to him, *A* knows that *P* on the basis of (let us say) being in reason-state *S* only if (1) *A* is consciously aware of *S*, (2) it is impossible that *A* should think he is in *S* without really being in *S*, and (3) it is impossible for *A* to be in *S* unless it is true that *P*; that the impossibilities here are logical impossibilities is indicated by Descartes's willingness to consider genuinely bizarre Evil Demon cases relevant to refuting knowledge claims. He requires condition *1* because for him any reason is a thought, and any thought is an item of conscious awareness. He thinks that condition *2* is easily satisfied, because he holds that our awareness of our own thoughts is immediate and hence diaphanous. This is the ultimate in reliability: a (para-) mechanism that cannot break down because it is absolutely simple and has no parts that could become disconnected. The difficulty Descartes sees is, obviously, the satisfaction of condition *3*, for which the Light of Nature is eventually invoked; "Properties *H*," for Descartes, must include one's belief's being clear and distinct, owing to illumination whose purity is guaranteed by the Author of the Universe Himself. (Fred Schmitt, however, has reminded me of Descartes's distinction between

With all these virtues in mind, let us begin to explore some alternative formulations of reliabilism. In later sections I shall make some use of possible-worlds semantics, but only for ease of computation and comparison: Readers persuaded of Armstrongian naturalism may dismiss it as metaphor. In the same interest I shall also standardize the reliabilists' notation a bit, perhaps at the cost of absolute exegetical accuracy.

II THE LOCUS OF RELIABILITY

Dretske's (1971) theory, remarkably close to Armstrong's in spirit and in motivation, differs from it in one conspicuous and important way: According to Dretske, what is "reliable" about a knower is not the knower's belief itself but, rather, the reason on which the belief is based. *A* knows that *P* so long as, by physical necessity, *A* could not have had the reason *R* that he does for believing that *P* were it not the case that *P*. Moreover, Dretske (1975) argues explicitly by counterexample against Armstrong's formulation. In his example, the ubiquitous *S* is staring directly at a Volkswagen Beetle ten paces away, in good light and under splendid atmospheric conditions, and so forth, and accordingly believes that the car is a Volkswagen. Now, although *S* is perceptually and cognitively in good working order, he suffers from the false belief that Saabs are Volkswagens (big, expensive ones). So *S*'s belief alone does not guarantee its truth, but certainly we should not deny on this ground alone that *S* knows. (Goldman [1975, pp. 129–30] makes an almost identical criticism of Armstrong.) Dretske adds:

Armstrong would doubtless retort that *S* is in a different *H* state when he is viewing a genuine Volkswagen than he is when viewing a Saab, and it is this difference in *H* state that will make *S*'s belief that the car is a Volkswagen, *when he is in the* H *state associated with viewing Volkswagens, a case of knowledge.* Certainly, but this is just the point; it is the *H* state itself, and not the consequent belief (if any) that figures in the determination of reliability. (p. 801)

The key element of *S*'s "*H* state," it seems fair to assume, is *S*'s sensory state or percept, which as Dretske construes it, is *S*'s *reason* for his belief that the car is a Volkswagen. Dretske concludes, in

scientia and mere *cognitio*, as illustrated by the example of the atheist geometer; in painting Descartes as history's most compulsive epistemic paranoid I have concentrated, perhaps unfairly, on the former.)

effect, that S's reason and not S's belief itself is what makes S a reliable Volkswagen detector in this case.

Consider a variation (cf. Dretske, pp. 800–1): S is looking at the Volkswagen, and it is producing the relevant perceptual state in him, so he has the same reason as in the preceding example. But at first S is not paying attention; he is listening to music, and since his attention is thus distracted, he does not form any belief about the car in front of him, even though he has reason to. Now, along comes a viciously irresponsible person, well known to be a pathological liar, who whispers to S, "There's a Volkswagen in front of you." S absently takes the liar at his word and comes to believe that the car is a Volkswagen – but not on the basis of his (S's) visual state. Surely we would not credit S with knowledge in this situation. And (I suspect Dretske would say) even if by some strange chance S's newly formed belief, taken together with some other facts about S, *were* nomically sufficient for the truth of the belief, we would not count it as knowledge. So it seems plausible to conclude that S's belief that P is a piece of knowledge only if it is based on a reason (here, S's visual state) that is itself reliable in the relevant sense.

Armstrong locates reliability in the belief rather than in the reason because he has already characterized noninferential knowledge (p. 77 and elsewhere) as knowledge that is not based on any reason at all; he has no such option. This characterization itself seems to me arbitrary, neologistic (I would have thought that noninferential knowledge was knowledge that is not based on *inference*), and obstructive, in that normally when we discuss the epistemic status of a subject's belief, we are forced to allude to some inner state of that subject, on which the belief is based, be the state another belief, a perceptual state, a memory trace, or something else, and the degree of warrant of the belief is determined in some way by the nature of this basing state and/or by the relation between the state and the belief (Dretske's case is just an illustration of this). Only when a belief is based on another belief do we speak of *inference*, but it seems always appropriate to describe any of the cognitive and perceptual states on which beliefs are based as being reasons in a usefully wider sense.[3] Moreover, if we accept this usage rather than

3 Following my discussion in Section IV of Chapter 3, let a "reason" of A's be a content-bearing psychological state of A that functions within A in a certain way to produce a belief. Thus, a reason might be a perceptual state, a sensory state

Armstrong's own, we can make some progress in adjudicating the present issue of the locus of reliability; so I shall adopt it from here on.

Now consider a slightly different example. As before, S is facing the Volkswagen and is in the relevant visual state but is not paying attention. The Volkswagen's horn beeps in a highly distinctive way, producing in S an aural state that is a completely reliable indicator of the car's being a Volkswagen. Still ignoring his visual state, for some perhaps perverse reason, S hears and attends to the distinctive beep and on that basis comes to believe that the car is a Volkswagen. In this case, presumably, S does know, but not on the basis of his visual state; he has a different reason. And here it is much more plausible than in the previous case to suppose that there is a lawlike connection between S's belief and the car's being a Volkswagen, although the nomic path passes through S's ears rather than through his eyes. This suggests that if O is a case in which a potential reason (R) for S's belief that P is either unreliable or not in fact the basis of the belief, but in which S's belief, taken together with other facts about S, still nomically guarantees that P, then in O, the "other facts about S" include some state R' of S that is a reason-state, is reliable, and is the basis of the belief. This supposition cannot be rigorously defended until we have a more definite explication of "reliable," but if it is true, then no belief that is reliable in Armstrong's sense will be unreliable in Dretske's.

Dretske has proved only half his case, however. I contend that we cannot now simply ignore our subject's belief and concentrate exclusively on the reliability of his reason, as Dretske does. Even though a belief counts as knowledge only if it is based on a reliable

of some other sort, a memory trace, a kinesthetic state, or what have you. My knowledge of my own pains, say, is noninferential, even though it is based on the pains themselves as reasons, only because they are not beliefs from which I infer my introspective beliefs, and I can have noninferential knowledge of my immediate environment based on perceptual states of me that produce my beliefs from which I infer my introspective beliefs, and I can have noninferential knowledge of my immediate environment based on perceptual states of me that produce my beliefs about it but are not themselves beliefs or premises in an inference.

If "basing" is whatever kind of functioning characteristically grounds a belief on its reasons, this notion itself demands analysis, and it has received a good deal, some from Armstrong himself in Chapter 6. See also Harman (1970), Lehrer (1974), Tolliver (1980), Swain (1981a, 1981b), and Pappas (1981a). Chapter 3 of Swain's *Reason and Knowledge* (1981b) gives an excellent overall account of reasons.

reason, the converse does not hold, because belief formation is a two-stage process (cf. A. I. Goldman [1975], p. 138). Something may go wrong *between* the reason, typically produced in us by receptor stimulation, and the belief, produced in us by the reason. This is most obvious when the reason itself is a belief and the new belief is produced by inference; inferences can be fallacious. But beliefs based on perceptual states can be defective too, through misinterpretation or just plain malfunction. A person suffering from an optical illusion does not know, even if his or her visual state is reliable and the "illusion" turns out to be accurate (we pull the stick out of the water and it *is* bent).

A first attempt at accommodating this is to insist, on Armstrong's behalf, that just as a reason must be reliable with respect to the fact of which it is a sign, the belief it produces must be reliable with respect to the reason. But exactly what this might mean is unclear. In the accepted epistemic sense of "reliable" it would mean that knower A (having properties H) could not be believing that P if A did not have her current reason R for believing that P; but nothing like that is true, since normally A *could* have formed her belief, and formed it justifiably, on the basis of some quite different reason. Rather, as Armstrong says, in extending his account from noninferential to inferential knowledge, we want the process of belief formation, *given* that A's belief is based on R, to be, in some strong sense, truth-preserving. It is tempting to express our requirement as, "A (having properties H) could not be believing that P on the basis of R unless it were the case that P," but as Dretske has observed in correspondence, this condition is fulfilled automatically provided that R itself is reliable: If A could not *have* R were it not true that P, than a fortiori A could not believe that P on the basis of R in that case either.

Let us have one more try: To say that A's belief that P is reliable with respect to R is to say that if it were not true that P, but A still believed that P, that would have to be because R was unreliable. (For now, I forbear cashing all the tricky subjunctive and modal terms here in possible-worlds jargon.) Thus, A's belief is *un*reliable with respect to R just in case, even given the actual reliability of R, the process by which R produced A's belief might have produced the belief that P in A, having received an unreliable but otherwise similar reason as input, even if it were false that P. This does seem to be the kind of situation we want to exclude; at any rate it captures the cases of fallacious inference and optical illusion.[4] We have arrived, then, at a two-stage theory, which requires reliability of both reason and belief. The locus of reliability is neither the reason alone nor the belief alone.

III RELIABILITY AND COUNTERFACTUALS

In expounding their views informally, reliabilists (Armstrong included) often express themselves in counterfactual terms: A's belief is reliable, it is sometimes said, if A *would* not be holding it unless it were true. Dretske (1971), in particular, flips back and forth between a nomic formulation and a counterfactual one without appearing to notice that these differ. A straightforward account of nomic implication would have it that X nomically implies Y just in case Y holds at every physically possible X-world; thus Armstrong's view, with details suppressed, is that in no physically possible world in which A has properties H and believes that P is it false that P. But on any standard semantics for subjunctives, this is visibly a stronger claim than the corresponding counterfactual one, which comes to saying only that some world in which A has H and correctly believes that P is "closer" to our world @ than is any world in which A has H and falsely believes that P. (I assume Lewis's [1973] semantics for convenience.) To satisfy a nomic requirement, the relation between a belief and the fact believed must hold throughout the entire set of physically possible worlds, whereas the counterfactual formulation requires only that there not be any very "close," similar, envisionable, or what-have-you world in which the belief exists but is false.[5]

---

4 It also rules out the counterexamples provided, respectively, by Christopher Murphy and Ken Waller that trouble Armstrong on pp. 178–9, as well as the obvious difficulty of self-fulfilling belief (pp. 180–1), sparing him the need to invoke his bulky notion of "nomic relevance" and his sign–cause distinction. On the other hand, parallel examples could be urged against the resulting account, attacking the reason rather than the belief. Schmitt (1981) urges plausibly that we scrap the notion of a reliable *indicator* entirely and speak just of reliable belief-forming *processes*, with the believer's reasons counted as elements of the processes and "reliability" defined with respect to the entire output of the processes. (Cf. also Nozick's [1981] appeal to "methods of coming to believe.") If Armstrong were to make this switch, he might avoid all the counterexamples, as well as our difficulties concerning the locus of reliability.

5 Note the felt difference in force between "A would not be believing that P unless

But it is no accident that nomic locutions and counterfactual locutions come to the reliabilist's tongue with equal ease. They tend to converge in an important way: Both Dretske and Armstrong qualify their nomic requirements by reference to circumstantial factors; Armstrong alludes to the believer's properties H, as we have seen, and Dretske relativizes his nomic necessitation to "the particular circumstances which in fact...prevail on the occasion in question" (p. 49). When we take these circumstantial restrictions into account, we notice that Armstrong's point 2, in particular, strongly suggests the traditional laws-plus-initial-conditions analysis of subjunctive conditionals (cf. Chisholm [1946]). On that analysis, to say that A's believing that P under the conditions collected in H implies by physical law that P, amounts precisely to saying that A would not be believing that P if it were not true that P. (Actually it amounts to the contrapositive of this, but conditionals do contrapose on this analysis, so long as H is held fixed.) Notice too that if a subject's believing that P together with the contents of H is ever really going to suffice nomically for the truth of the belief, a great deal is going to have to be loaded into H, although, as Armstrong rightly warns, we must stop short of maximal specificity. A well-detailed instance of point 2 is going to be a much weaker statement, owing to strengthening of its antecedent, than we might have thought at the outset.

I think, however, that complete coincidence between even a weakened nomic formulation and a counterfactual formulation is unlikely. For the traditional analysis of subjunctive conditionals in terms of nomic necessity is now, from the clearer perspective afforded by possible-worlds semantics, generally seen to be unduly restrictive:[6] The traditional analysans is harder to make true than is its English analysandum. So I shall continue to assume that a counterfactual is generally weaker than the corresponding statement that its antecedent, together with a less than maximally specific set of background conditions, nomically necessitates its consequent.[7]

P" and "A could not be believing that P unless P." And we can say, "A could be believing that P, even if it were false that P, but A would not be believing it in that case." Intuitively, "could" reaches out to more distant worlds.

6 For a brief but elegant discussion of the relations between laws of nature, the structures of worlds appealed to in current subjunctive semantics, and the traditional notion of "cotenability," see Lewis (1973), Secs. 3.1–3.

7 We can go some way toward articulating the actual connection. For the technical

99

That leaves us with another choice to make: Should we stick by Armstrong's official nomic formulation, or should we take the counterfactual option and leave it at that (as does, e.g., Nozick, 1981)?

Two factors bear in favor of remaining nomic. First, it is easier thereby to keep our theory naturalistic. What better way to fold knowledge and justification into the causal order than to define them explicitly in terms of laws of nature? Things are not nearly so straightforward if we analyze knowledge in counterfactual terms and quit there, because the ontology of counterfactuals is a notoriously tricky business. Suppose we treat the semanticists' appeal to "possible worlds" as being merely a pleasing and useful metaphor and do not take it as a serious, literal account of what makes a counterfactual true. Then what are we to propose as a serious, literal account of what makes our counterfactual true? The history of the *ontological* problem of counterfactuals is littered with bleeding bodies. Probably the most plausible pre–possible-worlds account is one that appeals to laws of nature, and that would bring us right back to Armstrong's nomic notion of reliability. Suppose, on the other hand, that we do take the possible-worlds treatment as a serious ontological account. Then (if we add nothing more) we will simply have abandoned naturalism; worlds distinct from ours are not part of the (our) causal order and cannot affect us causally in any way. (For more on the relation between possible worlds and nature see my essay "The Trouble with Possible Worlds" [1979b] and the appendix to my book *Logical Form in Natural Language* [1984a].)

The second reason for Armstrong, at least, to prefer the nomic formulation is that counterfactual ones do not quite answer to what I earlier called the "absolutist intuition." For on the assumption of noncoincidence between the formulations, the counterfactual theorist must concede that there is at least one physically possible world in which A has H and believes that P, even though it is false that P. Accordingly, the counterfactual theorist does not have as ready an explanation of people's tendency to say, "If I know, I can't be wrong." (I say just "*not as* ready" because some subjunctive semantics other than Lewis's do afford an explanation.)[8]

details couched in possible-worlds semantics, see my "Reliability, Laws and Counterfactuals" (1979).

8 I have in mind semantics that make subjunctive conditionals what I have called (1984b) "parametrically strict," rather than variably strict in Lewis's sense. Such

100

Despite these undoubted advantages of the nomic approach, I have some inclination to prefer the counterfactual. This mild preference is supported by four considerations.

1. Testability. Nomic theories are not easily testable against cases, since (1) we do not know what (applicable) laws of nature there are and (2) Armstrong can always block purported counterexamples by juggling the never-explicit contents of *H*. (For example, I presume he would accommodate Dretske's Volkswagen case by stipulating that *H* includes enough visual properties to rule out *S*'s belief having been produced by a Saab.) That does not show that Armstrong's theory is wrong or vacuous or even bad, but it is at least a mild drawback. It is shared by counterfactual formulations that mention circumstantial factors explicitly on their antecedents, as in "*A* would be believing that *P* in these very circumstances *C* only if *P*," but not by formulations that let the background information rip, as in simply "*A* would be believing that *P* only if *P*," where speaker and hearer fill in the background conditions tacitly for themselves. Counterfactual theories of the latter kind are testable at least against our intuitive judgments about the truth in the context of ordinary counterfactual statements, although when there is disagreement the various background assumptions will quickly be brought out. More on this will follow.

2. Laws of psychology. Armstrong's laws of nature are going to have to connect beliefs, or believings, to events in the believer's body and physical environment. Thus Armstrong is committed to the existence of psychophysical or psychological laws, and as we saw in Chapter 2, it is not obvious that psychology yields any genuine laws. In any case, the nomic theorist owes us an explanation of how there can be laws connecting subjects' beliefs to physical states of the world.

The nomic theorist has, I think, two possible moves. The first

a semantics determines, relative to a context of utterance, a special set of antecedent worlds and marks a conditional as true if its consequent is true in all members of the set; the distinctive inferential habits and mishaps of the subjunctive conditional fall out of the contextual shifting of the set-selection parameters. (Nozick [1981, p. 174n] also sketches a theory of this type.) On such an account, we can explain the "can't" in "If I know, I can't be wrong" as representing a lower-grade alethic modality than nomic impossibility: I am wrong at no world *in the selected set.*

101

is to develop a functionalist psychology (see again my "Form, Function, and Feel" [1981a] and *Consciousness* [1987a]) and then formulate psychofunctional laws that connect beliefs described in the usual semantical terms to physical objects qua macrofurniture (rather than describing the objects microphysically). If physical objects are characterized, not as by physics, but as by a much refined version of common sense, there may be lawlike statements of the following sort: "If a person S is thirsty and believes that the glass directly in front of him contains water, and has no reason not to reach for the glass, S will reach for the glass," or "If S is standing before a red object in good light with his eyes open and is functioning normally, S will have a visual impression of redness and will come to believe that there is something red in front of him." (Actually, the commonsense mental terms here would have to be replaced by successor technical terms drawn from a shiveringly futuristic function-computational jargon; see Section II of Chapter 2.) The trouble with this suggestion is that "laws" of this psychofunctional sort are open to falsification (and are often falsified) by hardware malfunction, unless they are rendered tautologous by undischarged appeals to "normal functioning" or the like. I do not see this as an embarrassment to scientific psychology (see again Chapter 2, and Cummins [1983]), but the matter of hardware breakdown is particularly pertinent to the issue of reliability: The "reliable" mechanisms that are supposed to be functioning within perceptual knowers and producing the knowers' beliefs are presumably neurophysiological mechanisms, and one thing we are concerned to require of knowers is precisely that they not be suffering relevant hardware breakdown. But a macropsychological "law" of the sort just described cannot rule out such breakdowns, since it does not mention hardware and would be falsified if a breakdown were occurring anyway (cf. Section VI of Chapter 2).[9]

The nomic theorist's second possible move is to presuppose a materialist theory of the mind that incorporates the Token Identity

9 Dretske (1981, Chap. 5) may be able to help Armstrong out here. He points toward an information-theoretically characterized way of walling off certain negligible breakdown possibilities, treating them in effect as idle, and allowing his probabilities to reach unity despite them (he even interprets such probabilities as constituting lawlike connections). Whether the unity thus achieved is more than nominal I cannot say. Goldman (1975) too, in his characterization of reliability, adopts the strategy of ignoring "irrelevant" or idle possibilities. (See note 16, this chapter.)

thesis and to understand the laws of nature demanded by reliability theory as connecting beliefs, not qua beliefs but qua the neurophysiological states with which they are identical, to physical states of the world. For example: Albert's belief that the cat in front of him is fat is identical with some neurophysiological state N_1 of Albert. (Let us even ignore, for now, the difficulties created for psychological description by extracalvarial factors (cf. Chapter 4). Albert's reason-state S is identical with a microphysical aggregate M whose structure is causally responsible for M's reflecting light waves toward Albert in just such a way as to have brought N_2 and then N_1 into being, and so forth. At this grittily concrete level of reality, we may fairly suppose that genuine and exceptionless laws are in force (though in fact this is not strictly so, even in neurophysiology).

But there is a remaining problem, that of the direction of causation. It is fairly easy to imagine that there might be laws to ensure that once the cat is reflecting waves of such and such frequencies smack onto Albert's retina and the retina is sending its resulting pattern of firings up the optic nerve, and so forth, Albert *must* go into N_2 and then N_1 and thereby come to believe that the cat is fat. But it is not so easy to imagine laws that go the other way, laws to ensure that if Albert is in N_1, owing to his having been in N_2 as a result of having been irradiated in such and such a way, then it must have been true that a structural feature F of aggregate M was doing the irradiating (where F is the microphysical feature we identify with the cat's fatness). One would have to pack an awful lot into H in order to rule out all the very effective and physically possible fat-cat-simulators there might be. Indeed, I see no reason to think that this can be done at all, even if we discount skeptical hypotheses such as evil-demon stories, which can be presumed to be physically impossible.[10] So I have no confidence that there are any laws of the sort Armstrong seems to need.

3. Skepticism. Even if there are actually a few cases of completely reliable belief, in Armstrong's sense (which, for the reasons just mentioned, I doubt), they will be tiny drops in a vast doxastic

10 Notice that one's favorite modern high-tech version of Descartes's global Evil Demon hypothesis – that is, the supposition that at this moment I am a victimized brain in a vat, being electronically stimulated by an evil scientist in a manner that causes experiences as of sitting at a typewriter, etc. – is not physically impossible at all.

ocean. The only beliefs that have even a remote chance of being absolutely reliable will be immediate perceptual beliefs under ideal conditions, perhaps along with some introspective beliefs and the contents of short-term memory. The overwhelming majority of what we ordinarily count as pieces of knowledge are beliefs that although they are conclusively well justified for all practical purposes and as well justified as are most of the beliefs used as examples of knowledge in philosophy books, admit nominal competitors that cannot possibly be assigned zero physical probability. Examples: I believe that I have just been downstairs, a few minutes ago, talking with two colleagues. I believe that behind me right now is a desk on which I have just placed a stack of books. I believe that at this moment Jay Rosenberg is in Chapel Hill rather than in Germany. I believe that I see a flower bed outside my window. I believe that there are songbirds outside. All these things are counted as items of knowledge both by common sense and (I think) by most philosophers; philosophers who do not grant that such things are known are called "skeptics." And I doubt that Armstrong's theory can allow that they are known. By contrast, the counterfactual approach has at least a shot at crediting me with knowledge. It does seem true to say that I would not now be believing that I had been talking with my colleagues downstairs if I had not been talking with them, and so forth.

Anticipating the charge of skepticism, Armstrong replies at length (pp. 187–90). First, he says, skepticism is truer than you think:

> The requirement that error be nomically impossible may condemn some using of the word "know" as over-optimistic. But so it should. Any "skepticism" about knowledge that results will be moderate and mitigated, like the skepticism which Hume advocated at the end of his *Inquiry*. It will not touch the paradigms. (p. 188)

Why will it not touch the paradigms? Armstrong only *asserts* (a few lines previously) that paradigm cases of knowing do satisfy his nomic requirement. I suspect he upholds the paradigms because of his expressly Moorean methodological reverence for the core truths of common sense (see his *Belief, Truth, and Knowledge* [1973, pp. 40, 44]); it is much more obvious that we have at least some contingent knowledge than that any particular philosopher's premise is correct. But if this is Armstrong's justification, I think it plainly will not do. One may not offer an analysis that *seems* to predict the nonexistence of Xs and then receive an objection based on our commonsense commitment to Xs by maintaining that since the analysis is correct and since there are indeed Xs, the analysis cannot, after all, imply otherwise. (If I am a Lockean representationalist, similarly, I cannot justly avoid the charge of skepticism by insisting that since we do know at least some empirical things, the objector is wrong in maintaining that my representationalism commits me to skepticism. I have to explain away the appearance of such commitment by pointing out *how* it is that we can have knowledge, despite the truth of representationalism – for example, by taking the explanationist line to be defended in the ensuing chapters of this book.)

By the way, I am not complaining that Armstrong's nomic view has a false consequence; I do not (here) maintain that skepticism is false. My objection is rather that an adequate theory of knowing should remain noncommittal on skepticism (cf. Goldman [1975, p. 144]). If an analysis puts so stringent a requirement on knowing that the requirement obviously is never or virtually never met, the analysis will not reflect our preanalytical judgments about knowing. A theory of knowing should not simply be an announcement that skepticism is correct. If one wants to spread skepticism, one has to argue on some principled grounds that it is correct. (Of course, Armstrong's appeals to the absolutist intuition and to the Lottery Paradox can be construed as arguments for skepticism, though surely inconclusive ones. Equally, suppose a theory puts only a very weak requirement on knowing, so that according to the theory knowledge is lying around all over the place.[11] Then it both fails to award the absolutist intuition the respect it deserves and makes the undoubted attraction of skepticism incomprehensible.)

It should be noted that Armstrong's view is solely a theory of knowing, not of doxastic justification generally. He gives little indication of how he regards all the countless beliefs we have that are entirely warranted even though no one would insist on counting them as knowledge. (For a hint, however, see pp. 189–90.) Other reliabilists have taken up this task. The usual move is to introduce probabilities short of unity – that is, the likelihood that one's belief is true given its existence and/or its provenance (Annis [1977]; Goldman [1981]; Swain [1981b]; Schmitt [1983]). Of course, in

11 I suspect Swain's (1981b) theory of being flawed in this way.

giving a general theory of doxastic justification as opposed to a theory of knowing in particular, one may not invoke an *unanalyzed* notion of probability, on pain of effective circularity. (What is the difference between unanalyzed conditional probability and an unanalyzed relation of doxastic warrant?) Goldman has attempted a modalized frequentist interpretation; Schmitt invokes Trenholme's (1978) propensity theory. More on this will follow.

4. Different topics of knowledge. For reliabilists, the paradigm of knowledge is immediate perceptual knowledge; rarely do they discuss any other kind in any detail. There it at least makes good sense to talk of nomic sufficiencies, propagated through mechanisms that are in flawless working order. Of course, as soon as we move any distance at all from this paradigm and consider all the much more numerous beliefs we have that are justified in looser and less mechanistic ways, things begin to go wrong much more frequently; not only do beliefs and their reasons lose any hope of absolute reliability, but actual performance error becomes prevalent: The inferences that people ought to draw and those they do draw come to differ considerably.[12] But quite apart from all that, there are (arguably) kinds of knowledge whose *topics* do not fit the perceptual paradigm, or at least do not fit it easily: for example, moral knowledge, mathematical knowledge, and whatever (other?) a priori knowledge there might be. It is hard to imagine laws of nature that would connect beliefs on these topics to the states of affairs that make them true. Armstrong or we might deny that they *are* true, precisely because we maintain that there are no states of affairs in nature that make them true, or we might counsel waiting until philosophy has settled disagreements about their truth-makers and only then seek to exhibit the reliable mechanisms that produce the beliefs.[13] For now, however, the counterfactual approach has a somewhat easier time allowing for them.[14] It is not at all unnatural to say that my acquaintance Ruth, a woman of great moral insight and thoroughly familiar with the intricate facts of the situation,

---

12 This raises a serious problem for naturalization programs, quite apart from theories of knowing; see note 12 to Chapter 2, this volume. For attempts at solution, see Sober (1978, 1981) and Chapter 7, this volume.
13 Kitcher (1980) sketches a reliabilist theory of a priori knowledge.
14 This is remarked on by Nozick (1981, p. 186). For useful discussion, see Schmitt (1982a).

would not believe that failing the student was wrong unless it was wrong, or that the mathematician Georg would not believe Goldbach's Conjecture unless it was true.

This fourth drawback to the nomic approach is the flip side of that approach's naturalistic advantage, just as the skeptical difficulty was the disadvantage of the effectiveness of the nomic approach in explicating the absolutist intuition. I do not claim that the counterfactual approach shows clear superiority. I have only tried to exhibit its merit as a live and vigorous contender.

If the counterfactual approach is adopted, we are confronted by further choices (I do not know whether this in itself is a virtue or a flaw). I shall mention two.

After introducing his original, very simple counterfactual formulation, Dretske (1971) goes on to weaken its consequent by explicitly building in his circumstantial condition C. (Alternatively, depending on contraposition, we could strengthen our counterfactual's antecedent.) I construe this as being less a specific attempt to define epistemic reliability than just the application to this particular issue of a much more general view of the "relevant background conditions" of subjunctive conditionals.[15] So even though his expressly weakened counterfactual is a more cautious statement than the original laconic one, we may want to return to the latter and go with our preanalytical intuitions about its truth-value relative to cases (cf. my discussion of testability in subsection 1 of this section), rather than try to second-guess the pragmatics of subjunctives in general. On the other hand, people's intuitions (particularly when the people have worked on conditionals for years) are tentative, theory-laden, and easily upset. If we are presented with a hypothetical case and asked whether a given subjunctive is verified, falsified, or left cold by the case, we usually try to sharpen and firm up our intuitive judgment by pressing the questioner for background conditions or for advice on what facts are to be held fixed in determining closeness of worlds. And so we should press, since the more of these things we know, the clearer idea we will have as to the truth-value of the conditional.

Therefore, I think reliabilists should try to specify the background conditions of their conditionals, rather than let them rip – for this

---

15 Accordingly, we can understand Pappas and Swain's (1973) attempt to counterexample his analysis as mobilizing a different subjunctive pragmatics.

is what we would inevitably and rightly do anyway. But we must doubt (pace Dretske's attempt on p. 50) that any such set could ever be completely specified, and we may also bear in mind that our laconic or unqualified counterfactual formulations will always still be available for use as an intuitive check.

A second choice that faces us is that of selecting a preferred semantics for subjunctives. In this chapter I have simply imposed Lewis's theory, because of its familiarity and its general adequacy, but subsequent work on the semantics and pragmatics of conditionals has produced powerful competing analyses and has also revealed some various types of conditional to which Lewis's account does not apply. One major result of recent investigations (Harper et al. [1981] offer a marvelously clear and thorough survey) is a fairly sharp distinction between objective and epistemic conditionals, the former depending for their truth merely on the relevant states of the world, and the latter depending on speakers' subjective probabilities or other doxastic states. (See particularly Gibbard [1981].) If Armstrong were to go counterfactual, I presume his subjunctives would be interpreted in the objective way, but even that option alone admits several subchoices. Until the botanizing of conditionals and the comparison of analyses is finished, there is nothing we can do to choose the optimal explication of a counterfactual version of reliability. Of course, we may just bypass both laws of nature and English conditionals by cashing "reliability" directly in terms of possible worlds. Goldman (1975) proceeds in essentially this way.[16]

16 Goldman's view ends up looking superficially not much like Armstrong's or Dretske's, but this appearance is deceptive. According to Goldman's analysis, Albert (say) knows that the cat in front of him is fat only if there is no possible state of affairs of the type that Goldman calls "relevant," in which a percept that is "equivalent to" Albert's actual percept is producing Albert's belief that the cat is fat, but in which the cat is not fat.
    We can simplify the analysis a bit, in order to see more clearly what it comes to, by identifying Goldman's "percepts" with our reason-states and then speaking of state-types rather than of state-tokens. We have been thinking of Albert's reason-state as being of whatever the relevant type of belief-causing state is: being appeared to fatly, or having his visual field suffused with fatness, or perhaps just his being in a certain psychofunctional or physiological state. But let us incorporate Goldman's notion (1975, p. 130) of a "sufficiently similar" percept into our identity condition for the perceptual state, whatever percepts are taken to be. Let our "reason-state S" now denote an equivalence class under the sufficient-similarity relation (or, if the latter is not transitive, take instead the

In this section I shall present one case[17] that I think causes some embarrassment to externalist theories generally (including my own; I shall bring my explanationist view to bear on it in Chapter 8). Suppose that Albert is looking at his cat, as before, and that everything is going perfectly, so far as cat, light, retina, perceptual mechanisms, and perceptual experience are concerned; let us even suppose that the likelihood of error is actually zero. But this time suppose also that Albert has good reason to think that his perceptual mechanisms are *not* functioning reliably. A very trustworthy friend (with a strong interest in stimulants) has just told Albert that the champagne they are drinking has been infused with a powerful hallucinogen that produces visual experiences as of household pets. (He says their host is playing a nasty practical joke on an ailurophobic guest.) Perhaps Albert has even seen the host doctor the

class of state-tokens that bear it to Albert's actual state), so that Albert will be said to be "in state S" whenever he is perceptually in whatever condition he is actually in now or he is in any "sufficiently similar" condition. Now we may understand Goldman's analysis as demanding that there be no "relevant" state of affairs in which Albert is in S (which is producing his belief that the cat is fat) but in which the cat is not fat.

What is a "relevant" state of affairs? Goldman suggests picking out this class, from context to context, on the basis of considerations of likelihood, similarity to the actual situation, and so forth. This ties in rather nicely with my own preferred analysis of conditionals (1974b), mentioned in note 8 (this chapter), which represents conditionals as being parametrically strict. Roughly, a conditional $\ulcorner A \rightarrow C \urcorner$ comes out true on it just in case C is true in every possible state of affairs in which A is true and which is an "envisioned, real, and relevant" possibility in the context. (Membership in this class of possibilities is determined by surface grammar, plus a mixture of objective and epistemic contextual factors.) Now, if we may assimilate Goldman's reference class to mine (call it R), then his analysis reduces to

(G) Any world R in which Sa is one in which Fc

a dead ringer for Dretske's original conditional, parametrically interpreted. (Nozick, 1981, p. 209n, also hints at this convergence.) And if we manage to build enough detail into Albert's set of properties H, which detail itself specifies a class of real and relevant possibilities and thereby takes the place of R, (G) will come very close to the Armstrongian requirement (modified to include mention of Albert's reason-state) as well, though Armstrong would insist on the "relevance" of some physical possibilities that Goldman would dismiss as idle.

17 It is structurally similar to an ingenious one put to me by Robert Vishny and also not unlike one of Bonjour's (1980) and Kornblith's (1980); Schmitt (1982b) discusses this type of case sympathetically but without abandoning externalism.

champagne. Yet Albert irrationally forms his belief about the cat anyway. Now, unbeknownst to Albert, he happens to be immune to the drug; still, it seems, he does not know.

Manipulation of Goldman's (1975) or Dretske's (1981) Peircean distinction between "relevant" possibilities and idle ones would handle this case perfectly: Since the possibility of hallucination has been explicitly called to Albert's attention and indeed been made highly probable on his evidence, it ought certainly to count as a "relevant," "real" possibility (although it still is not realizable in the present hardware of Albert's visual system, owing to Albert's immunity), and this would explain why Albert does not know. But Armstrong allows no such distinction, and according to his analysis, Albert does know; his belief is an absolutely reliable sign of the cat's fatness, whether he himself knows that or not.

I am troubled by this case, despite my own firm sympathy with Armstrong's externalism. But perhaps what we should conclude is simply that the KK thesis is even more radically false than granite-jawed externalists have urged.

V   WHY I AM NOT A RELIABILIST

I shall indicate in Chapters 7 and 8 why I esteem my explanationist view of epistemic justification as superior to reliabilism. But I should summarize here a few objections to reliabilism that are independent of my alternative theory.

First, there is the problem alluded to in Section III: Reliabilism is *at best* a theory for mad-dog empiricists. Even if perceptual mechanisms are really nomically or counterfactually reliable (which I doubt), they produce only immediately perceptual beliefs, which constitute a minuscule subset of all the beliefs we have and rely on daily. Most of our ordinary beliefs, and certainly our scientific and other theoretical beliefs, are fairly dramatically inferential and ampliative. Any definition of "reliability" tailored to such beliefs would be either de facto frequentist – and so inaccurate – or modalized, and so both arbitrary and nonnaturalistic. In addition, the reliabilist who invokes a notion of probability or degree of confirmation must specify which such notion is to serve, and it is hard to find any particular one that will do. (On this as well as the following point, see Pollock [1985].)

Then there is the problem of the *range over which* a belief-forming process is reliable. It is process-*types* that are "reliable" in any probabilistic sense (frequentist or modalized); how is the relevant type or reference class to be chosen? We cannot simply specify "perception" or "memory" or the like as a belief-forming process-type and let it go at that, for perception and memory are reliable only in certain normal circumstances; when they are in working order, when ambient conditions are good, and (if the aforementioned granite-jawed externalism is wrong) when no other cerebral information has intervened. So reliabilists must individuate "processes" more finely. They must hyphenate, and talk of perception- or memory-under-circumstances-*C*, where '*C*' includes all the material needed to rule out whatever potential counterexamples loom. The problem is to do this ruling out without specifically or tacitly including the brute stipulation that the subject's belief be *true*. (Although truth is, of course, required for knowledge, it is not required for justification alone.) And there is no obvious way of doing that that is not arbitrary.

Reliabilism is too narrow, in its concentration on immediate perceptual knowledge, and even in extension to ampliative and theoretical knowledge it is profoundly unsatisfactory. There must be a better way, and there is.

6

Occam's Razor

In this chapter I am concerned to show that explanatory inference is fundamental to philosophical thought and that deduction and ordinary induction (so far as the latter occurs in philosophy) are either abbreviated forms of explanatory inference or merely tools used in the tightening of explanatory coherence. I shall also argue that simplicity, power, and the other explanatory virtues are fundamental to all inference, not dubious frills that may be pointed to after, or instead of, the more robust and concrete and empirical marks of truth. Finally, I shall invite the reader to extrapolate these conclusions from philosophical thinking to all of thought.

I shall begin by considering a paradigmatic appeal to simplicity and elegance: Occam's Razor.

I THE RAZOR

Probably the most prominent and popular modern application of Occam's Razor ("Do not multiply posited entities beyond explanatory necessity"[1]) is the one that figures in the philosophical elimination of irreducibly mental entities. Possibly the most straightforward example of this particular application is to be found in J. J. C. Smart's "Sensations and Brain Processes" (1959),

> If it be agreed that there are no cogent philosophical arguments which force us into accepting dualism, and if the brain-process theory and dualism are equally consistent with the (observed) facts, then the principles of parsimony and simplicity seem to me to decide overwhelmingly in favor of the brain-process theory. As I pointed out earlier, dualism involves a large number of irreducible psychophysical laws (whereby the "nomological danglers" dangle) of a queer sort, that just have to be taken on trust, and are just as difficult to swallow as the irreducible facts about the paleontology of the earth with which we are faced on Philip Gosse's theory (of the earth's origin). (p. 172)

1 But see Smart (1984).

Smart appeals precisely to Occam's Razor: To deny that the mind is the brain is to multiply entities (and/or laws) beyond necessity.

We may well admit that from time to time in philosophy, Occam's Razor or something like it has at least tended to curb our inclinations toward muddled extravagance in metaphysics. But it has never been obvious that the Razor supplies a test for truth.[2] Are we to believe that Smart's Identity Theory is true because it asserts the existence of only half as many entities as do its competitors? Why should this be a reason? What is the argument? If Smart has given an argument, it has as a major premise the "principles of parsimony and simplicity" (hereafter, the "PS principles"), and what reason have we for accepting these? They are not straightforward a priori truths, nor do they seem to be supported by any particular empirical evidence. (Don Gunner suggests that, for all Smart has shown, we might be just as well justified in adopting the claim that "nature is lush, prodigal, messy, wasteful, sexy, etc." [1967, p.5].) Perhaps the Razor's sheer venerability gives us some slight reason for siding with Smart, but the many problems that have been raised for the Identity Theory and for each of the other current forms of materialism have given us at least equally good reasons not to do so.

Smart has replied in various places to criticisms of this kind. He would, I think, object to my treating the PS principles as premises in a deductive philosophical argument. ("I am now doubtful whether there are compelling arguments in philosophy anyway," he remarks [1967, p. 85].) Possibly the PS principles, being rather methodological directives, have no truth-values at all. What, then, warrants their invocation and backs up their imperative force? The answer, for Smart, seems to be that they constitute part of the conceptual framework of science itself. Without them we would have no science as we know it, and it would be self-evidently irrational to do away with science tout court.

Less pompously, we might say only that the adoption of the PS principles is just good scientific methodology;[3] scientists know that,

2 Cornman (1966, 1972), among others, expresses skepticism concerning the philosophical use of Occam's Razor.
3 A brief and compelling, though not entirely conclusive, way of showing this proceeds from the model of curve fitting. Given any finite set of data represented by points on a standard two-dimensional graph, there are indenumerably many curves that can be drawn through the points. The relevant PS principle ("Draw the smoothest curve you can") is our *only* guide to framing a hypothetical curve;

113

even if philosophers do not. Discovering the nature of the mind is a scientific enterprise, so provided the Identity Theory or some other materialist theory continues to be confirmed by neurophysiology and has all the "purely observational" advantages its competitors have, and fares as well apropos the PS principles as they do, that theory must be the best hypothesis to accept.

This is all very well, Smart's opponent will say. Considered from the neurophysiologist's viewpoint, Smart must be right. But the issue concerning token identity is not just a scientific one. It is conceptual or philosophical as well. And there is no reason to assume, just because the PS principles partially constitute scientific method, that they have very much to do with philosophical method.[4] Scientists tell us "the nature of" things only in a certain restricted way; tables and chairs they say, are collections of molecules, lighting is electrical discharge; minds are brains. We can understand and appreciate these claims as being informative in a way appropriate to the high-school classroom, but so far we have learned nothing from the scientists about the ultimate metaphysical nature of physical objects, flashes of lightning, or minds. (Some philosophers might complain, in this connection, that science does not tell us necessary, eternal, and immutable truths; philosophy, which does at least attempt to tell us things, demands more rigorous demonstrative methods than those afforded by the PS principles, principles that smack, in any case, of appeals to convenience, not to say corner cutting, and a quasi-aesthetic attitude toward learning the truth. This view has a long history and has swayed many.) Things must be conceptualized, it might be said, before scientific theories about them can be framed and philosophy is the study of how this is done: It precedes science logically, if not temporally.

if we were denied appeal to this principle, we would never be able to make a choice at all. (This argument can be generalized to finite sets of data and indenumerably infinite sets of explanatory hypotheses generally.)

There are at least two objections to this line: (1) It is sometimes denied that the enterprise of curve fitting is a good model of scientific inquiry in general; but I think it is a good enough analogue for our purposes here. (2) It may be said that we *could* make a choice among curves without recourse to the smooth-curve principle: we could decide to choose the curve that had the most horizontal tangents, or some such, rather than the smoothest. In actual cases, however, things would begin to go wrong (all else being equal) if we were to do so; this can be tested.

4 Carnap (1956) can be construed as making this distinction, in his writings on the positing of abstract entities in semantics.

114

It is just this distinction that Smart wants to erode, and here, I think, we get down to the basic outlook that motivates his support of the invocation of the PS principles in philosophy. Replying to similar criticisms put by Gunner (1967), he writes:

> I do not think that philosophy can be as sharply demarcated from science as [Gunner] does, nor do I accept his view that people's competences are determined by the university departments which they inhabit. That is, I cannot accept Gunner's dictum that philosophers have no qualifications for determining what sort of things exist, whereas scientists are competent to do this. Certainly philosophers commonly operate at a more general level than virologists and icthyologists. . . . Nevertheless might there not be more general questions of existence which are the objects of inquiry both by people that university administrators label "philosophers" as well as by people that university administrators label "scientists," and may there not be even more general questions of existence that only those labelled "philosophers" happen to attack? (1967, p. 87)

Other passages make it clear that he denies that philosophy comes to anything more than very general, high-level science. (In this he concurs with Quine.) So he sees no sense in the philosopher's question of why we philosophers should take the scientist's methodological word.

Smart's support of the Identity Theory then, ultimately stems from a fairly well-developed but unsupported metaphilosophical view. The trouble now is that one is hard put to see how to begin adjudicating between the Smart/Quine position and more traditional views of philosophy. Both seem, at this point, to be articles of faith; one feels that a meta–metaphilosophy is called for. It is not yet clear what sorts of considerations would show whether or not Smart is right.

Even so, I think we can say something, based on forms of argument that philosophers of both persuasions will acknowledge, about the relative merits of the two seminal methodologies. I shall defend a version of Quine's famous claim that *there is no first philosophy*, and so no autonomous and autocratic philosophy.

II A DEFENSE OF EXPLANATIONISM IN PHILOSOPHY

Let us begin by characterizing the position of Smart's opponent a little more fully. Some philosophers hold, or appear to hold,[5] that

5 To the best of my knowledge, this view (like most other metaphilosophical views)

proper philosophical argumentation consists in the construction of valid arguments with true premises, or, more specifically, deductively valid arguments whose premises are obvious, self-evident, indisputably true, or at least uncontroversial. This is the way in which, according to this metaphilosophical view (let us call it "deductivism"), philosophers arrive at conclusions that are guaranteed to be as indisputably true as the original premises, once the ingenious deductive arguments have been hit upon. This attitude has pervaded the rationalist tradition, and survives among those who are commonly called "analytic" philosophers in a correctly narrow sense of that expression.[6] Of course, the quality of self-evidence that the deductivist's premises are supposed to have and to transmit to his conclusion has been variously described (as for example, analyticity, a priority, clarity and distinctness, mere obviousness, or just the property of having been agreed upon by all concerned).

Some deductivists do recognize what they call "plausibility arguments" – arguments in which two or more claims are compared with respect to their antecedent plausibility, after we have found by deductive means that we must give up at least one of them. A choice is then made, on various pragmatic and intuitive grounds, including those of what we are inclined to think, what it seems simpler or more natural to believe, and so forth. Such arguments, though sometimes appealed to and acknowledged as such by deductivists when they cannot think of a deductive proof, are generally considered to be of an inferior order ("Of course, this is only a plausibility argument, not a conclusive demonstration").

In any case, the deductivist holds that philosophy and science differ in that deductive argument from self-evident premises pervades the former but not the latter. (Some deductivists have held a particularly strong version of this view, identifying the philos-

has not been widely articulated. But many contemporary philosophers behave dialectically as if they accepted it, and make patronizing remarks about argumentative strategies that do not appear to meet the standards I shall outline. I shall try to avoid mentioning names, since I do not wish to spark subtle exegetical dispute. But certain well-known "analytic" philosophers come to mind, very much in the tradition of Descartes and Spinoza.

6 Admittedly such philosophers are now, in the 1980s, very few. (I myself know one or two, I suppose.) In the introduction to his *Philosophical Explanations* (1983), Robert Nozick pungently ridicules the idea, but he also seems to think that it is a majority position.

ophy/science distinction with the a priori/empirical distinction.)
Now Quine (1960, 1963, 1970) has a rather special reason for rejecting the dichotomy between philosophy and science, or, to put
the point more accurately, between philosophical method and scientific method: He rejects the analytical–synthetic distinction, and
thus the proposal that there are two kinds of truths ("conceptual"
or "a priori," and "empirical" or scientific), one of which is the
province of philosophy and the other the province of science. This
is an impressive way of undercutting a bad old reason for scoffing
at the Smart/Quine position, though I am not sure that by itself it
commits us to that position.

I side with Smart and Quine against the deductivist, but for what
I think is a more fundamental and compelling reason, one that does
not depend on the rejection of the analytical/synthetic distinction.
If my argument is sound, then, one can countenance that distinction
and still be forced to the conclusion that the Smart/Quine meth-
odologial view is correct.

Suppose we try to take a strict deductivist stance. Now, as is
common knowledge, one cannot be committed (by an argument)
to the conclusion of that argument unless one accepts the premises.
Upon being presented with a valid argument, I always have the
option of denying its conclusion, so long as I am prepared to accept
the denial of at least one of the premises.

Thus, every deductive argument can be set up alternatively as
an inconsistent set. (Let us, for simplicity, consider only arguments
whose premises are internally consistent.) Given an argument

$$P$$
$$Q$$
$$\therefore R$$

the cognitive cash value of which is that R follows deductively
from the set of P and Q, we can exhaustively convey its content
simply by asserting that the set $\{P, Q, \text{not-}R\}$ is inconsistent, and
all the original argument has told us, in fact, is that for purely
logical reasons we must deny either P, Q, or not-R. The proponent
of the original argument, of course, holds that P and Q are true;
therefore, she says, we are committed to the denial of not-R, that
is, to R. But how does she know that P and Q are true? Perhaps
she has constructed deductive arguments with P and Q as conclusions. But, if we are to avoid regress, we must admit that she relies

ultimately on putative knowledge gained nondeductively; so let us suppose she has provided nondeductive arguments for P and Q. On what grounds, then, does she accept them? The only answer that can be given is that she finds each of P and Q more plausible than not-R, just as Moore found the statement "I had breakfast before I had lunch" more plausible than any of the metaphysical premises on which rested the fashionable arguments against the reality of time.

Even if we try to be deductivists, then, we seem to be stuck with the conclusion that all philosophical arguments are really explicit or implicit *comparisons of plausibility*.[7] This, I think, is what Smart and Quine must mean in contending that there are no "compelling" arguments in philosophy. Considerations of various different sorts, of course, may contribute to plausibility: ordinary inductive support, explanatory power, coherence with antecedently accepted theories, coherence with our linguistic intuitions, parsimony, fruitfulness, failure to give rise to embarrassing and difficult questions, accessibility to rigorous systematization, and so forth. All of these can probably be subsumed under the juxtaposed rubrics of simplicity and explanatory effectiveness (which I take to be the two primary marks of pragmatic serviceability, though much more elaboration and defense is called for in this regard, for some of which, see Chapters 7 and 8).

But these are just the sorts of considerations to which the theoretical scientist appeals. If what I have said here is (more or less) right, then we appear to have vindicated some version of the view that (1) philosophy, except for that relatively trivial part of it that consists in making sure that controversial arguments are formally valid, is just very high-level science and that consequently (2) the proper philosophical method for acquiring interesting new knowledge cannot differ from proper scientific method. This joint thesis would suffice to refute the objection ("Why should a philosopher care about parsimony?") raised against Smart, since parsimony is an important canon of scientific theory-preference.

It may be felt that there are still two lacunae in my reasoning up to this point. Granted that all philosophical arguments are "plausibility arguments" – that the difference between what the deduc-

---

7 And a *paradox* is an inconsistent set, each of whose members is equally (and quite) plausible.

tivist would consider a "conclusive" deductive proof and what he would term a (mere) "plausibility argument" is purely one of degree – then (1) why does it follow that the considerations that make for plausibility in philosophy are the same as those that make for plausibility in science? And even if it can be shown that the two are the same and thus that as Smart and Quine contend, philosophical method and scientific method are one, (2) why does it follow that "philosophy is just very high-level science"?

I shall now present an argument designed to fill the first lacuna.

1. The interesting principles of rational acceptance are not the deductive ones (even in philosophy).

This is because: (1) Applications of deductive rules are almost always totally uncontroversial. (2) In any case, any deductive argument can be made valid in a perfectly trivial way (by the addition of inference-licensing premises). (3) In an obvious sense, deductive inferences do not accomplish the expansion of our total store of explicit and implicit knowledge, since they succeed only in drawing out information that was already implicit in the premises. And (4) as I argued earlier, a deductive argument can always be "turned on its head" by an opponent.

2. There are, roughly speaking, three kinds of ampliative, nondeductive principles of inference: principles of self-evidence (gnostic access, incorrigibility, a priori, clarity and distinctiveness, etc.), principles of what might be called "textbook induction" (enumerative induction, eliminative induction, statistical syllogism, Mill's Methods, etc.), and principles of sophisticated ampliative inference (such as the PS principles and the other considerations of theoretical elegance and power mentioned earlier, which are usually construed as filling out the "best" in "inference to the best explanation").

This taxonomy, despite its crudeness, seems to capture a distinction that is exhaustive.

3. Principles of textbook induction are not the interesting principles of rational acceptance in philosophy.

At least four reasons support this third point: (1) The literature contains relatively few explicit appeals to textbook principles, and it is plain that few philosophers ever carry out textbook inductions in support of their premises. (2) Even if they were to do so, the inductive arguments themselves would have premises, which would stand in need of justification (we can mount the same ob-

119

jection against the textbook inductivist that we did against the deductivist). (3) Any philosophical theory, if its subject matter is sufficiently broad and if its author has sufficient ingenuity, can be rendered immune to ordinary inductive attack (e.g., Berkeley's theory of the physical world, Cartesian dualism, or Quine's counterintuitive views about semantics). Finally, (4) it can be contended powerfully that the textbook principles themselves are not autonomous but are only special or degenerate cases of the "elegance and power" principles. (I believe Mill held this view. See also Harman [1965] and Chapter 9 of this book.)

4. Principles of "self-evidence," though popular throughout the history of philosophy and hence considered "interesting" principles of rational acceptance, cannot be used to settle philosophical disputes.

Point 4 is defended by Quine and Putnam on more or less Duhemian grounds; they argue that the demise of the analytic/synthetic (and a priori/a posteriori) distinctions brings with it the end of the idea that there is a class of sentences that are immune to revision and cannot be given up under any circumstances. But I have promised to defend the Smart/Quine methodological view without criticizing the analytic/synthetic distinction. I shall put the latter task off for a few paragraphs.

5. If there are any interesting and decisive principles of rational acceptance in philosophy, they are the elegance principles.

And the elegance principles are to be extracted mainly from the history of science. To obtain precise and useful statements of such principles, we can look only to the histories of science, philosophy, and logic, in order to see exactly what considerations motivate the replacement of an old theory by a new theory. The answer to our question *1* – "Why does it follow that the considerations that make for plausibility in philosophy are the same as those that make for plausibility in science?" – is that there is nowhere else to turn.

Suppose someone offers a principle P_r, which he claims is a non-scientific but (in philosophy) overriding canon of theory-preference. P_r is of the form, "Whenever you are in situation *r* with respect to a sentence *s* you should accept *s*." (*r* might be, "*s* is self-evident for you"; "*s* seems analytic"; "*s* is a commonsense judgment"; "*s* is announced to you by an angel in a dream"; "*s* is about the contents of your own mind and seems to be true"; etc.) It would seem that almost any such P_r as one finds in the writings of philosophers who do not share the Smart/Quine approach can be refuted in the following way: We look at the history of science and find a clear case in which an antique and baroque theory that could not seriously be held today (e.g., the flat-earth theory) was replaced by a theory, the basics of which we still accept, and that is by now regarded as an obvious truth; then we point out that anyone who accepted the antique view, certain other common background assumptions, and P_r would have been committed to sticking by the antique theory rather than joining the enlightened in switching to the modern view. This should convince the proponent of P_r that P_r is a treacherous principle of acceptance. The technique (reminiscent of Feyerabend, Kuhn, and Laudan) is most easily applied to appeals to common sense, to tendentious pleas of obviousness, to putative cases of a priori, necessary knowledge, to claims that one's thesis is "axiomatic," and so forth, to say nothing for appeals to religious dogma.

This last argument of mine may well be charged with implicit question begging, because (as we know perfectly well) the staunch deductivist will reply, "I agree that scientists should not accept P_r for the reason you give, but it doesn't follow that I shouldn't accept P_r; I'm a philosopher, not a scientist." (My inability to avoid some tacit question begging here is a predictable symptom of the possible need for a meta–metaphilosophy, remarked on earlier.) But I am at a loss to say how the deductivist's reply could be supported. It would seem to be just as reasonable to insist on the principle "Whenever s has exactly sixteen words, you should accept s" and, being sternly confronted with the history of science, to reply, "Well, I'm not doing science; I'm doing 'phepsiology,' which is also a cognitive discipline whose avowed purpose it is to find out the truth about the world but which uses the 'sixteen-word' principle instead of scientific principles."

It is important to note that I am not here abjuring such principles of rationality as "Accept at the outset what seems to be true (obvious, self-evident, etc.)." Explanatory hypotheses must have some data or phenomena to explain. (This fact will soon prove initially troublesome but will ultimately be helpful. Chapter 8 will be devoted entirely to it.) The point is, rather, that such principles, though sound, are defeasible; they can conflict with the more general elegance principles in particular cases, and often lose.

I shall now support point 4 in a somewhat different way. I believe that we can discredit at least two popular appeals to nonscientific principles of acceptance.

III AGAINST PRIVILEGED PREMISES

The deductivist has a fairly standard reply to my original infinite-regress argument. He can say that arguments having contingent or synthetic premises are none of the philosopher's business anyway. (This rather startling view, or something quite like it, is no longer popular, but it has quietly been espoused by a number of modern theorists. E.g., Taylor [1967–8], Lazerowitz [1955, 1964], and still other philosophers, particularly in the Chisholmian tradition, write exactly as if it were true. Interestingly, proponents of this position are the most determined opponents of any metaphilosophical outlook that permits appeal to science in any form.) That is, the deductivist may agree that all arguments whose premises and conclusion are contingent are indeed only "plausibility arguments," but deny that the same is true of arguments whose premises are necessary or a priori or analytic or whatever. The philosopher's job is to analyze concepts or to explore fundatmental metaphysical structure anyway; so arguments of this latter kind will be more interesting and important to the philosopher in the first place. We may, then, still write fascinating books containing deductive proofs whose conclusions take the form "Theory T is necessarily true," "Theory U is incoherent," and perhaps others.

Although demonstrations of incoherence are sometimes philosophically interesting (skepticism, time travel, ethical egoism, theism, and possibly even materialism), necessary truths that do not bear on these issues usually are interesting only because they can be used to license inferences in more daring lines of reasoning about empirical (or at least admittedly contingent) matter; look at all the arguments from contingent facts about how certain words are learned or used, how we identify and reidentify, how things look to us, how humans sometimes behave, and so forth. But there is a deeper question to be put to the retreating deductivist: What warrants reliance on the allegedly analytic premises of a deductive argument? (For the sake of argument, let us continue to allow the deductivist to beg the analytic–synthetic issue against Quine, for now.) He will probably respond that the prized virtue of analytic

122

truths is that one is justified in appealing to them (one knows them) simply by virtue of knowing the language in which they are stated; one need not present any empirical evidence or gather any information in their support.

The difficulty here is that in order to be justified in believing a premise to be necessarily or analytically true, and hence true, I must at least tacitly assume that I have my words right, that I do know their meanings, that I do have the appropriate concepts, or the like. And these presumptions are all facts of a familiar stripe: They are testable empirical truths about the middle-sized world, not themselves even putatively necessary truths. And I must therefore have justifying grounds for presupposing them. Of course, it is almost always overwhelmingly reasonable for a deductivist to believe that we do in general have our words right, or that he on a particular occasion has his words right; but this is only because my belief that I have my words right is one of the most plausible empirical beliefs that I hold – plausible for reasons of just the same sort that I listed earlier (coherence, simplicity, explanatory power, etc.).[8] Thus, even the deductivist who takes the present line must rely ultimately on considerations of elegance, even if, *pace* Quine, there is such a thing as a valid argument with analytic or necessary premises.

The same sort of objection can be marshaled against a second common kind of deductivist, a philosopher who holds that there is a class of assertibles that are incorrigible or unimpeachable, given that the speaker knows the language and so on. (Russell and Ayer are probably the two most notorious modern defenders of such a position.) Introspective (particularly sense-datum) sentences seem to fill this bill admirably: I cannot be nonverbally wrong about whether or not I am being appeared to greenly, though I can be wrong about there being any actual green thing that is causing me to be appeared to in that way. The deductivist might well hold that these incorrigible introspective sentences can safely serve as the unsupported premises he is looking for, in order to be able to launch his deductive arguments without any appeal to the PS principles or their ilk. (Or he might pick out another class of sentences that he takes to be incorrigible. Austin, I believe, held that at least some sentences about physical objects are sometimes incorrigible to us.)

---

8 For a brief but convincing account of the ways in which these notions apply to our knowledge of our own language, see remarks by Richard Henson (1964). A somewhat similar view is espoused in Searle (1969, p. 12).

In any case, the invocation of incorrigible sentences helps the present type of deductivist out of the problem of substantiveness: Incorrigible sentences have certainty, plus the extra advantage of being synthetic and therefore ampliative or informative.

The trouble is, as few incorrigibilists have seen, that one can still be mistaken in asserting introspective sentences, just as mistaken as one can be in making physical-object claims, other-minds claims, and so on. Although the incorrigibilist shrugs off verbal error as being unimportant, I still presuppose, in reporting a sense-datum, that I have got my words right; as before, this presumption is required in order for me to be justified in advancing my allegedly incorrigible premise, even if the latter is synthetic. (If I have, as is possible, got my words or concepts wrong, then I am not justified in accepting my premise.) Thus, the incorrigibilist meets the same fate as the ordinary deductivist.

Besides, incorrigibility doctrines are themselves now widely rejected, on the basis of arguments like those of Armstrong (1968, pp. 100–15) or Lehrer (1974, Chapter 4). Armstrong's "Electroencephalogram Argument," in particular, carries a good deal of weight. I have not the space to rehearse it here (see, however, Chapter 6 of my *Consciousness* [1987a]), but it casts nearly terminal doubt on the idea that we have logically indubitable knowledge of our own inner sensings.

IV SUBJECT MATTER

It appears, then, that philosophical justification cannot proceed exclusively or even primarily by deduction, even though in an obvious way deduction is philosophy's primary tool. Nor can justification proceed exclusively by deduction plus textbook induction; nor can it proceed by appeal to self-evidence, obviousness, analyticity (even if there is such a thing), or incorrigibility. If, as it seems reasonable to think, our only other canons of theory-preference, the elegance principles, come more or less exclusively from science, and if we continue to admit that there is a rational philosophical method, it seems to follow that that method and scientific method are one.

But this brings us back to lacuna 2, mentioned in Section II. It is possible that philosophical method is scientific method but that philosophy and science deal with entirely disparate subject matters. If so, then our conclusion about methodology does not entail that

124

"philosophy is just very high-level science." It does sound strange to say that *ethics* is just very high-level science. (See Chapter 11, however.)

First, it may be replied that there is no clear boundary between the two subject matters; in particular, there is no boundary at all that I can discern between physics and metaphysics: The difference is one of degree of generality and degree of "remoteness from raw experience." The subject matter of both is the structure of the physical and/or nonphysical universe and everything in it.

Also, more generally: We can take the term "science" in this connection more restrictively or less restrictively. If by "science" we mean just the study of the behavior of the basic furniture of the world (i.e., more or less, physics), then it may be true that ethics, and at least some other philosophical disciplines, is not high-level science; although philosophical and scientific methodologies are the same, the subject matters differ – assuming, not very controversially, that ethical theses cannot be meaning-analyzed in physical terms. (Of course, in this strict sense, the same an be said of psychology and even of biology.) And by similarly restricting the applicability of "science" to the study of physical objects generally, we can prove with equal force that neither arithmetic nor even electromagnetic theory is part of science. But these restrictions seem entirely arbitrary.

If, on the other hand, we mean by "science" just the attempt to say everything it is true to say about the universe on the basis of scientific method, then lacuna *2* is blocked after all.

V   FROM PHILOSOPHY TO REASONING OF ALL SORTS

As I broadly hinted in the preface and in the opening section of this chapter, I intend my explanationist view of philosophical method to be extrapolated to reasoning generally: scientific, commonsensical, ethical, or what have you. My main argument in Section II, from the possibility of turning any deductive argument on its head, applies across the board: *We are always and everywhere stuck in the business of making comparisons of plausibility, and such comparisons are made only by weighing explanatory virtues.*

The by no means original picture of knowledge acquisition that I shall defend is roughly this: We begin with lists of things that seem to be true (perceptual judgments, linguistic intuitions, rules of inference, and the like). We then advance theories (however primitive) that purport to explain these data or phenomena and to incorporate them into a coherent overall picture of the world. We choose, in each case, the theory that best explains the data; the desiderata that select the better of two competing theories are just the elegance and power principles (however their slogan formulations are to be cashed). Sometimes the principles require us to reject some of the phenomena, either because the phenomena in question do not cohere with others or because they are incompatible with a theory that the elegance principles rate extraordinarily highly. (Putting anomalies down to sensory delusion, lapse of memory, or faulty computation is both easier and more prevalent than might be thought.) Deductive reasoning helps, crucially, both to keep our overall theory coherent and to expand our explicit body of knowledge by revealing tacit consequences of what is already accepted, but logical axioms and rules of inference themselves are accepted only because the elegance principles rate them so highly.

This picture, in turn, suggests a sketch of a refutation of skepticism, or at least a response to a certain (perhaps uncommon) sort of skeptic. Consider a Humean skeptic who maintains, "We are never justified in accepting claims about the physical world, about other minds, or about the future, because we are caught in the egocentric predicament; our only direct acquaintance is with the contents of our own minds. As has just been shown, our only ultimate reasons for accepting any claim about any other sort of thing are reasons of elegance, which are purely aesthetic and hence not (epistemically) justifying. Consequently, our vulgar beliefs in physical objects and so on are illegitimate." This skeptic (epistemically) *blames* us for holding the beliefs in question. From the standpoint of the ethics of belief, he says, we *ought not* to hold them. If we reply that they are justified by the elegance principles, he will rejoin that we ought not to embrace the elegance principles, or at least ought not to form beliefs on the basis of them.

Now I suspect that it is biologically necessary to a sentient organism's survival that the organism organize its experience in the simplest, most coherent and expedient, and yet most powerful and comprehensive way that it can. An organism (say, a human child) that lacked the drive to do this would not even form the concept of a physical object, recognize its mother and other benefactors, or acquire any of the other abilities necessary to its getting about in

126

the world without mishap.[9] Such a type of organism would surely be selected against, in evolutionary competition. It thus comes to be lawlike that a viable organism operates, epistemically, according to the elegance principles (including PS principles) or something relevantly like them. This position and its details, of course, need much confirmation and spelling out by biologists, psychologists, and anthropologists; I shall expand it philosophically in the next chapter.

If the suspicion I have expressed is well founded, the point is this: A normal human being cannot keep from forming beliefs in ways that have survival value, or from making use of the elegance principles in doing so – at least up to a point. And if that is so, then no one is obligated in any way to refrain from following those primitive procedures. (I assume here that the "'ought' implies 'can'" principle, familiar and almost irresistible in moral theory, applies in the ethics of belief as well; that assumption will be relaxed in the next chapter.) And if all this is right, the normal human being cannot epistemically be blamed for acquiring beliefs on the basis of the elegance principles; in that sense, *at least*, he or she is justified in holding those beliefs.[10] We shall shortly see that even better evolutionary defenses against skepticism are available.

9 This account is suggested by the last few paragraphs of Quine (1969).
10 In its present crude form, this approach overlooks obvious problems. E.g., sometimes it is biologically (or at least psychologically) necessary to a human being's sanity (and hence his ability to function) that he or she accepts some belief that is flagrantly unwarranted by any principles of rational acceptance. Our theory will have to be modified to take account of this and will be so modified in the next chapter.

7

Epistemic value

The key notions of epistemology are normative through and through. "Justification," "warrant," "rationality," and the like are all matters of what one *ought* or *ought not* to believe.

Epistemic obligation and permission seem to be sui generis – in particular, they do not coincide with moral obligation and permission – but they are as fully evaluative as are their moral counterparts. For this reason, their place or ground in the closed causal order we call "nature" is not at all clear; the business of "naturalizing" them (and simultaneously protecting them against facile skepticism) is as difficult on its face as is the much better publicized task of naturalizing moral goodness. It is interesting that this parallel goes generally unremarked. Moral subjectivism, relativism, emotivism, and the like are rife among both philosophers and ordinary people, yet very few of those same people would think even for a moment of denying the objectivity of epistemic value – that is, of attacking the reality of the distinction between reasonable and unreasonable belief. I wonder why that is.

If one upholds the objectivity of epistemic value and if one is also inclined to think that there are no real differences that are not at bottom natural differences, then one must try to say what it is in nature that distinguishes reasonable belief from unreasonable belief.[1] I propose to attack this problem from the stance I have been maintaining throughout, the theory of epistemic justification that is commonly, if clumsily, called "explanationism": crudely put, the doctrine that all justified reasoning is fundamentally explanatory reasoning that aims at maximizing the "explanatory coherence" of one's total belief system.[2] I shall sketch a fuller version of the view,

---

1 This conception of the "naturalization" of epistemology is roughly the same as Alvin Goldman's (1980, 1981) and Armstrong's (1973, 1978b). It differs rather sharply from the conception originally intended by Quine (1969); see note 5, this chapter.
2 Explanationism has guided the works of W. V. Quine (beginning as early as the

128

defend it at some length against certain skeptical challenges, and then show that it affords a fairly plausible reduction of epistemic value to value of a naturalistically more tractable sort.

I EXPLANATIONISM

The explanationist's basic mode of ampliative inference[3] is given by the following schema, or something like it:

$F_1, \ldots, F_n$ are facts.

Hypothesis H explains $F_1, \ldots, F_n$. ["Explains" here is to be read in its nonsuccess sense, as "would explain if true."]

No available competing hypothesis explains the F_i as well as H does.

∴ [probably] H is true.

This characterization of abduction, explanatory inference or "inference to the best explanation" raises any number of immediate questions: What are "facts" and where do they come from? What exactly is meant by "explain"? What makes one explanation a *better* explanation than another? In the rest of this book I shall concentrate on the third of these questions, since the explanationist's epistemic value predicate attaches specifically to this comparison of competing hypotheses.

A mechanism for selecting the *best* from among a number of available explanations must take the form of a set of rules or canons of theory-preference. No small and simple set will suffice, alas, theory-preference being the difficult and controversial business that it is. Ideally, we would discover the set of canons that do govern justified theory choice by looking painstakingly through the history of science, collecting a large sample of justified theory choices and a large sample of actually or counterfactually unjustified theory

papers collected in *From a Logical Point of View* (1953a) and of Wilfrid Sellars (e.g., 1963a). The most vigorous articulator and defender of the view is Gilbert Harman (1965, 1973 and elsewhere). Criticisms of explanationism are to be found in Lehrer (1974, Chap. 7), and in Cornman (1978); for a rehabilitated view, see Cornman (1980).
3 In concentrating on the basic mode of ampliative inference, I am ignoring three other key components of a justificatory apparatus: (1) deduction; (2) forms of ampliative inference that I consider to be *derived* from enthymematic forms, such as enumerative induction (see Harman [1965] and Chapter 9, this volume); and (3) whatever epistemic procedure it is that produces our ultimate explainees. These are topics that I shall take up at length in Chapters 8 and 9; the present chapter constitutes only one small element of a global defense of explanationism.

choices, and trying to articulate the features that in fact distinguish the two. Short of doing that, for my purposes in this chapter, I shall just offer from the comfort (and safety) of my armchair a few sample rules that can serve as examples for metatheoretical discussion:

1. Other things being equal, prefer T_1 to T_2 if T_1 is simpler than T_2.
2. Other things being equal, prefer T_1 to T_2 if T_1 explains more than T_2.
3. Other things being equal, prefer T_1 to T_2 if T_1 is more readily testable than T_2.
4. Other things being equal, prefer T_1 to T_2 if T_1 leaves fewer messy unanswered questions behind (especially if T_2 itself *raises* messy unanswered questions).
5. Other things being equal, prefer T_1 to T_2 if T_1 squares better with what you already have reason to believe.

This list is laughably oversimplified, in several ways. First, the individual "rules" are just slogans that gloss fantastically complex procedures: Rule *1* is a notorious culprit, since "simplicity" comes in many different kinds and respects that overlap and cut across each other and are hard to compare. Second, there are undoubtedly more rules than those I have listed, other ones dealing with fruitfulness, accessibility to rigorous formulation, and similar refinements. Third, the rules themselves often conflict – tradeoffs between simplicity and explanatory power are particularly common – and so we need a set of metarules to show how we are to balance the difference features we favor against each other. Fourth, it is not clear that all of the rules are conceptually independent of one another (I suspect, for example, that rule *2* is just a special case of rule *1*, applied to global belief systems). Fifth, it may be that not all the rules apply at the same stage of inquiry; there is some evidence that rule *5* actually should be stated as a metarule or weighting principle rather than as a first-order rule.[4] Sixth, I have yet to specify the exact relation between the rules and people's doxastic behavior. This last is a crucial task, to which I now turn.

There are at least three importantly different roles that our set of canons might be supposed to play in a theory of justification, or rather, there are three different types of "theory of justification"

4 We may need a metarule of conservatism in order to account for our ultimate explainees in the way I want to; also, as Don Loeb pointed out to me, such a metarule can play an important tie-breaking role. See the next chapter.

that the set of canons might be supposed to constitute. (1) The rules might be intended merely as a description of the reasons people in fact have for their choices of hypotheses, a purely causal explanation of the choices they do in fact make. This is the nonnormative role that Quine sees for epistemology to play.[5] (2) The canons might be intended to characterize the distinction between rational and irrational theory choices, between warranted and unwarranted explanatory inference. Thus, the set of rules would serve as a normative theory of what beliefs are justified and why. (3) The rule might be intended to constitute what Alvin Goldman (1980)[6] calls a "doxastic decision procedure" (DDP), that is, a (recursive) recipe that real people could look up in a book and act on as practical advice in forming their beliefs. As Goldman points out, it is important to distinguish this use of our set of canons from the preceding one. A perfectly good normative theory of justified belief may be correct (may accurately tell a disinterested party which of someone's beliefs are in fact justified and which are not) and yet be quite useless as a DDP, owing to a subject's inability to tell from within his or her own, first-person–present epistemic situation whether or not the conditions laid down by the normative theory of justification are satisfied in his or her case. For example, suppose a plausible normative theory imposes a causal requirement on justification, or a requirement to the effect that a justified belief have been produced by the operation of a "reliable" mechanism; a subject cannot normally tell from within the first-person–present perspective whether a present belief satisfies either of these conditions, and so cannot use the theory's normative rule as a practical guide to determining whether he or she ought to be holding that belief.[7] If our set of rules is to serve as a DDP, subjects must be able to tell on the spot whether the features mentioned by the rules are present or absent in the theories they are evaluating.

If our set of rules were intended as reportive psychological description, they would be hopeless. There is no set of rational guide-

5 Quine (1969) argues directly from the futility of Cartesian epistemology to this purely descriptive conception and does not seem to consider alternative 2, perhaps because he conflates it with 3.

6 Here and elsewhere I am indebted to Alvin Goldman's writings.

7 Another example: Any acceptable normative theory of justification will entail that no Gettier victim is nondefectively justified. But no acceptable DDP could entail this or make use of it, since from within one's own epistemic situation one has no way of telling whether or not one is being gettiered.

lines for theory choice (and certainly no accompanying deductive logic) that accurately describes the actual formation of beliefs by real people. This is because "real people" include lunatics, bigots, wishful thinkers, drooling morons, lust-crazed undergraduates, lust-crazed philosophers, and the like; what people believe and what they ought to believe all too often diverge. So, unless one makes a fairly heroic competence–performance distinction,[8] our canons of theory-preference cannot serve as a plausible descriptive psychology of belief formation. A much more interesting question is that of whether they could serve as the core of a DDP.

It is plain that they are not often used in that way, at least self-consciously, because most people do not often think consciously in terms of explanatory virtues at all, and besides, no one has ever formulated an authentically complete and articulate set of canons. For the same reason, it is doubtful that they will ever be used by many people in that way, though in argument scientists and philosophers sometimes make crude appeals to "simplicity" and "power" and "elegance" (and philosophers, at least, can do no other, or so I argued in the preceding chapter). *Could* any manageable version of our set of canons serve as the core of a DDP? That depends on whether their first input requirements could be "accessible" in Goldman's way, mentioned earlier: Could I be *able to tell* which of two theories is simpler, which explains more, which is more testable and so forth? Sometimes I think I can tell, and sometimes scientists evidently think they can too. We may be making vague judgment calls, relying on instinctive simplicity- or power- or whatever-metrics, or we may be relying on some explicitly (and presumptuously) articulated versions of the canons in question, versions that leave lots of room for error of formulation. If I were setting out to build myself a DDP based on my initial intuitive ideas about theory-preference, all I could do would be to try some first approximations, see how well or badly they fared for a while, revise them, see how well the revised versions fared, and so on. This itself would be theorizing on my part, analogous to constructing a logical theory (later to be proved sound and complete) in an attempt to capture our basic individual logical intuitions

---

8 This is roughly the line taken by Cohen (1981); related arguments appear in Sober (1978). For an explanationist comment on Cohen's strategy, see my " 'Is' and 'Ought' in Cognitive Science" (1981b).

and reveal whatever internalized *Ur*-logic is responsible for them. As is shown by examples drawn from the history of logical theory, such theorizing can easily go wrong. (I have in mind particularly the theory of conditional logic.)[9] In effect, to seek a DDP based on our canons of theory-preference is to do philosophy of science – specifically, to give advice on scientific method, to make methodological recommendations to working scientists. This is a worthy project, but one far too ambitious for a plain old philosophical epistemologist such as myself. So our set of canons is best construed, as I have meant it to be construed all along, as a normative theory of justification (option 2) and nothing more. In my theory, the role of canons is simply to distinguish those beliefs that are justified (to whatever degree) from those that are not, regardless of whether the canons ever are or could be used explicitly in human doxastic practice.

The sorts of arguments put forward by explanationists are designed to show that whatever ultimately justifies a belief is a matter of the explanatory contribution of that belief. If this is true, then we have built-in or tropistically acquired measures of explanatory goodness. What are those measures? That is an empirical question. On the basis of superficial observation,[10] it seems to me that the measures are something like, or are something barely glossed by, the crude rules that I have listed. The job of a full-fledged and detailed normative theory of justification (let alone a DDP) would be to articulate the measures in full and without counterexample, but fortunately no epistemologist need offer so fine-grained a theory as that. For my purposes of stiff-arming the skeptic and of naturalizing epistematic value, slogan proxies for whatever are the real probative principles of theory-preference will do. I assume merely that there is some such set of canons of theory-preference that does accurately distinguish justified from unjustified theory choice, and of which my stated list of rules is but a crude illustrative parody.

9 For correction on the semantical side, see Stalnaker (1968) and the immense subsequent literature on conditionals. On the syntactic side see Geis (1973) and my "Syntactically Motivated Theory of Conditionals" (1984b).
10 And occasional guidance from the literature; see particularly Quine and Ullian (1973) and Thagard (1978).

I have suggested that something like our rules of theory-preference comprise the foundation of ampliative infererence; for me they are ultimate, not themselves justified by any more fundamental epistemic norms. And this raises the specter of skepticism, in both a general and a more specific way.

The general worry is that if the canons are ultimate and cannot themselves be justified, then it seems they are epistemically *arbitrary*; they are the rules that human beings happen to use, perhaps even the rules that human beings are built to use, but that does nothing to justify them in the normative sense appropriate to epistemology. We sport no epistemic halos when we use them; they are, at best, devices of convenience. And if they are arbitrary in this sense, no belief licensed solely by them is justified or, at any rate, an item of knowledge. But as an explanationist I hold that any belief is licensed solely by them: Global skepticism ensues.[11]

The specific worry is that our rules of theory-preference key on features of theories that seem quite unempirical. Simplicity? Absence of mess? Why not prettiness and niceness? Why should these virtually *aesthetic* properties, which smack in any case of laziness and corner cutting, be thought to count in any way toward *truth* (John Keats notwithstanding)?

Explanationism comes straight out of the pragmatist tradition, and the explanatory virtues on which our canons key are pragmatic virtues that make beliefs *utile*. It is this fact that will help us turn aside the two skeptical arguments. Let us recast the issue slightly by costuming the characters in a more stylized way: Imagine a generic Scientist-Laborer, working away in her laboratory or her vineyard or her machine shop, achieving visible technological progress as she works. She builds houses, makes clothes, invents airplanes, finds cures for disease, and so forth. In aid of all this useful activity she forms theories, beliefs, which serve her as tools by guiding her decisions in relation to her goals. And when she uses them correctly, they serve her well; hence all the technological

11 Note that this general worry would apply to *any* supposedly basic form of ampliative inference, not just to the explanationist's canons, so it constitutes an argument for skepticism about inferential belief tout court. A skeptical challenge that counts equally against any account of nondeductive, nonbasic knowledge is no embarrassment to explanationism in particular.

progress. How does the Scientist-Laborer form these beliefs? According to certain methods, epistemic procedures, such as our canons of theory-preference. These methods are tools with which to make tools, then. And when the Scientist-Laborer uses them correctly, the beliefs they produce are utile ones.

A happy proletarian scene. But in the midst of all this productive activity, a singular event occurs: A gleaming epistemic Rolls Royce glides up beside the Scientist-Laborer's workplace, and there alights an Epistemologist (suitably attired in morning clothes, with white gloves and halo), who observes the Scientist-Laborer's activity for a few moments and then addresses her in a condescending tone, asking whether she thinks she is *justified* in holding the belief she has formed. The Epistemologist suggests that despite all the practical value of the methods by which the Scientist-Laborer forms them, there is something lacking. The beliefs are not really *justified*, or at least, though they are vindicated in some sweaty and purely utilitarian way, they are not truly *top-drawer*. They do not qualify as items of "knowledge."

The prephilosophical Scientist-Laborer reacts blankly to this. What is wrong? What, exactly, is lacking? What does the snooty Epistemologist want from her? The answer is unclear, and we might spell out the Epistemologist's challenge in any of several different ways:

1. "It's been admitted, in print [earlier], that your basic epistemic procedures are not validated by any *proof* or evidence, since you say all 'evidence' rests ultimately on the procedures themselves. Doesn't this show at once that they are unjustified?" It may seem paradoxical that any beliefs (or inferential methods) that are justified in the epistemological sense are justified ultimately on the basis of beliefs and/or methods that are not susceptible of proof, but the alternative *is* paradoxical: On pain of circularity or regress, we know that some epistemic methods or procedures (whether explanatory methods or others) are going to be fundamental; so if a theorist is claiming to have discovered some such fundamental epistemic method, it is a fortiori inappropriate to respond by demanding a justification of it, in the sense of a deduction of it from some more fundamental principle – indeed, it is contradictory. As Bentham says, "That which is used to prove everything else . . . cannot itself be proved" (1789/1961, p. 19). Basic epistemic norms, like moral norms (and logical norms), are justified not by being deduced from

135

more fundamental norms (an obvious impossibility), but by their ability to sort specific, individual normative intuitions and other relevant data into the right barrels in an economical and illuminating way. The present skeptical observation is tautologous, and the attendant demand is contradictory.

2. "Your methods my be utile faute de mieux, but they don't produce beliefs that satisfy Descartes's demands of absolute reliability. It's always *possible* for a belief to be produced by your method and still be false, so no such belief counts as an item of Knowledge and none is really Justified in the full-fledged epistemological sense of the word." This seems to me to be a word game. It is (relatively) uncontroversially true that few if any beliefs, especially beliefs formed on the basis of our loose-living rules of theory-preference, are either incorrigible in the strong Cartesian sense or deduced by indubitable inferential steps from beliefs that are incorrigible in that sense. If that is what the snooty Epistemologist means by "Known" and "Justified," let us agree forthwith, and give him the terms "Known" and "Justified." Certainly there is a sense – the capitalized one – in which our beliefs are not items of Knowledge. But whoever thought they were? Descartes only hoped they might be, and (as he himself showed in *Meditation* I) he hoped in vain. The ordinary terms "known" and "justified" are *our* words, applied according to our much weaker and more casual standards,[12] and they considerably predate the advent of the chauffeur-delivered Epistemologist. The Scientist-Laborer was wont to distinguish what was "known" from what was "just a theory" – albeit in a highly context-dependent way – long before anyone came along and proposed, for whatever unexpected reason, that those terms be used in a new and stricter sense. The Epistemologist's skeptical suggestion is either unsurprising (in its neologistic sense) or prima facie false and in need of further argument.

3. "As I said, your methods are all very well from a practical point of view, but that still doesn't answer why they might be thought to count toward *truth*. Granted that beliefs produced by correct application of the methods are utile and tend to promote success in goal seeking, what independent reason have we for think-

12 For an examination of these standards and a probing of certain key context-dependencies in knowledge claims, see Kilgore and Lycan (1982). However, Armstrong (1973) argues at least obliquely to the contrary.

ing that they *correspond to reality?* We can't step out from behind the iron curtain of our first-person perspective, out from behind our perceptions and beliefs, and compare those perceptions and belief with reality laid bare; we can't look at the beliefs and also look at the reality and then observe in some God's-eye, diaphanous, non–theory-laden way that they *match.*" This observation seems pointless, and I think it betrays at least one of two confusions. The first confusion, a common one, is the tendency to spell "true" with a capital 'T.' Suppose someone says (I have heard this now and again), "I see you have evidence for your belief that P, but what evidence do you have that that belief is *really true?*" The coherence of this question is dubious, at best. To believe that P is precisely to believe it is true that P, and for that matter to believe it is really true that P. My evidence for believing it is *really true* that P is exactly my evidence for believing that P in the first place (plus, perhaps, my evidence for the quasi–T-sentence, "The belief that P is a true belief iff P"). One has evidence that one's belief that P is *really true* when one has evidence that P; one need not in addition perform some spectacular feat of stepping out from behind one's perceptions and conceptual scheme and eyeballing naked reality in some humanly impossible way.[13] (The other relations between explanationism and "realism" are the topic of Chapter 10; see also section V of this chapter.)

It may be that what is bothering the objector is, rather, the fact that from within our first-person perspectives we cannot always tell whether our evidence is adequate or whether our epistemic methods are as utile and reliable as we would like to think. But to infer from this that the beliefs produced by the methods are inadequately justified and/or that they are not items of knowledge is to fall into the second possible confusion that I mentioned earlier: That I cannot tell whether my evidence is adequate does entail that I do not know that I am fully justified and hence that I do not know *that I know,* but one can infer from this that I do not know (at all) only if one tacitly presupposes the nefarious KK thesis ("Neces-

---

13 Some philosophers attempt to preempt skepticism by relativizing "truth" and "reality" to one's overall view or conceptual scheme. This amounts to abandoning "realism," in the none too clear sense of that term currently made fashionable by Dummett, Putnam, and others; it is a line that does not attract me at all; see Chapter 10.

sarily, if you know, then you know that you know"), which thesis is widely granted to be false, for each of several reasons (see Lycan [1982]).

Incidentally, we may wonder why people have so strong an urge to swallow skeptical arguments that pass illicitly through the KK thesis or its contrapositive. I think Goldman's distinction between DDPs and ordinary normative theories of justification yields an explanation: The urge comes from confusing the two types of device. Seeing that the subject's ability to tell whether the input condition of a doxastic rule is satisfied is a strict requirement on DDPs, we come to think that it is a strict requirement on theories of justification generally; but this inference is fallacious, since the differing purposes of DDPs and ordinary normative theories naturally generate differing sets of requirements and adequacy-conditions. One might think of arguing independently that any normative theory of justification *must* meet all the requirements of DDPs; that would lead almost immediately to skepticism. (In fact, that is essentially what Descartes did; he was seeking a method of forming beliefs that one could apply – ultrareliably – from within one's own epistemic situation, and this is just a DDP.) There is an idea that we are *obligated* to start from an epistemic position of zero: holding no beliefs and trusting no epistemic methods that have not been epistemically guaranteed in advance. But this idea, taken literally as it stands, is a contradiction. If you have no beliefs and no epistemic methods to start with, you cannot epistemically justify or guarantee anything or perform any other doxastic act. If that is what the snooty Epistemologist is demanding of the Scientist-Laborer, we can ignore him; we cannot be obligated to perform contradictory tasks.

4. "All very well. But you still haven't faced up to the charge of arbitrariness. Of your fundamental canons of theory-preference you still end up saying just 'These are the ones we use.' And it's no good invoking justification by convention, à la Wittgenstein, since our fundamental epistemic methods are rooted in psychology, not in social custom." Even if our rules of theory-preference are not themselves epistemically justifiable, we must guard against supposing that we could simply see the error of our ways and stop using them. We never made a conscious choice to use those rather than others, and I doubt psychology will ever reveal that as children we make unconscious choices to use them either; probably they are

hard-wired. (Of course, this does not mean that we use them correctly at all times. More on this follows in Section IV of this chapter.) Now, as I conceded in Chapter 6, one difference between epistemic and moral obligation is that " 'Ought' implies 'can' " does not hold so obviously in epistemology as it does in ethics, and I doubt that any particular belief draws much warrant from our inability not to hold it, but it makes little sense to say that we are somehow epistemically to blame for using fundamental *methods* or canons that are wired into our belief-forming apparatus. The canons are not arbitrary in that sense.

5. "Still, it's just a fact of our psychobiology that we happen to operate in the way we do. So even if it's not arbitrary with respect to our psychobiology that we use the canons we do use, it's still arbitrary with respect to the class of possible cognizers generally; there might be alien creatures who operated according to entirely different and superior wiring diagrams." This observation on the Epistemologist's part is both true and significant. My response to it will point to what I think is the real, natural ground of epistemic value.

III EPISTEMIC GOODNESS

We still want to ask, *Why* is simplicity in a theory better than lush, Byzantine complexity? *Why* is testability better than immunity to refutation? And so on. We still feel that there is point to these "why" questions, even though we are agreed (I hope) that the "why" in them is not the kind of "why" that asks for further epistemic justification. It remains to see what kind it is instead.

I suggest that the question of why we use the particular set of canons we do use is best understood as having the force of asking *why it is good or utile or desirable* for us to use those canons, to operate according to those epistematic principles rather than others. This question does have plenty of point and admits of a substantive and illuminating answer. I shall try to bring out the answer by means of a thought experiment.

In many ways we are as if we were the products of a benign developmental process that had our welfare, survival, and propagation at heart. This is a common and useful way of thinking of the results of biological evolution, whether or not one supposes that evolution was set in motion and guided by a Great Designer.

I will suppose that we were fashioned by a skillful and benevolent Mother Nature. And let us continue to see beliefs as being tools that we use in making our environment safer and more comfortable for ourselves, and epistemic methods as being tools that we use in forming beliefs. Now, we may ask, what cognitive habits would a skillful and benevolent Mother Nature have given us in order that we might go on to form beliefs of the most utile kind?

It is essential to grasp that there are a number of empirical constraints to be respected here. By the time she thought of giving us minds, Mother Nature had already made a large number of decisive and very consequential choices: Our hominid ancestors occupied a certain sort of environment; they had a certain general shape and size, and were made of certain chemicals, and so on. When Mother Nature started in on higher brain functions, she had left herself only a comparatively small space within our skulls and a limited range of materials with which to fill it; into this space, using those materials, she would have to have fit all the cognitive resources she could provide. She would be able to allow us only a small, very manageable stock of basic mechanisms that would do the job of amplifying and extrapolating our immediate environmental input. These mechanisms would have to achieve great efficiency, at some cost in reliability and detail. In particular, the following hypotheses seem plausible.

1. Mother Nature would have built us to prefer simpler hypotheses to complex ones.

There are several reasons for this. (1) Simpler hypotheses are more efficient to work with. A simple handbook of rules, such as the *Boy Scout Manual*, is easier to use than is the 1976 U.S. tax code. (2) As Russell observed, in defense of his version of Occam's Razor (1957), complexities incur greater risk of error. A simpler device has less that can go wrong with it (think of a simplified phonograph turntable or automobile engine).[14] (3) Simplicity is *itself a form of* efficiency. The whole point of obtaining simple and unified hypotheses in science is to achieve plenitude of result (in the way of

14 See also Elliott Sober's remarks on the "informational fitness" conferred by detector economy (1981, pp. 106–7). Some of the ideas in the present section are not unlike those developed independently by Sober in that paper, but they will diverge a bit in Section IV and V.

data explained and results predicted) with parsimony of means.[15] If we were not able to mobilize a few simple hypotheses and thereby obtain maximally informative analysis of the news, especially in the way of experimental predictions, we would be far less competent in coping with environmental developments; the world would present us with too many surprises, and they would overwhelm us.[16]

I have already quoted D. L. Gunner's (1967, p. 5) protest that principles of parsimony and simplicity are excessively and arbitrarily restrictive. His pungent remark about nature's being lush, messy and so forth suggests that what epistemic principles we ought to use depends on prior metaphysical facts about the overall nature of the world. I believe this suggestion must be firmly resisted. In particular, my own defense of our preference for simpler hypotheses is not based on any metaphysical assumption to the effect that "nature is simple" or any such thing (rule *1* is not a factual claim to that effect either); I am not even sure what such an assumption would mean. When we look for explanations, using our canons of theory-preference, we are not either seeking or presupposing any sort of *report* as to the state of the world. An explanation is not a report of any kind, but an interchange or transaction between our minds and the world, and the canons are devices that mediate and

15 On such matters, and particularly on the relation between simplicity and informativeness, see Sober (1975). He writes, "Our desire for simple theories turns out (at least in part) to be a desire for 'efficient' deductive networks between the members of different families of natural predicates. We want any given link to have logically minimal input conditions while at the same time yielding outputs of great logical strength; we want to be able to say a great deal about the properties of any individual in our world without first having to find out very much about its special features. The degree to which this goal is attained is a measure of how well we have succeeded in rendering particular experience redundant" (p. 23).

16 More abstractly, suppose we are faced with a fairly well marked-out selection of apparently (but questionably) related phenomena and someone puts forward a statement *H* that logically implies the occurrence of all these phenomena but is very convoluted and messy; indeed, let us suppose *H* is internally no more elegant or economically organized than is the collection of phenomena itself (a limiting case would be that in which *H* is simply a seriatim description of the phenomena themselves). What reason would we have for calling *H* an *explanation*? (It seems built into our notion of "explanation" that somehow a range of superficially diverse observables get brought together under a unifying principle or systemic underlying mechanism – not that this remark is much of an *argument* for the rule of simplicity.) If *H* does not show by more streamlined, parsimonious means that the data were to be expected, then presumably *H* effects no reduction in uncertainty concerning the future.

expedite this transaction.[17] Simplicity, in particular, is a desired feature of the transaction for the reasons I have mentioned; it is a way of doing things, not itself a belief or assumption of any sort, and rule *1* is as utile a tool as it is no matter what reality is like.

2. Mother Nature would have built us to prefer hypotheses of greater explanatory power to narrower ones.

The same considerations that motivated her drive for simplicity apply here (as I said, I think rules *1* and *2* are of a piece). Also, it is much more efficient to use one powerful device than to have to select constantly from among a collection of weaker ones (assuming, of course, that the more powerful hypothesis is not very cumbersome or so powerful that it keeps getting us into trouble).

3. Mother Nature would not have wanted to waste storage space on beliefs that have little or nothing to do with our immediate interactions with the environment, unless they have enormous unifying, simplifying, and systematizing power.

This is simply because beliefs are primarily guides to action.

4. Mother Nature would build us to prefer neater systems of beliefs to messy ones full of pathways that lead nowhere.

If we think of belief systems as maps or charts, it is evident that neat ones allow us to find our way about the environment more surefootedly. Also, a particular belief that raises awkward questions thereby causes distraction; at least some mental time and energy have to go into pondering the questions, and that energy might be put to better use elsewhere.

5. Mother Nature would not want us to change our views capriciously and for no reason.

Arbitrary and gratuitous changes of belief, like arbitrary and gratuitous changes of a political institution, come only at a price; they draw on energy and resources. Also, the instability created by a habit of capricious belief change would be inefficient and confusing.[18] (Hypothesis *5* is not meant to preclude certain useful generate-and-test strategies; of course, we may sometimes want to try a series of working assumptions in turn to see which might pay off

17 On this, see Sober (1975, p. 169) and Walsh (1979).
18 These facts are overlooked by Keith Lehrer (1974), who prefers an anarchical open-mindedness. See Chapter 8, this volume.

the best. But I want to distinguish in the end between things we adopt merely as working assumptions and things we actually believe to be true.)

Our five hypotheses about the choices that would be made by a skillful and benevolent Mother Nature should sound familiar; in effect, they predict that when we are in top epistemic form we shall operate according to the canons of theory-preference gestured at in Section I. And whatever more detailed rules we are in fact wired to use, I should think some such evolutionary reason will be available that will answer the question why we are wired in that way. Even when we demythologize Mother Nature, herself, we will still be left with some convincing reason why it is good and desirable for us to be designed to use the methods we do rather than being designed in some other way. And this explains the most important sense in which our use of those methods is not arbitrary, thus answering the last of the Epistemologist's skeptical challenges.

The foregoing Panglossian reflections are not intended, please note, as an answer to any of the four preceding skeptical challenges – particularly not to the first or to the third. I am not claiming either that our basic methods' adaptive utility justifies them in the epistemological sense or that it *per se* provides any guarantee of true beliefs as output. Epistemology, in the official, normative sense, leaves off at our Benthamite answer to the first challenge in Section II. In the present section I have been trying to answer what I hope I have persuaded you is a different kind of question but worth investigation in its own right.

The Mother Nature story yields another benefit. I have said that it is *good* for us to have been designed in roughly the way we are. *Goodness* (so they say) is an evaluative property. And this may explain why, in epistemology, we trade in normative terms such as "warrant" and "justification." I suggest that the normative force of epistemologial terms comes from the value notions explicit or implicit in design-stance psychology. What Mother Nature provides is *good design*, and it is that evaluative notion that is the ultimate source of our ordinary superficial evaluative ideas of "better explanation," "rational inference," and so forth. As Dennett has observed (1978, 1981a, 1981b), our having survived as long as we have and indeed achieved dramatic preeminence in a hostile world shows decisively that we are well designed, especially so far as

143

intellectual matters are concerned. We may want to presume that our fundamental epistemic principles are, in particular, as utile as they can be, given Mother Nature's antecedent choices of environment, materials, and overall anatomical structure. If so, we are fully rational when our optimally selected epistemic mechanisms are working as well as they can – working as they do when they are not flagging owing to lack of energy, or jammed by conative noise, or the like.

But this is not quite the whole story, and not quite correct so far as it goes, either. Several objections remain to be answered.

IV   OBJECTIONS AND REPLIES

1. Isn't this Vitalism? Are we not positing occult, weirdly sentient forces in or behind nature that somehow endow inert physical matter with teleological properties and with an epistemic destiny? In calling a cognitive design a "good" or "optimal" design, do we not presuppose a supernatural Designer, or at least some being whose desires and purposes are being served by the design?

No. The notion of a good design is no more mysterious here than it is in virtually any branch of biology or biochemistry. I am proposing to reduce the evaluative notions of epistemology to the teleological notions of the theory of organ systems. The latter are considered respectable by biologists, even if there are philosophical problems about how they can best be understood – and there are philosophical problems about how *anything* can best be understood.

2. Even so, how are these teleological notions themselves to be naturalized? This is really two questions: What are we to make of teleological talk per se (as in "The function of the kidneys is to clean the blood")? And what, in particular, are we to make of teleological *value*, as in *"well* designed"? The force of the question is this: Even if no one is a vitalist anymore, how are the biologist's functional notions to be fitted into the causal order? What have they to do with the underlying level of ultimate reality, namely, atoms and the void? After all, traditional epistemology never claimed to be a description of a part of nature; it is we that are imposing on it the biting constraint of naturalism. But biology does claim, and always has claimed, to be a theory of (one level of) nature; so its constitutive notions do have to admit of naturalization.

Fortunately, there are at least two very productive lines of inquiry

144

that show strong promise of cashing the teleological notions in terms of atoms and the void. First, the work of W. C. Wimsatt and other philosophers of biology encourages and supports the prospect of explicating the teleological notions of biology in terms of evolutionary theory, population genetics, and the like.[19] Second, Jerry Fodor's and D. C. Dennett's ingenious way of "discharging" homunculi in pschychology, step-by-step as one descends through the organizational hierarchy of an "intentional system," is at the same time a way of discharging teleological notions, or so I have argued elsewhere (1981a, 1987a, following Fodor [1968a] and Dennett [1978, especially Chaps. 1, 5, 9]). So there is positive reason to think that the teleological notions of biology will not resist naturalization in the end.

What about teleological *value*? It seems clearly to be a species of instrumental value, à la Aristotle; a thing is well designed – or, more generally, good at its job – if it in fact promotes its telos efficiently, where "efficiency" may be spelled out in cost-benefit terms of some kind. Thus, teleological value judgments are a species of factual judgment, even though they are also evaluative.

3. Our epistemic methods are good and desirable supposedly in that they are "utile" – but utile for whom, and as regards what? Clearly the welfare of an individual organism, that of its genes, and that of its species can diverge; and just as clearly, an entity's welfare can be improved in one respect by an event while being diminished in another by the very same event. Can we put a name to the recipient of our supposed utilities and to the nature of the utilities received? If population genetics is to serve as the mechanism by means of which Mother Nature moves (her wonders to perform), then presumably the recipient is the individual organism and the uility in question is reproductive fitness or potential for passing on one's genes. (Alternatively, the recipient is the gene type, and the utility is its potential for being passed on.) Thus, my claim should be that our operating according to customary rules of theory-preference maximizes our reproductive fitness. But this may seem false. Indeed, one can easily think of instances in which individuals' use of rational methods leads straight to reproductive disaster: We use sophisticated means to prolong our own lives well past the age of fertility,

19 See Popper (1972), Wimsatt (1972, 1976), Wright (1973), and Neander (1981). However, for critical views, see Cummins (1975) and Bigelow and Pargetter (1987).

145

if we can, draining our species' resources at colossal rates; worse, we practice birth control and even voluntary sterilization in order to limit the number of our offspring, for reasons of our own personal convenience; and in defense of our national wealth and security we deliberately set events in motion that we know may well result in global thermonuclear extinction. If reproductive fitness is what Mother Nature cares about, then how can I still maintain that the brand of rationality she has given us is as good at its job as my program must suppose?

The objection evidently assumes that rationality *alone* produces the genetically undesirable effects I have listed. But, where "rationality" means simply our basic epistemic methods, this assumption is clearly false. As I shall return to emphasize later in this chapter, our epistemic methods are *topic-neutral*. They are insensitive to subject matter in the same way logic is; and in particular, they themselves make no (nonepistemic) conative presuppositions when it comes to practical reasoning. If Mother Nature overshot a bit in building in our instinct of self-preservation (then deftly compensating for it with the time bomb of aging), that is no reflection on the design of our cognitive methods per se. If for cultural reasons we form and pursue a desire to limit our families, whether or not that desire has any adaptive function, that is no fault of our all-purpose canons of theory-preference.[20] And if we are going to destroy ourselves in an eschaton of our own ingenious making, that is because our aggressive territorial instincts have outlived whatever adaptiveness they may have had when we were hominids, not because there is any fault in the structure of our ingenuity itself. The fact remains that other things being equal, hominids who were by chance disposed to use epistemic methods like ours lived long enough to have more children than did hominids who were not so disposed.

20 It is important to keep in mind, besides, that evolutionary theory does not predict success in perpetuity for every species. Mother Nature sometimes overshoots, or practices overkill, in her original design and previously adapted traits sometimes become obsolete as environments change. The complexity of brain that developed in early man may simply have run amok and caused us to value individual members of our species (particularly ourselves) for their own sake, without regard to inclusive fitness. (Andrew Oldenquist has emphasized this point to me.) So much the worse, perhaps, for the welfare of our genes, however strenuously someone might try to argue that increased egoism or self-concern on the part of individuals really promotes reproductive fitness too.

There is a temptation at this point to relativize the utility of the epistemic methods to specifically cognitive goals: A method would be an instance of good design iff it produced an optimal balance of truth over error, we might say. But what balance of truth over error *is* optimal, and for what purpose(s)? One way of answering this question is to collapse our explanationist theory into a reliabilist theory of the sort proposed by Goldman (1979): A belief is justified iff it is produced by a process (for us, a method of theory-preference) that is reliable in that it generally produces true beliefs rather than false ones; the probability of the truth of such a belief, given the type of process that caused it, is high, "probability" here bearing an essentially frequentist interpretation. Indeed, people who are skeptics concerning simplicity and our other quasi-aesthetic desiderata often ask, "Why does a theory's being *simple* make it more *likely to be true?*"

The immediate answer is that it does not, at least not in any straightforward way. To begin with, a theory that goes beyond its data in order to systematize them in a simple and economical way is of course less probable than is the conjunction of all the data sentences alone.[21] If high probability were our only cognitive concern, or even our main concern, we could just limit the contents of our beliefs to tautologies, protocols, and perhaps meter readings, as some philosophers have urged. But although likelihood of truth and avoidance of falsehood matter, they are not the only features of belief that matter, because beliefs are not merely consulted but mobilized as guides to action, often sudden and streamlined action. For the latter reason, efficiency of internal cognitive organization matters too, and so does predictive power.

But the question was: Of two theories, *both* of which outrun the data, why is the simpler more likely to be true? And I have not yet addressed that question. (I thank Alan Musgrave for pressing me

21 Cf. Sober (1975, Sec. 5.2); on p. 167 he points out that although in some instances we may hold that theories that are simple in certain respects are therein *un*likely to be true, we hold this on the basis of second-order inductions that themselves presuppose the value of simplicity considerations.

In any case, I do not see how a simple frequentist interpretation of "likelihood" in the formulation of reliability theories can succeed. That a certain process has never in historical fact led us astray is not by itself much of a recommendation; one would have to move, as Goldman suggests, to a modalized or counterfactual notion of "frequency," which is just to move to a subtler interpretation of probability.

on this point.) Actually, I *reject* it as stated, for two reasons. (1) As I said, following Bentham, earlier in this chapter, if one has isolated what is in fact an epistemically fundamental form of amplitative inference, one has isolated an epistemically *fundamental* form of inference, a fundamental epistemic method, and cannot properly be asked for a further "justification" of that method, even for an extrinsic link between that method and truth. I may of course be wrong in thinking that there is some magnitude called "simplicity" that is what drives some of our justified theory choices. (In that case there is some other detectable feature that does drive them, and in time we can detect it.) But if I am *not* wrong, and appeal to simplicity is in fact a fundamental epistemic method, then it is fundamental; no further question can arise regarding its "connection to truth." (I shall have more to say on this point in the next section of this chapter.) (2) For that matter, I do not in the first place accept the a priori assumption that epistemic justification must be a matter of quantitative relation to truth. Rationality is a many-factored value, and its component factors trade off against each other in complex ways that have evolved over all these millions of years. Although one may go on about the "optimal" balance of truth over error, *optimality* is an open-ended magnitude, and the balancing respects mobility and cost-effectiveness, as well as reliability in any easily specified narrow sense.

But this observation brings us to a final objection, more serious than any considered so far.

4. Aren't we simply falling in with Dr. Pangloss? What makes us think this is epistemically the best of all possible worlds? I began my argument for my claim that our canons of theory-preference are the ones that a skillful and benevolent Mother Nature would have given us by maintaining that Mother Nature had to work within certain serious though self-imposed constraints. In this sense, her choices were suboptimal. Yet more than once, later on, I sneaked in the suggestion that our being wired to use the canons we do use is a happy consequence of our being *optimally* designed; that suggestion has already been criticized by Stich (1985) and by Sober (1981, 1985).

At best, our design is optimal only relative to the constraints imposed by Mother Nature's prior choices anent general anatomy and the structure of our prerational crocodile brains. That still allows us a fairly clear sense in which it is *good* (and hence not arbitrary) for us, who do satisfy the constraints, to use the rules of theory-preference we do use. But there are at least four ways Mother Nature's choices are at the same time to be deprecated:

1. She could have built a much more successful cognizer if she had used better materials in the first place. We could have had far greater storage capacity, better memories, and so forth, if we had bigger heads. (The problem of the birth canal could have been alleviated by making us marsupials, which I have always thought should have occurred to Mother Nature in any case.) If we were made of durable hardware, we should be subject to fewer malfunctions due to tiredness, cerebral accident, or the like. And most obviously, if we had more sensitive receptors we would be less prone to sensory illusion. However, I do not see how any of these potential improvements in reception or in storage, within bounds of evolutionary feasibility, would affect the utility of our basic epistemic methods; perceptual and memory data would still fall well short of omniscience.[22]

2. Susceptibility to false beliefs of certain sorts may serve important noncognitive evolutionary needs. We systematically deceive ourselves in any number of useful ways: We quickly forget the painfulness of certain otherwise useful activities; we tend to overestimate the attractiveness and other admirable qualities of our own children; and so forth. Of course, these habits in no way impugn my characterization of warranted belief in terms of the epistemic methods that would have been selected by Mother Nature, since the unfounded though adaptive beliefs are presumably

22 Ron Laymon points out that in a way we are becoming radically superior cognizers, by developing sophisticated perception-magnifying instruments such as electron microscopes, as well as computers for massively increased storage and computation. This does somewhat reduce the importance of efficiency; we now have "inelegant grind-it-out techniques" that are more useful and accurate than their more efficient predecessors. But my basic point stands: Even after all the rich instrumentational evidence is in and stored and after all the feasible computations have been performed, a staggering amount of theorizing and hypothesis formation remains to be done, and all that avails is a set of methods of theory-preference.

On the other hand, our comparatively recent, explosive cultural evolution has affected both our self-conscious reasoning and our goals, thus enabling us to articulate and adopt various formal, explicit patterns of (e.g., statistical) reasoning for special purposes such as gambling. In this way, Mother Nature has (perhaps inadvertently) provided us not only with our basic epistemic methods but with the means to refine them, sharpen them, and even override them in the service of special pursuits.

not products of the operation of our basic epistemic methods but have psychological extraneous sources. It is important to keep in mind that the *methods* are what justify reasonable beliefs on my view, not the adaptiveness of the beliefs themselves. *If a belief is not sanctioned by the methods in light of its explanatory virtues, then it is unjustified, no matter how adaptive and/or psychologically compelling it is in itself.* The same point applies to the observation that false theories are frequently more useful, in the day-to-day sense, than their competitors.[23] Such a theory's handiness is indeed a significant explanatory virtue and thus, on my view, a mark in favor of believing it, but this virtue is outweighed in the end by the presumably deeper explanatory advantages of the competitor that replaced it. (Remember again that for me *epistemological* justification comes to rest with the final weighing of the explanatory advantages; there is no further tribunal, not even an evolutionary one.)

3. Mother Nature is a *satisficer* and has made many design shortcuts. As Dennett has put it, a human cognizer is a "passable jury rig," a "bag of tricks" (1981, p. 43–4).Some of our inductive methods themselves, for example, are over generalized in the interest of simplicity and fast action. A tendency to jump quickly to conclusions may be more useful, on the whole, than a scrupulous respect for textbook adequacy of sample size; at the same time, as Dennett and Stich have both mentioned, it may be better to err on the side of prudence in some matters. Now, how should we describe these satisficing results in normative terms? Stich is inclined to brand them as irrational or at least "normatively inappropriate" (1985, p. 126), even though they have adaptive value. But it is not clear to me that any sound and unequivocal notion of "rationality" is in play here, for in one sense it *is* plainly rational for us to use the heuristics and short-cut methods that Mother Nature has given us; they work out better for us in cost-benefit terms than would obsequious pursuit of academic perfection.[24] Sometimes it is rational

23 Ron Laymon offers the examples of Ptolemaic astronomy versus Copernican astronomy, as regards navigation; Newtonian astronomy versus the general theory of relativity, as regards launching satellites; and ray optics versus quantum physics or electrodynamics, as regards lens design.

24 Dennett (1981a) takes the position that "the concept of rationality is systematically pretheoretical" and that "rational" functions "as a general-purpose term of cognitive approval" rather than being tied unrevisably to any particular epistemic method or procedure. I am more inclined to think that we simply have at least two or three different notions of rationality.

in the cost-effective sense to be irrational in the textbook sense. Independent confirmation of this slightly surprising point is provided by at least one plausible approach to Newcomb's Problem.[25]

But to return to our main concern, are our beliefs *epistemically justified* when they are produced by one or another of Mother Nature's short-cut devices? Stich mentions three specific examples: Garcia's phenomenon, of rats' forming the belief that a certain food is dangerous on the basis of just one misleading instance of eating that food and subsequently becoming ill (Garcia, McGowan, and Green [1972]); Alcock's (1979) case of the toad that eats BBs until it is unable to move; and the "representativeness heuristic" posited by Nisbett and Wilson (1977). These examples may damage the argument of Dennett's that Stich uses them to criticize, but I do not see that any of them impugns the view that I am now developing. Considerations of space prohibit a detailed discussion here, but let us take just the typical case of a beneficially overcautious, or "Better safe than sorry," heuristic. By its nature, such a heuristic has a subject-matter; "Better safe than sorry" invites the query, "Safe from what?" Garcia's rats' heuristic conduces to safety from toxic foods, for example. But a heuristic that has a specific subject matter in this way is not topic-neutral, and so it is not a *fully general* cognitive method (indeed, we may question whether it is properly a *cognitive* method at all). It is an override, one that produces beliefs (perhaps) and inclinations that would not be sanctioned by an all-purpose and hence topic-neutral epistemic device. Since my view is that a belief is justified only when it is (in some way) the output of one of our basic, topic-neutral canons of theory-preference, I am not stuck with the unwelcome judgment that Garcia's rats are rational believers.

4. There is no factual guarantee that evolution has succeeded optimally, even from the cost-benefit point of view. Even within our original constraints, chance events have probably prevented desirable developments that would otherwise have occurred; and as Sober (1981, 1985) has emphasized, it is not obvious when a trait

25 See Gibbard and Harper (1981). They express what they take to be the moral of Newcomb's Problem as follows: "If someone is very good at predicting behavior and rewards predicted irrationality richly, then irrationality will be richly rewarded" (p. 181). However, we might add that if I *know* that someone is very good at predicting behavior and rewards predicted irrationality richly, then it is rational for me to act irrationally.

is the product of selection rather than of random drift, mutation, or migration. If our basic epistemic mechanisms are in fact not the products of an indefatigably optimific process of natural selection alone, what is the relevance of our appeal to evolutionary considerations? Sober says:

> We might have to revert to our optimality arguments and argue that it is optimality *rather than* actual genesis which explains what makes our mental equipment rational to whatever degree it is. We would then have to grant that the evolution of rationality – i.e., its actual history of emergence – has *no* bearing on the question of why our cognitive apparatus is rational; we would have to grant that the actual sequence of evolutionary events leaves absolutely opaque why the traits which emerged were any good. (1981, p. 111; italics mine)

Of course, my own argument is stated as an "optimality argument" in Sober's sense, since it begins by asking what cognitive mechanisms a skillful and benevolent Mother Nature *would have* bestowed on us under such and such conditions and lets alone the historical question of where our basic cognitive traits really come from. Does it follow that an answer to the latter question "leaves absolutely opaque why the traits which emerged [here, our basic cognitive methods] were any good"? If so, I should think the same argument would apply to any hypothetical evolutionary explanation of the emergence of a trait designed to exhibit the adaptive value of that trait. But let us consider Sober's problem a little more closely.

We must distinguish, as so far I have neglected to do, among (1) the cognitive mechanisms we in fact use, working as they do under normal combat conditions; (2) those same mechanisms, working as they do under epistemically ideal conditions (i.e., working as well as they possibly ever can, unimpeded by fatigue, noise, etc.); and (3) the cognitive mechanisms Mother Nature *would have* given us (relative to her original constraints) had she been in full control of her materials. As I understand it, Sober's point is that since selection is only part of the whole etiological story, there is no reason to think that item 3 coincides exactly with point 1 or even with item 2. Thus, in promoting item 3 as the locus of epistemic value, I am precisely *not* defending the epistemic mechanisms that we actually have and use, but am in effect comparing them unfavorably with rather better ones that we could have had but do not. Some readjustment is required; how can we make our theory predict the epistemic value of the procedures we do use (understood ideally as item 2)?[26]

We must now think of Mother Nature as being in less than full control of the development of species. (Perhaps this is heresy, but here I stand.) Mother Nature works through selection, we may suppose, but she is somewhat at the mercy of chance events, mutation, drift, and so on. So perhaps we should simply effect another relativization of our original notion of optimality: Mother Nature does the best she can for her creatures, within her self-imposed constraints *and* given the vagaries of her medium. Now, as before, we may ask what cognitive methods Mother Nature would have bestowed on us under such newly complicated conditions. I think it is still plausible to suppose that she would have given us something like the rule of theory-preference I have listed. This is now plainly an empirical suggestion, since it amounts to saying flatly that the effect of nonselectional factors in the evolutionary process has not (in actual historical fact) been great enough to deflect Mother Nature's basic strategy of maximizing cognitive efficiency in the ways I sketched in Section III. I am inclined to accept this empirical claim for two reasons: First, the strategic preferences I have ascribed to Mother Nature are so general and so basic that we would be unlikely to have survived in as handsome style as we have if those preferences had not been realized at least in large part. Second, the resulting rules of theory-preference are virtually environment-neutral, in addition to being topic-neutral; it is hard to imagine an earthly environment, no matter how bizarre, in which they would not serve well. Thus, it seems reasonable to retrodict selection pressure toward them, no matter what normal chance events may have intervened or twisted the evolutionary path.

Perhaps, despite this, the campaign for optimality will fail in some way; but if we must drop "optimal," we may substitute "pretty damn good." All's for *nearly* the best, in this next-best of all possible worlds.

26 I overlooked this point in my " 'Is' and 'Ought' in Cognitive Science" (1981b). But I still think that the relativity of "optimality" and "suboptimality" to sets of background conditions is what lies behind the current controversy over psychological experiments designed to reveal systematic and pervasive patterns of "irrationality" in human reasoning. (Cohen [1981] is a summary and critique of some of these experiments.) I suspect the dispute will turn out to be largely verbal.

The worries of this section might be taken to encourage skepticism again. Given all the respects in which our cognitive capacities are *sub*optimal, should we not conclude that we are epistemically lowly and unworthy beings who stumble along as well as we can but never succeed in doing what a futuristic supercomputer, or God, or another superbeing could do? At the very least, should we not stop claiming to *know* things and say merely that to the best of our feeble ability to probe at reality, using our pathetically primitive equipment, we suppose that such and such is true? I do not see why. As I have mentioned, the word "know" is *our* word, invented by humans for humans and geared to human standards of efficiency and reliability. The fact that we are subject to certain limitations and that our equipment is not adequate to every possible epistemic task does not entail that the equipment is not adequate to *any* epistemic task. There are some things, it seems, about which our instruments are adequately efficient and reliable by the standards that govern the ordinary use of the word "know." The fact that there could be beings who were epistemically superior to us in a general way does not affect the fact that about some things we are sophisticated enough to satisfy the common standard.[27]

V   A FINAL CLARIFICATION

Bas van Fraassen (1980) and other contributors to the recent philosophy of science literature (Hacking [1982], Cartwright [1983]) have expressed a distinctive and appealing sort of doubt about explanationism.

When a theory is advocated, it is praised for many features other than empirical adequacy and strength: it is said to be mathematically elegant, simple, of great scope, complete in certain respects: *also* of wonderful use in unifying our account of hitherto disparate phenomena, and most of all, explanatory. Judgements of simplicity and explanatory power are the intuitive and natural vehicle for expressing our epistemic appraisal. What can an empiricist make of these other virtues which go so clearly beyond the ones he considers pre-eminent?

27 This material was first formally presented to Peter Machamer's workshop in epistemology at the University of Pittsburgh in 1981. I am indebted to all the participants for their many useful comments, which helped me to improve this chapter. I am especially grateful to Larry Laudan for a set of insightful criticisms that I do not know how to answer; rather than try to take them up before press time, I hope to expound them and deal with them in a future paper.

There are specifically human concerns, a function of our interests and pleasures, which make some theories more valuable or appealing to us than others. Values of this sort, however, provide reasons for using a theory, or contemplating it, whether or not we think it true, and cannot rationally guide our epistemic attitudes and decisions. For example, if it matters more to us to have one sort of question answered rather than another, that is no reason to think that a theory which answers more of the first sort of question is more likely to be true. (van Fraassen [1980, p.87])

Two arguments are encapsulated here. The first I have already touched on in the preceding section: Why is an explanatory virtue such as simplicity or power supposed to make a theory more likely to be true? The second argument may be put as follows. Truth and empirical adequacy are relations between theories and the world, or at least they involve the world as a crucial determinant. But explanatory goodness is a relation purely between theories and minds, to which the world seems irrelevant; explanation has to do with the role a representation plays within a subject's private cognitive economy, not with anything external to the subject. Why, then, would explanatory goodness be a mark of truth? Or, as Ian Hacking (1982) puts it, what "warrants of truth" could be offered by "what makes our minds feel good," per se?

Let me revisit the first argument and then turn to the second.

Some philosophers evidently think that a proposed epistemic method must be defended in a way that (either historically or a priori) *connects the method to truth.* My own appeal to the history of science in Section I of this chapter may seem to suggest that we look back at that history and try to pick out the methods of theory choice that have most often *led to truth.* Such an enterprise would presume that we already (now) have access to truth independently of establishing any epistemic methods. I am not sure that the circularity or regress implicit in that presumption is vicious, but I would prefer to avoid it, and I officially shun it here. Rather, just as the logician starts with a set of intuitively valid inferences and a set of intuitively invalid ones, the epistemologist starts with a set of intuitively rational theory choices and a set of (actually or counterfactually) irrational ones.

Nor, please note, do I understand "rational" here as "likely to yield truth," for this would be both to take "likely" as primitive, and to introduce "true" at the beginning of our epistemological quest rather than see it fall out at the end. It seems to me that the

155

idea of rationality or warrant is more accessible to everyday intuition than is any particular notion of "likelihood" or probability,
and as we shall see, I think no formal probability relation can
exhaust epistemological justifiability. Also, introducing "true" at
this point would both threaten circularity or regress again and invite
questions of the form "But what reasons have you to think that U
leads to truth?" where U is a posited ultimate principle of theory-
choice. Such questions have answers, but the answers can only be
given after our system of epistemic principles is in place; they cannot
properly be demanded at the outset. In the beginning, "rational"
is a primitive term used to evaluate epistemic acts; particular principles are later seen to "tend toward truth," because the beliefs they
produce are rational – not the other way around (see argument _3_
in Section II of this chapter).

A similar response may be made to our second version of van
Fraassen's argument. The question is, Why should a relation between theories and minds (that of the former making the latter feel
good) ground or serve as a mark of an apparently quite separate
relation between theories and the world? But the question can be
taken in either of two ways: (1) Why should we as epistemologists
think that the explanatory virtues are what underlie all justified
belief? (2) Can we demonstrate either historically or a priori that a
connection obtains between the explanatory virtues and truth (or
empirical adequacy)? And here we can divide and conquer. Query
_1_ succumbs to our Benthamite strategy; if the explanatory virtues
seem after exhaustive reflection to be what all justified theory choice
has in common, that is as good evidence as one could have that
they do in fact underlie all justified belief. Query _2_ has already been
answered firmly in the negative, but I have repudiated the skeptic's
right to the demonstration demanded. We can no more "prove"
the truth-conducingness of the explanatory virtues than we can
prove that of Modus Ponens, but there is no embarrassment in
either inability. Some set of epistemic methods or other must be
seen to be epistemologically primitive. I may be wrong in thinking
that my favorite explanatory virtues constitute that set of methods,
but the primitiveness I claim for them cannot possibly be _itself_ an
epistemological objection.

8

Conservatism and the data base

I have been much concerned that so many people today with Conservative instincts feel compelled to apologize for them. Or if not to apologize directly, to qualify their commitment in a way that amounts to breast-beating.

So wrote Barry Goldwater in *The Conscience of a Conservative*. (He went on to quote Richard Nixon, then vice-president of the United States, as saying that although Republicans should be conservatives, they should be "conservatives with a heart.") I have conservative instincts, not in building societies but in building belief systems, and so do you. I am not going to apologize for my doxastic conservatism, and let us not beat our breasts either. My purpose in this chapter is, rather, to show how a policy of conservatism is justified and how it helps in solving each of two difficulties for the explanationist theory of epistemic justification I have been defending.

I   THE VIRTUE OF CONSERVATISM

As we have seen, the explanatory virtues are easily enumerated, at least in slogan form. But what reason have we to think that these humble, conventional virtues are really what determine epistemic justification or *warrant*? How do simplicity, power, coherence, fruitfulness, and so forth count toward truth?

Again, this question really splits into three questions, which are sometimes confused with one another. (1) What reason have we to think that these humble conventional virtues are really what control our intuitions about the justified–unjustified distinction; that is, is it really this list of virtues that captures that intuitive distinction? (2) What justifies any particular appeal to one or more of the virtues? If I say, "T_1 is simpler than T_2, and other things are equal, so let us adopt T_1 rather than T_2," what justifies this use of simplicity as a criterion of theory-preference? (3) Is it a good thing that we do use these particular virtues as criteria of theory-preference, and if so, why?

As I tried to show in Chapter 7, these three questions have different sorts of answers. In answer to question *1*, I would compare epistemology to logical theory and to ethics, as a discipline that begins with some clear intuitions about cases – cases of justified conduct and cases of unjustified conduct – and tries to formulate general principles that will sort the cases into the right barrels and also settle other, disputed cases in a reasonable way. On this view, the epistemologist and the philosopher of science look back at the history of science (broadly construed) and try to spot the factors that distinguish intuitively rational theory-preference from irrational theory-preference. Note that this is a job for professionals, epistemologists and philosophers of science; it is not something that must be carried out by any ordinary person in order for that person's own everyday beliefs to be justified. The answer to question *2* – "What justifies any particular appeal to one or more of the virtues?" – is "Nothing," if the question is taken to mean, "What *more general and fundamental principle* mandates simplicity or conservatism?" Obviously, some epistemic principles are ultimate; what is used to prove everything else cannot itself be proved, as Bentham says. Once a final answer to question *1* has been given, question *2* does not arise. (What justifies Modus Ponens? What is good about happiness?)

A reminder apropos question *1*: I have not suggested that we look back at the history of science and try to pick out the methods of theory choice that have most often led to truth. Rather, we are to start with a set of intuitively rational theory choices and a set of (actually or counterfactually) irrational ones, and extrapolate. Nor, again, do I understand "rational" as "likely to yield truth."

Question *3* is more interesting and admits of a more illuminating answer. I have tried to spell out the answer in Chapter 7 by adopting a form of epistemic rule-utilitarianism, with the aid of some grossly vulgarized Darwin. Crudely, the idea is again that it *is* a good thing, in cost-benefit terms, that we choose theories on the basis of simplicity and the other explanatory virtues. Specifically, these methods of theory choice are the ones that a wise and benevolent Mother Nature would have given us, subject to the constraints imposed by her prior choices of materials, overall anatomical structure, the nature of our prerational crocodile brains, and the very general

158

shape and characters of our environment, because our having these methods rather than others has survival (and welfare) advantage. For example, Mother Nature would want us to organize our receptor input as efficiently as possible and also to incorporate it into our standing belief set. Simplicity is itself a form of cognitive efficiency (plenitude of result, in the form of data explained and events predicted, with parsimony of means); besides, simpler hypotheses are easier to work with, and complexities incur greater risk of error. Similarly, Mother Nature would have us prefer theories with greater explanatory power to narrower ones (efficiency of organization again) and would not want to waste storage space on beliefs that have little or nothing to do with our immediate interactions with the environment, unless they had enormous unifying and systematizing power, simply because beliefs are primarily guides to action; hence our attachment to explanatory power and testability. She would also have built us to prefer neat belief systems to messy ones full of pathways that lead nowhere, since messy ones would be harder to apply to our environment in footing our way about it, and mental time and energy would be wasted by the distraction of awkward questions and loose ends.

It is important to remind ourselves[1] that these hasty Panglossian reflections are not intended as an answer to our earlier question 2. That is, I am not suggesting that our customary canons of theory-preference are *epistemically justified* by the adaptive utility of our habit of using them; I have already denied that they are justified in the epistemological sense by anything at all. Certainly I am not suggesting that Pascal's Wager is epistemically warranted, even if it is prudentially warranted. I am only saying why I think it is a good thing that we do operate according to those canons, although I do contend that the goodness, in the cost-benefit sense, of Mother Nature's design for cognizers is the ultimate ground of the value notions of epistemology ("justification," "warrant," "good reason," "legitimacy," "license").

Even so, I must reiterate the qualification expressed in Chapter 7. By way of doing so, let us back up and look at a simpler putative connection between belief, justification, and utility or adaptiveness.

1 Pardon my repeating this from the preceding chapter, but I have found in discussion that heavy repetition and emphasis of the present point is necessary.

Someone might think that an individual belief could be justified by *its own* adaptive utility, particularly if, following Peirce, one thinks of beliefs as tools or instruments. But there are obvious counter-examples to the thesis that all and only beliefs that themselves have adaptive value are epistemically justified; all sorts of patently unreasonable beliefs may enhance reproductive fitness(!). That is why I am an epistemic rule-utilitarian rather than an act-utilitarian and hold that beliefs are justified by their explanatory virtues alone. The adaptive value that figures in my theory inheres rather in the *methods* of belief formation, in the tools with which we make cognitive tools (and at that, it does not confer justification of the epistemic sort upon those methods).

But I cannot stop there, for more counterexamples loom: It is easy to imagine cases in which, for some specific purpose, Mother Nature endows us with a belief-forming method, perhaps a heuristic for use in situations of a certain specific type, which might have great adaptive value despite being totally irrational. Indeed, as we have seen, Stich (1985) has offered examples culled from cognitive psychology and from animal studies in which subjects seem to operate according to a "Better safe than sorry" heuristic, rather than by rational assessment of the evidence. What seems to me distinctive about such cases is that these heuristics are not *all-purpose* belief-forming methods; they are geared to certain types of purposes, such as the evading of predators or the avoiding of toxic foods. It seems reasonable to regard these methods as *overrides* of the subjects' more basic epistemic mechanisms, installed by Mother Nature for reasons that are obvious in particular cases. Therefore, I must tie my account of justified belief to the belief-forming methods that are all-purpose and fully general. That is why I have proposed that a belief is epistemically justified if and only if it is rated highly overall by the set of all-purpose, *topic-neutral* canons of theory-preference that would have been selected by Mother Nature for creatures of our general sort, where "topic-neutral" means being subject-matterless. I will stick to this proposal, for present purposes.[2]

2 Actually this will not do. William Harper has pointed out to me that a belief-forming method can be an "override" in my sense and still be subject-matterless or "topic-neutral." E.g., the members of an exotic tribe might be hard-wired to believe anything told them by a child so long as they are in the child's presence, because, due to other twists in the evolutionary path, the children are abnormally

As I have said, a Just-So story of the sort I have sketched can also be told about a rule of epistemic conservatism: Mother Nature would not want us to change our minds capriciously and for no reason. Any change of belief, like any change in social or political institution, exacts a price, by drawing on energy and resources. A habit of changing one's mind on a whim or otherwise gratuitously, like a habit of unrestrained social experimentation or a national disposition toward political coups or other sudden power and real estate grabs, would be inefficient and confusing; the instability it would create would be poorly suited to a creature whose need for cognitive organization in aid of sudden and streamlined action is great. (My wife points out that it does help, in the morning, not to have to reason your way to the bathroom.)[3] This point is missed, I believe, by Keith Lehrer, who writes:

The overthrow of accepted opinion and the dictates of common sense are often essential to epistemic advance. Moreover, an epistemic adventurer may arrive at beliefs that are not only new and revelatory, but also better *justified* than those more comfortably held by others. The principle of the conservation of accepted opinion is a roadblock to inquiry, and, consequently, it must be removed. (1974, p. 184)

and

Such [conservative] epistemology favors the sentiments of . . . defenders of the status quo in both philosophy and politics. And the principle that, what is, is justified, is not a better principle of epistemology than of politics or morals. (1978, p. 358)

sensitive to epistemic criticism and would sicken and die of rejection if disbelieved. So topic-neutrality alone does not suffice to distinguish "all-purpose," basic epistemic method from overrides; another condition is needed. Jarrett Leplin has pointed out to me in conversation that natural selection could never favor children of Harper's hypersensitive sort; I agree, but regretfully take that to be a plainly empirical and contingent fact that cannot bear the weight of our explanationist reductive program.

3 My defense of a canon of conservatism is very like that fashioned by Sklar (1975, 1981). Indeed, what I have to say improves on Sklar's discussion in only one way: As he says (1975, pp. 385–6), "In trying to decide if conservatism is a justifiable rule for rational belief we are in deep water, for what is required is a general account of justification in epistemology." My project here is to set conservatism within the context of such an account, one that I have devised and defended antecedently.

William James describes the conservative attitude nicely in "What Pragmatism Means" (1954, pp. 148–50), but he there ties conservatism into the analysis of truth; I reject pragmatic and other epistemic theories of truth.

161

One cannot disagree with Lehrer's premises, but they hardly vindicate epistemic anarchism. Political reformers, indeed political anarchists, push for social change because they think there is something wrong with the status quo or at least that it can be improved. Epistemic adventurers similarly think that new beliefs will exceed present beliefs in overall explanatory goodness, and quite often they are right. A theory's coherence with what we already believe is only one virtue among others, and it is easily outweighed. Indeed, I shall emphasize in the next section that it is the least significant of the conventional epistemic virtues; the two roles that it plays are humble, though essential.

In my original list, I stated the mark of conservatism as "coherence with what one already has reason to believe." Actually a stronger conservative rule is both available and endorsed by our Mother Nature story: "Other things being equal, prefer the theory that coheres best with what one already *believes*," period. This bolder principle is vindicated by our earlier considerations of the inefficiency and instability of gratuitous changes of mind. But it has a slightly startling consequence. Consider my present belief set B, and three theories T_1, T_2, and T_3. T_1 is logically equivalent to B; T_2 is logically stronger than B; and T_3 is incompatible with B, though T_3 and B may have a large intersection. Now, T_3 may outweigh T_1 and T_2 in explanatory advantages, in which case we should reject those theories in favor of T_3. But suppose this is not so. Then we should prefer either T_2 or T_1, according to our strengthened canon of conservatism. T_2, by virtue of its greater strength, may have an explanatory advantage over T_1, or it may not, but in either case our rule of conservatism justifies us in accepting one of the two, *absent* any competitor other than T_3. But either entails B, my present belief set. It follows that I am justified in accepting B, merely in virtue of my already holding B. Our rule of conservatism, then, is tantamount to the claim that the *bare fact of one's holding* a belief renders that belief justified, to some degree; any belief at all is at least minimally warranted.

Descartes would be appalled. He thought that without some additional guarantee, the beliefs that one happens to find oneself holding are subject to the severest skepticism.[4] (Paul Feyerabend would

---

4 Although it is currently fashionable (and correct) to attack Descartes on *externalist*

go farther and suggest that the fact of one's now presently holding a belief is considerable evidence that the belief is *false*.) Yet I think the strengthened rule of conservatism is correct, complacent consequence and all. I shall now argue that our conservative policy helps explanationism out of some difficulties and shall then answer a few objections.

II   ESTABLISHING THE DATA BASE

According to the explanationist, a person S at a time t has many beliefs that are justified by their ability to explain other beliefs. But at t, S must have some beliefs that are justified on some other basis. There are three reasons why this is so. (1) Otherwise there would be either an infinite regress or a vicious circle of explanations. (2) It is easy to give examples of beliefs we have that are justified but explain nothing, such as (to take an example put forward by George Pappas) my belief that my visual field contains little moving spots. It is possible to maintain that that belief really is justified by a secret explanatory achievement that is inaccessible to my consciousness, but I cannot think of any independent motivation for such a claim. (3) Explanation is asymmetric, in that it proceeds from stronger propositions to weaker propositions. (In a paradigm case, when P explains Q, P entails Q but is not entailed by Q.) It is hard to imagine how a lot of little, weak propositions could band together to explain a big, strong general proposition; so it is hard to see how there could be even a nonvicious *circle* of explanations. But any finite or nonfinite regress of explanations would produce weaker and weaker explanations as explananda, and it seems clear that we will come to a point at which one of our explainees will be so weak and obvious and uninteresting that one could not plausibly think it justified by its ability to explain some even weaker proposition.

How, then, can an explanationist account for the warrantedness of beliefs that are justified but not justified by their ability to explain other beliefs? (This is the problem of the "explained unexplainers," raised by Sellars and by Lehrer.) Two suggestions come to mind.

1. Some beliefs are justified by being (logically) deduced from more

grounds, I shall attack, instead, his presumption that nothing can be taken for granted at the outset – that everything is, simultaneously, open to question.

general beliefs that have been justified antecedently on explanatory grounds. It is unquestionable that some beliefs are justified in this indirect way. As a trivial example, take my belief that either the molecular theory of gases is true or Jesse Helms is in Tanzania. As a less trivial example, I suggest that we are justified in believing that there are numbers, including irrational and imaginary numbers, because the existence of numbers is entailed by certain theorems of kinematics and other sciences that do explain things, even though it is not obvious that the belief that there are numbers explains any other belief on its own hook.

Unfortunately for the explanationist, this suggestion will not solve the problem. For if a belief is justified *only* by its deduction from an explainer, then it is justified only if the explainer is antecedently justified on the basis of its ability to explain something else. So there must still be some other kind of ultimate explainee.

2. Some beliefs are justified by being explained by justified explainers. This suggestion is investigated by Lehrer and by James Cornman. I think it holds more than a grain of truth, as I shall argue later on, and it has some prima facie appeal. To return to Pappas's example, I believe that my visual field contains little moving spots. Now, why would I believe that my visual field contained such spots if it did not? I could make up some desperate hypothesis suggesting some other reason why my visual field seems to me to contain the spots, even though it really does not – for example, that invisible Martians were tampering with my introspector – but no such hypothesis is equal in explanatory goodness to the simple supposition that my visual field seems to me to contain the spots because it does contain them. If pressed, we can go farther and give a deeper explanation of the presence of the spots, in terms of corneal imperfections or particles floating in my aqueous humor or whatever. (If you are put off by this reification of a "visual field," change the example to that of your favorite noninfer ential perceptual belief. Lehrer's favorite is that he has blood on his shoe.)

But this account incurs a difficulty not unlike the one I raised against the preceding suggestion. Unlike the deductive consequences mentioned there, the explainees in question are presumably going to be the ultimate explainees themselves; that is, they are going to be the initial data that get the whole explanatory enterprise started in the first place. And that, essentially, is our question: How *does* the whole explanatory enterprise get started in the first place?

The present suggestion is that we begin with a set of initial data, explain these by making certain hypotheses, defend the hypotheses on the basis of their ability to explain the data, and then defend the initial data on the ground that they are explained by a set of justified explanatory hypotheses. Right: Any elementary logic student would spot the circularity.

As I see it, the problem for the explanationist is to break into the circle by finding independent justification for the initial data ("independent" in the sense of being epistemically prior to their being explained by justified explainers). This is just a special case of the problem that C. I. Lewis and others have raised for coherence theories generally; others have wrestled with it too, notably Nicholas Rescher.[5] One simple solution would be to appeal to an unrevisable given. But Quine and Sellars have argued persuasively against this idea. If we accept their arguments and return the given to sender, we must find a *defeasible* independent justification for the initial data. We must also delimit the class of data propositions: Which beliefs of mine at t are my initial data or ultimate explainees at t? (Lehrer [1974] and Cornman [1980] have both pointed out that if no class of beliefs is thus selected before we begin to measure explanatory coherence, "coherence" can be maximized at no cost by our simply throwing out almost all our perceptual beliefs and memories, or at least all that are in any way troublesome. I mean to block this maneuver.)

Let us begin with the fact that we have *spontaneous beliefs* that are produced in us by a number of sources. We find out what those sources are only after engaging in some theory construction, so I cannot appeal to the sources yet. I am pointing only to the fact that at any given time, I find myself holding beliefs that are not (at least consciously) inferred from other beliefs. Typically these will be beliefs about my immediate environment, perhaps about some of my own mental states, or perhaps about something else.

I want to propose the following Principle of Credulity: "Accept at the outset each of those things that seem to be true." That is, I hold that each of the spontaneous beliefs I have mentioned is prima

5 Cf. Rescher (1973, Chap. 3; 1976; 1977; 1980); the problem has also been raised by Lehrer (1974) and Cornman (1980, pp. 147–50). The theory I am developing is structurally similar to Rescher's but differs in detail. On the present point, he speaks of "data-directed coherence" (1973, p. 65). See also Alan Goldman (1979, 1981).

facie justified and therefore available as a candidate for explanation to get our explanatory enterprise off the ground. Now, why should anyone accept the Principle of Credulity? (Might it not just as well be called the Principle of Stupidity?) Is doxastic behavior of this sort not just arbitrary at best, as Cornman (1980) charges?

Not if my general theory of justification is right. Conservatism as a canon of theory-preference has no justification in the epistemological sense, but neither have simplicity, testability, fruitfulness, and the other explanatory virtues. What they have instead is their respective Just-So stories to back them, and as we have seen, the canon of conservatism has one of those too. The rule of conservatism has just the same epistemic authority as any reason we can ever have for preferring one member of a pair of empirically equivalent theories to another. Of course, the Principle of Credulity is a very degenerate instance of the canon of conservatism, since it makes no reference to competing hypotheses and so is not on its face a canon of theory-*preference*. But (1) I argued in the preceding section that if, like the positivists, we allow a logically equivalent axiomatization of our belief set B to count as an explanation of B, the conservative canon of theory-preference entails (in effect) the Principle of Credulity anyway. (2) We knew – or should have known, in any case – that we were going to need some epistemic principle (or principles) that would apply to beliefs other than those that happen to be members of pairs of competing hypotheses (this is made obvious by the asymmetry of explanation and the consequent inevitability of ultimate explainees). (3) As we shall see in the next section, the rule of conservatism itself is not an entirely ordinary canon of the theory-preference but has a mildly distinguished role to play. (4) The Just-So story I told about the canon of conservatism would back the Principle of Credulity as well, in exactly the same way. So it seems that the principle itself has as sound epistemic credentials as has any of our conventional canons of theory-preference.

Nevertheless, both the canon of conservatism and the Principle of Credulity are *highly defeasible*, indeed (as I shall maintain) they can be defeated by almost anything: new input, noncoherence with other beliefs even in a minimal way, slight explanatory advantage to be gained elsewhere, or whatever. The justification conferred on a spontaneous belief by the Principle of Credulity is flickering and

166

feeble. Many of our spontaneous beliefs get thrown out almost instantaneously.

Does it not follow that, since our explanatory chain is only as strong as its first link (the ultimate explainees), all of our subsequent explainers will be only very weakly justified as well, and that although our beliefs may be made very minimally reasonable in this way, they are still not justified in the strong sense required for knowledge, or anything approaching it? It would follow, if that were all there was to it. In fact, I think, the minimal justification conferred on spontaneous beliefs by the Principle of Credulity can be and is *reinforced* in several ways by the superadded explanatory structure. This is where explanatory "coherence" comes in. There are (at least) three kinds of coherence that help to reinforce the justification of spontaneous beliefs.

First, there is ordinary logical consistency. Some spontaneous beliefs are logically inconsistent with other spontaneous beliefs and will be dropped for this reason. (Which of two incompatible spontaneous beliefs should be dropped, however, is a question that requires appeal to overarching explanatory considerations.) Second, there is consistency, and perhaps "fit" in a looser sense, with previously justified explanatory beliefs or with explanatory beliefs conjoined with other spontaneous beliefs. Some of our initial data will be thrown out as hallucinations, misperceptions, inaccurate memories, and miscalculations, because they do not square with the empirical predictions generated from other, firmer bodies of data by justified explainers. A spontaneous belief that has survived each of these two tests of coherence is much more strongly justified than is a spontaneous belief that has yet to face them. To put a name to it, we might say that a survivor of this sort is not only prima facie justified, but is *tenable*.

The third kind of "coherence" I have in mind is the most important. It is (I think) the one that Lehrer intends when he suggests that ultimate explainees are justified by being explained. This suggestion is still true, and is even more effective, now that we have removed the threat of circularity that bothered us earlier. Suppose we have a spontaneous belief that is coherent with our other beliefs in each of the ways just discussed. Suppose, in addition, that our total body of beliefs and theories yields an idea of how that specific spontaneous belief was produced in us – perhaps even a mechanical

167

explanation of how it was. Finally, suppose that according to this idea or explanation, the mechanism that produces the belief was (as we say) a reliable one, in good working order. Then, I submit, our spontaneous belief is fully justified, and we may want to count it as an item of knowledge.

(Qualification: I am not suggesting that in order for the spontaneous belief to be fully justified, or to count as knowledge, the believer must know or be justified in believing *that* his or her belief was produced in him or her by a reliable mechanism in any very technical sense, and I do not mean to require knowledge of multiply iterated counterfactuals, objective physical propensities, or other such exotica. Such principles would threaten to launch a regress and, consequently, a dive on our part down the coal-scuttle that leads to the black pit of skepticism. What is required, for the spontaneous belief to be fully justified, is only that the believer be aware of the source of the belief and recognize that the source is a generally trustworthy one. I think my four-year-old satisfies this condition; if asked how she knows that there is a guinea pig in her playroom, she is quite capable of replying that she can see that there is, and she knows that she sees with her eyes.)

It is in this way that a spontaneous belief gets swept up into a coherent explanatory structure; surpassing mere testability, the belief is incorporated into an entire doxastic system that includes beliefs about the sources of our beliefs. Perhaps there is circularity here, but the circle is large, satisfying, and *data-directed* (in Rescher's phrase), anchored rather than floating free.

Coherence of the third kind will rule out what we might call "wild" spontaneous beliefs. The spontaneous beliefs that I have focused on so far are of familiar, lovable sorts, produced by perceptual mechanisms, memory, and the like. But we acquire lots of other spontaneous beliefs as well, some of which survive the first two coherence tests and so achieve tenability. For example, we all have primitive, superstitious forebodings of various kinds – eerie feelings that such and such is so, fits of inspiration, tricks of memory, such as déjà vu. Some people unquestionably have religious feelings and experiences. All these sorts of things (and more) can qualify as or produce spontaneous beliefs that may be tenable – logically consistent with all one's other spontaneous beliefs and with one's other theories as well, however suspicious they may seem even to the believer. We do not want such beliefs to count as fully justified. I suggest the reason is that typically they do not achieve coherence of the third kind. Either we simply do not find any information-transmitting mechanisms that are producing them, no matter how hard we look or how much we know about our minds, or we find positively discrediting evidence – minor or major disorders whose presence explains the wild beliefs away.[6] Thus, although these beliefs are tenable, the ability of other hypotheses to explain them will not count much in favor of those hypotheses.

There are many interesting borderline cases here. One very robust one is that of our *logical intuitions*. Where do logical intuitions come from, and do logical theories *explain* them? Grammatical and other linguistic intuitions raise similar questions, already debated by philosophers of linguistics (see, e.g., Stich [1975] and Rosenberg [1986]). (Note that such intuitions, along with more arcane metaphysical and epistemological intuitions, are the philosopher's stock-in-trade.) Religious experiences are also an interesting borderline case, especially since their owners customarily apprehend the subject matter of the experiences being the output of a very Reliable mechanism indeed.

What about ground-level moral intuitions? The question of their epistemological status is crucial for metaethics. Gilbert Harman (1977, p. 4) has addressed it in a directly relevant way: "If you round a corner and see a group of young hoodlums pour gasoline on a cat and ignite it, you do not need to *conclude* that what they are doing is wrong; you can *see* that it is wrong." In my terms, you have a very firm spontaneous belief that it is wrong. The belief is tenable – that is, consistent with other spontaneous beliefs and with all your other theories (unless you happen to be a moral nihilist or a puddle of moral slime, or both). The interesting question is that of whether it achieves coherence of the third kind. Moral intuition does not work in the straightforward way that perceptual mechanisms do; for, as Harman says, we can discover no genuine moral sense that in some definite way delivers moral facts to our consciousness; it is not obvious that any property of feline incineration affects anything in our brain (organ or not) whose function

6 I do not mean to suggest that all "wild" spontaneous beliefs are the product of disorder. There may be types of wild belief that are the products of useful mechanisms other than our standard sense organs. For example, ordinary human beings have an uncanny ability to tell, without visibly glancing about, when someone is looking at them; this ability is left over, I presume, from more parlous times.

is to detect moral wrongness. But there may still be some system of explanation that sweeps up moral intuitions and endows them with coherence of the third kind, especially if we find some plausible a posteriori reduction of moral properties to sociological and/or evolutionary ones. (Note that as I have set up the problem of conservatism, our task is not to explain *people's having* moral intuitions but to explain the purported facts that they intuit: not *why* we feel that immolating the cat is wrong but why it *is* wrong. As Harman observes, the former task would be much easier to carry out without appeal to moral properties of actions. But the latter is parallel to explanatory procedure in standard cases; we explain why the spring stretched just 15 centimeters, not why it seemed to us to do so. I shall have much more to say on this issue in Chapter 11.)

That moral intuition and moral theorizing are epistemologically borderline in this way may explain why people seem so unable to agree on cognitivism or on noncognitivism in ethics. Against cognitivism there is the doubt that moral intuitions can be coherent in the third way; against noncognitivism there is the *insistency* of spontaneous moral judgments. Spontaneous moral judgments are almost impossible to ignore or to write off. Some people perhaps try to therapeutize themselves into genuine amoralism, and possibly a few succeed, but it takes drugs or some other very powerful alienating force. Moral intuitions can seem as hard to disdain as are perceptual appearances, and in the perceptual case this difficulty is felt to indicate the presence and activity of delivery mechanisms. Perhaps, as in the perceptual case, there are sound evolutionary reasons for the existence of a moral delivery mechanism. But this is not obvious, and so one retains the idea that noncognitivism may be true after all.

III FOUNDATIONS

We may compare my Principle of Credulity (as it applies to the data base) to a number of similar proposals, such as "Accept all the propositions you have been conditioned to believe"; "Accept all the propositions belief in which would have survival and/or reproductive value"; "Accept all propositions that seem to be correct descriptions of your current mental state" (this last is actually a special case of my principle). My own proposal bears some similarity to Chisholm's principle B, in his *Theory of Knowledge* (1977, p. 76): "For any subject S, if S believes, without ground for doubt, that he is perceiving something to be F, then it is beyond reasonable doubt for S that he perceives something to be F."[7] But Chisholm's principle is quite differently motivated. He believes in it because, according to him, perceptual beliefs in particular are "self-presenting" and therefore can serve as (part of) the foundation of knowledge. I am not a foundationalist – at least not as "strong" a foundationalist as Chisholm is. Also, Chisholm is seeking a ground of certainty, not merely trying to establish a credibility marginally greater than .5. The main differences between principle B and the Principle of Credulity are (1) that the latter applies to any belief whatever, not just to perceptual beliefs, phenomenal beliefs, or beliefs of any other special kind, and (2) that my principle confers nothing like certainty or "epistemic" justification but only a credibility value of $.5 + \epsilon$, where ϵ is vanishingly close to zero.

It is because my principle is doing only this very humble job (the rest of the work being heroically performed by explanatory coherence) that I am able to avoid the convincing objection made against Chisholm by Alvin Goldman (1980, p. 42), concerning telepathy and clairvoyance. On my view, ostensibly telepathic spontaneous beliefs and spontaneous ostensible clairvoyances do receive minimal justification, along with spontaneous perceptual beliefs, but unlike the latter they get knocked out almost instantaneously by being coherent in the second or at least in the third way (unless, of course, the subject *is* a genuine telepath or clairvoyant). Although each wild spontaneous belief is born with a flicker of presumption in its favor, this minuscule presumption is immediately and overwhelmingly defeated.[8]

---

7 A revised and elaborated version of this principle appears on p. 272 of Chisholm's essay "On the Nature of Empirical Evidence" (1978). In "A Version of Foundationalism" (1980) he also adopts a strong conservative rule, but not on explanationist grounds.

8 I have not yet considered Cornman's own proposal for characterizing the data base. On page 150 of *Skepticism, Justification, and Explanation* (1980) he says that we must give up explanationist justifications of ultimate explainees and seek a nonexplanationist account of their *prima facie* acceptability. In the earlier paper from which his Chapter 6 is drawn, ("Foundational Versus Nonfoundational Theories of Empirical Justification," 1978) he had focused on "singular, categorical observation reports" and "psychological reports" and proposed that each of these be "tested individually and either confirmed or disconfirmed by observing or experiencing what occurs on the appropriate occasion" (p. 248). This was puz-

Even if my theory of the initial justification of ultimate explainees eventually fails, we could always fall back on a straightforward reliability account, since our ultimate explainees tend to be the very sorts of beliefs for which a reliability theory works well. Now that the preexplanatory nature of the Principle of Credulity has been made clear, it is not so obvious that my overall characterization of the data base differs much from the one that Alvin Goldman (1976, 1980) would give – something like "Accept all propositions believed by you as a result of the proper functioning of a reliable mechanism" – except for being less simply organized. Goldman would just begin by accepting the propositions that were spit out by reliable mechanisms; I would begin by accepting all sorts of spontaneous beliefs but go on to eliminate (almost?) all of these except the ones that had been spit out by reliable mechanisms. Why not simply stick with Goldman's view, instead of struggling to defend my oily conservative principle?

There are at least four reasons. The first is modest: My principle can serve, as Goldman's cannot, as part of a doxastic decision procedure (DDP), a laboratory manual that a subject can follow from within his or her first-person epistemic perspective. The subject knows what seems true to him or her at any given time but does not know which of his or her then current beliefs are the products of reliable mechanisms (until the subject has done some theorizing). This seems to me an advantage, though certainly not decisive.

The second reason is that for Goldman reliability confers "epistemic" justification – that is, the sort of justification that if "non-defective" in the post-Gettier sense, suffices for *knowledge*. But I do not want to limit the data base, even after the wild spontaneous beliefs have been pruned away, to propositions that are known. Surely some ultimate explainees will be propositions that are quite reasonably believed but not known.

The third reason is that I want to allow at least the possibility that some spontaneous beliefs achieve their coherence of the third

---

zling. How does one confirm or disconfirm reports such as "I see something brown" or "I am hurting"? We could do this only if we already had some general background assumptions about what is supposed to happen if I am seeing something brown or if I am hurting, but these observational and psychological reports are (by hypothesis) our initial data. Besides, any *pre-explanationist* notion of inductive confirmation is so far unexplicated, and I do not think that any nonexplanationist (nonenthymematic) inductive inference pattern is even a legitimate form of inference, unexplicated or not.

kind purely through the roles they play in a maximally coherent explanatory system and not because of anything in particular to do with the mechanisms that produced them (unless, trivially, one wants to say that the subject's tacit canons of theory-preference are themselves a mechanism that is "reliable" in a weaker sense than Goldman's). In this respect I am not so fierce an empiricist as Goldman and at least can make a gesture toward meriting the epithet of "Hegelian fellow traveler" that has been applied to me at one time or another.

The fourth reason is that I am able to handle cases of the sort put forward in Section IV of Chapter 5 as an embarrassment to purely "externalist" epistemologies, in which a subject has a de facto reliably functioning mechanism inside but also has overwhelmingly good reason for thinking that he or she does not have such a mechanism. (See again Bonjour [1980] and Kornblith [1980].) I suggest that the reason one is not justified, in a case of this Bonjour/Kornblith type, is that even though one's belief is in fact the output of a nomically reliable mechanism, the belief does not cohere in the third way – perhaps not even in the second.[9]

IV THE REMAINING PROBLEM

I turn now to the second of my two difficulties for explanationism. According to Lehrer:

[Explanationism] has a defect characteristic of coherence theories, to wit, inconsistent statements turn out to be completely justified. Two systems of beliefs may each have a maximum of explanatory coherence, and yet be inconsistent with each other. (1974, p. 181)

This sounds bad, but just in itself it is not. If the two explanatory systems are tied for first place, then neither is the *best* available explanation, and we are not justified in accepting either at the other's expense, but only their disjunction. Lehrer, however, goes on to argue that "there are *always* conflicting theories concerning some aspect of experience that are equally satisfactory from the standpoint of explanation" (p. 181; my italics), and if so, then there will never

9 Goldman has an independent way of handling these cases: He relativizes his notion of "reliability" to a set of "relevant" possibilities, and presumably our subjects' good reasons for self-doubt make the possibility of error a "relevant" one, even though it is not a nomological possibility.

173

be a best explanation and no one will ever be justified in believing anything on explanatory grounds.

A first response here is to recall that we are told to infer the best *available* explanation, the best explanation that can be devised at the time (always assuming that it meets minimal standards of plausibility). If the molecular theory of gases, for example, has an equally meritorious competitor, the competitor is still hiding in the Heaven above the Heavens; no one has brought it down and put it forward as a rival to the molecular theory. So its existence does not count against the letter of explanationism, at least. Yet suppose (as I believe Lehrer means to hint) that someone could construct an alternative-theory–generating algorithm, a device that takes a theory as input and somehow permutes it into a distinct, conflicting theory, without loss of overall explanatory merit. If such an algorithm were ready to hand, then, given an available explanation, that explanation's cranked-out rival would be available too. So if it is true *and provable* that every belief system admits of competing alternatives that match it in explanatory merit, as some philosophers contend, then explanationism is in trouble after all.

We can imagine a puckish sort of person, a funster, who gets hold of an algorithm of this sort, or a device purporting to be one, and goes around heckling serious theorists with it. He stands and watches in the shadows while a worthy scientist constructs a theory with much sweat and toil and ingenuity. The funster waits until the scientist finishes at last and then walks over, saying, "Well, well, what have we here?" He aims his algorithm at the scientist's theory, turns it on, and cranks out a "rival theory."

It is pretty obvious that something is amiss here, for there is a compelling (if not entirely clear) sense in which the scientist has done all the work. The funster has not really achieved anything or made any advance of his own. Now, there are three possibilities, depending on how successful the funster's method proves to be: First, if the funster is not careful, he may create a *notational variant* of the original hard-won theory, and if he has, he has not produced a genuine rival. Case 2: He does create a genuine rival, and it improves on the original theory. His theory wins. True, the funster did not do all the work himself – indeed, he did hardly any. So he gets little *credit* for his achievement, but his theory should be adopted. It is hardly rare that a great theorist's own version of a great theory is improved on by a lesser mind.

174

Case 3 is the hardest: The algorithm is genuine, and the resulting rival theory (not a notational variant) is *exactly* as good as the original, according to all standards but that of conservatism. What to do?

I say, *keep the original*, without shame, *because it was there first*. The original scientist constructed the theory, found further evidence for it, and so forth, and came to believe it justifiably, on the basis of all the evidence and our criteria of explanatory goodness. It would be irrational for him and for us simply to drop the theory and move to the funster's theory, gaining no explanatory advantage, because we would have changed our minds for no reason.

Before defending this rock-ribbed policy against a few final objections, I should note that our discussion so far has granted, for the sake of argument, the existence of a funster algorithm. But this concession is an enormous one, for why should we suppose that there is any such algorithm? Even if all scientific theories were regimented into first-order logic, the devising of a procedure that would spit out uniformly genuine rival theories precisely equal in explanatory merit would be no trivial task (especially since the measures of explanatory merit are likely to remain imprecise themselves until shortly before the heat-death of the universe). Lehrer's problem would arise, of course, for such ties in explanatory goodness as may happen to occur in real life.

In closing this chapter I want to make a few disclaimers and address two final problems. The disclaimers are redundant, but I have found in discussion that reemphasis is needed:

1. Conservatism is nothing to be dogged or stubborn about, nothing to hold out for. At the first sign of new evidence or of theoretical advantage, the enlightened conservative is as ready to relinquish his or her current view as is anyone else. The conservative policy I defend is only that of not giving up one's view *without some reason, however tiny*.

2. Conservatism has no force at all when even the slightest explanatory differential is in view; it is outweighed by every other epistemic virtue. Beyond its use in generating the data base, it has only its tie-breaking role.

3. Even when conservatism does have justificatory force, this

force is *only* justificatory; it has nothing to do with exploration, with data-seeking or discovery. Thus the conservative maxim in no way discourages exploration or hampers research efforts. So far as I can see, it has no effect on scientific practice at all.

The first of my two final problems was put to me by Robert Vishny: Even if the force of conservatism is vanishingly small, why does it go *nonexistent* in the face of compensating explanatory advantages? Could we not face a situation in which two theories differed so slightly in their other explanatory virtues that conservatism managed to bring the lesser just precisely up to the level of the former in overall goodness? In that case, we would have a tie again and no conservative rule left to break it.

It is for this reason that we cannot regard conservatism as a first-order rule on a par with simplicity, power, and the rest; it must be a metarule, to be invoked only after the first-order rules have been applied and weighed against each other. This is already signaled by the formulation, "Do not change your view *for no reason*," because that last qualification is recursive; "reason" has to mean "advantage in terms of the other epistemic virtues." Thus conservatism occupies a slightly specialized place in our cognitive design.

Our final objection is more troublesome.[10] Suppose again that a genuine scientist comes up with an excellent theory. But this time another genuine scientist (not a funster) comes up independently with a rival theory of the same phenomena, and this rival theory is precisely equal in merit to the first scientist's theory. The two scientists meet at a national convention and compare views. How says the canon of conservatism? It seems that on my view, the first scientist is justified in rejecting the second scientist's theory, indeed ought to reject it, in favor of her own, and the second scientist is justified in rejecting the first's theory in favor of *his* own. Each of two mutually incompatible theories is positively justified; each has (however marginally) a greater than .5 credibility. Does that outcome not straightforwardly reduce the conservative policy to absurdity and so devastate it?

I believe that this result seems, or should seem, absurd only to someone who looks at epistemology in a certain way, a way that

10 The objection was first put to me by Marshall Swain. It is also forcefully emphasized by Goldstick (1976) and by Kaplan and Sklar (1976).

is of a piece with the Cartesian zero-base policy that I have tried, in the preceding chapter, to impugn. A "zero-base policy," as I use the term here, is the view that justification starts from blank slate and proceeds in stages, according to fixed formal probabilistic or confirmation-theoretic relations among propositions considered in the abstract. On this view, an evidential proposition simply confirms or supports a hypothesis to a certain fixed degree, quite regardless of any subject's actual cognitive background. Now, we know that justification cannot really begin from a blank slate; that is why the problem of the data base arose in the first place. I want also to suggest that the support lent to a hypothesis by a subject's evidence depends in part on what else the subject believes and on the subject's cognitive history. If this is right, it is not surprising that two subjects with the same evidence should both be justified in accepting conflicting theories.[11]

What of confirmation theory? Must we give up the principle that a hypothesis and its negation cannot both be more probable than not? I prefer a less destructive revision in our epistemological thinking: Let us keep confirmation and probability theory for use where appropriate but admit that confirmation and formal probability do not tell the whole story of epistemological justification. It seems not unnatural to say of the two scientists in our example that both of their theories are confirmed to the same degree by their evidence, but that each is rational in cleaving to his or her own theory and rejecting the other's, until new evidence comes along.

I have tried to persuade you that a policy of conservatism is both needed and justified in epistemology. I hope I have also persuaded you that we can pursue conservatism without bigotry or small-mindedness – conservatism *with a heart*.

11 Kaplan and Sklar (1976) offer a useful comparison: Two agents faced with recurring situations of a particular type always act differently – "incompatibly" – in situations of that type. Their moral grounds are equally good but lead them to conflicting conclusions. Does it follow that they cannot both be morally justified in acting as they do? Surely not, for the cost to each (and to innocent bystanders) of switching habits might be prohibitive, in which case each should go on doing what he is doing.

I think the present point, if sound, also suffices to answer the related case urged against conservatism by Foley (1983, pp. 176–7), a sort of cross between the Vishny and Goldstick objections.

177

9

Induction and best explanation

I am a rabid explanationist, eager to defend the claim that *every* justified form of ampliative reasoning is a special case of explanatory inference. In this chapter I examine each of the most prominent forms of inductive and statistical inferences and try to show how to reconstruct it (to its advantage) as a type of explanatory inference. This particular project was inaugurated by Harman (1965), and I hope to advance it here, although we shall be running into a nasty obstacle in Section II.

I ENTHYMEMES

My thesis is that all justified ampliative inference is a matter of increasing the explanatory coherence of one's total belief system. It follows that no standard form of inductive or statistical reasoning is legitimate unless some background explanatory assumption is in play. I firmly accept that consequence, and in this chapter I try to defend it, though without complete success. I lift a few arguments from Harman; the rest are my own.

1. As Harman (pp. 89–90), points out, explanatory inference is rife in any case. There are scads of paradigmatically rational ampliative inferences that are clearly not species of correlational induction or statistical reasoning, notably inferences to the existence of unobserved and perhaps unobservable objects as standing causally behind observed empirical regularities. Thus (or so I have argued in Chapter 7) we have independent grounds for supposing that explanatory inference is a legitimate *and primitive* form of reasoning. This provides a motive, though no specific reason, for supposing that other ampliative inference patterns are enthymematic forms of explanatory inference.

In fact, it seems to me that, as strictly and literally construed, Humean skepticism about induction is simply right. The bare fact that the sun has risen on every one of the past *n* mornings is *by itself* not the slightest reason to think that the sun will rise every morning in the future or even that it will rise tomorrow. I suppose one might make some a priori argument in favor of the contrary claim, either a conventionalist argument à la Strawson (1952, Chap. 9) or a more ingenious dialectical one (e.g., Stove [1986]), but it is hard to be convinced by such an argument when the qualification "by itself" is firmly emphasized and the Grue paradox is simultaneously kept in mind. *Something* must be going on in the background, besides the brute fact of a Humean regularity, where "regularity" itself is already known to be relative to our human choice of a particular style of predicate. And, I maintain, something is going on: explanatory virtue.

2. Enumerative (straight-rule or Mickey Mouse) induction has two characteristic associated fallacies. Its reconstruction as inference to the best explanation shows why those fallacies are fallacies.[1] By "enumerative induction" I mean the inference pattern

$$\frac{N\% \text{ of all the observed } Xs \text{ have been } F.}{\therefore \text{[probably] Roughly } N\% \text{ of all } Xs \text{ are } F.}$$

According to explanationism, this argument is an enthymeme, assuming in particular that its conclusion *is the best available explanation of* its premise.

The besetting fallacies of enumerative induction are those of *insufficient sample* and *biased sample*. "Insufficient sample" is committed if not enough *X*s have been observed. "Biased sample" is committed when we have antecedent reason to think that the proportion of *X*s in our sample that are *F* differs from the proportion of all *X*s that are *F*.

I submit that the former fallacy is a fallacy because the suppressed assumption of best explanation fails: When a sample is grossly insufficient, the inductive conclusion is by no means the best explanation of the meager data. If I were to ask just two Carolina students what they thought of President Reagan's support of the Nicaraguan Contras and the two split 50–50, the hypothesis that "Carolina students generally split 50–50 on the Contra issue" would hardly be a contender. That hypothesis has virtually no explanatory

---

1 I trust that no one will balk at my use of abduction in defending abduction. "Defending abduction," in the present context, means defending explanatory inference *as fundamental*, not as legitimate in the first place. The latter has been disposed of in Chapter 7.

force in that context, even if true. I do not know what *would* explain our two-person data, depending on the researcher's interests and purposes; I suspect that without elaborate stage setting and background assumptions, nothing would count as explaining it. But certainly the proposed statistical conclusion is not a candidate.

The case of biased sample is even clearer. When we see that a sample is biased, we see precisely a *better explanation of its distribution* than the hypothesis that the general population is distributed that way. If only registered Republicans are consulted in a poll concerning approval of Reagan's performance as president, the best explanation of a markedly positive rating is that Republicans tend to support Reagan, not that a marked majority of Americans do.

3. Harman (1965), reminding us of Gettier cases, points out that our reluctance to impute knowledge to Gettier victims normally stems from the fact that their subjects' reasoning passes through a warranted but false premise (whatever the deeper basis of that reluctance may be). Harman then describes several cases in which we do not impute knowledge, but which, if construed as involving simple (nonenthymematic) induction alone, would seem to be quite nondefectively justified true belief. Here is just one case:

Consider what lemmas are used in obtaining knowledge from an authority. . . . When an expert tells us something about a certain subject . . . we are often warranted in believing that what we are told . . . is correct. Now one condition that must be satisfied if our belief is to count as knowledge is that our belief must be true. A second condition is this: what we are told . . . cannot be there by mistake. That is, the speaker must not have made a slip of the tongue which affects the sense. Our belief must not be based on reading a misprint. Even if the slip of the tongue or the misprint has changed a falsehood into truth, by accident, we still cannot get knowledge from it. This indicates that the inference which we make from testimony to truth must contain as a lemma the proposition that the utterance is there because it is believed and not because of a slip of the tongue or typewriter. (p. 93)

If our arguments from authority were simple enumerative inductions devoid of explanatory considerations, the falsity of an explanatory assumption should make no difference to our assessment of the strength and probity of the evidence; but it does, in this and a wide range of other cases (the fallacy of biased sample is itself another example). Harman concludes that inductions of all the sorts he surveys involve "lemmas" about the best explanation of the initial data.

180

It is sometimes claimed that a subject can be gettiered even when his or her inference occurs in one step and does not pass through any lemmas, true or false, at all. For example, I wake up some morning to find my digital alarm clock reading 6:30. I infer directly that it is 6:30 A.M. It is 6:30 A.M., and since my clock is in itself ultrareliable, my belief is fully justified. But in fact my clock has been unforeseeably stopped (twelve hours before) by a freakish burst of Q-radiation from the sky and reads 6:30 only by the merest chance.[2] I have been gettiered, in a reasonably broad sense of the term, even though I have not – or not obviously – reasoned through a false step.

But even this case confirms Harman's point. Suppose I did *not* believe that the clock read 6:30 *because* it was in good working order and was correctly registering the time. In fact, suppose there was an available alternative explanation that was a strong competitor, such as that my wife (having tired of making remarks about my ties) had been fooling with the digital clocks lately, setting them at 6:30 as part of a routine for getting them to emit realistic cuckoo noises. Obviously I do not know, presumably because the hypothesis that the clock is correctly registering the time is not – or not by much – the best explanation of the clock's reading.

4. Although I cannot go into detail here, explanationism helps mightily to resolve various paradoxes of confirmation. Goodman's (1955) New Riddle of Induction is a case in point (cf. Sober [1981]). Why is it rational to "project" "grue" rather than "green"? That is, why is it rational to suppose that all emeralds (now and forever) are green rather than that they are green-and-examined-before-the-year-2000-or-blue-and-not-examined-before-that-year? Formally speaking, both hypotheses are equally well confirmed by the fact that all observed emeralds have so far been green, yet the hypotheses are incompatible. (And any inductive inference can be grued in this way.) The answer seems obvious to an explanationist who disdains mere bloodless inductive or confirmation-theoretic relations: The "green" hypothesis is plainly and massively simpler than the "grue" hypothesis and has other explanatory advantages as well in the way of coherence, fruitfulness and the like. One could and should argue

---

2 I owe the basics of this example (and the lovely commemorative gift of a broken watch) to Marshall Swain, who swears that except, perhaps, for the burst of Q-radiation, such an occurrence actually happened to him. It was one of the happiest occasions of his life.

about what exactly these notions and alleged advantages come to, but intuitively the point seems clear enough. Similar points can be made, I believe, about Hempel's (1945) Raven paradoxes and others.

5. Until a few years ago, justification was conceived in purely formal terms. It was thought that to be justified in believing that *P* is just to believe some proposition *Q* that bears some logical or quasi-logical relation to *P*, a relation of probabilifying or confirming-to-a-degree or what have you (where *Q* was either "self-justifying" or justified in turn in the same formal way), and that was that; no further psychological considerations were esteemed as relevant. That situation began to change when Harman, Lehrer, and others began to think about the *basing* of beliefs on reasons (see the references in Chapter 3). But it needs to change more. As the pragmatists emphasized, the characteristic *value* of a belief qua belief is a function of what beliefs are *for*, and I have been concerned to argue that the real, natural ground of epistemic value is teleological value in organism design. So a *warranted inference*, in particular, should have the positive value it does in virtue of the role it plays in our inner strategy that gets us successfully around in the world.

This (very vaguely) is why I think that an abstract, formal inductive-argument form is by itself unimpressive, why Hume was perfectly right in supposing that a body of observations *alone* lends no support whatever to a hypothesis about the unobserved, and why paradoxes of confirmation will always remain intractable so long as they are tackled purely formally, without psychologistic intervention: The inductive relations in question have not been connected up in any way with psychological notions such as systematizing, simplifying, streamlining, and *understanding*. A virtue of explanationism as a reductive program is that it does make precisely this connection.

II ENUMERATIVE SYLLOGISM AND STATISTICAL SYLLOGISM

So far I have concentrated on just one stereotypical form of inductive inference: the straight rule. Other forms are not so amenable to explanationist treatment. For example, Ennis (1968) has offered a number of putative counterexamples to the claim that all inductive and statistical reasoning can be reconstructed as special cases of explanatory inference. The first interesting one of these is that of "regularity in the next instance" (p. 527).[3] Suppose M.D.s have always been found to be right when they have predicted that a child was about to come down with the measles. (Moreover, "We realize that M.D.s have given years to the study of the diagnosis and treatment of the disease . . . and that [the relevant] . . . stud[ies] had a scientific basis.") Then we may infer that the next time an M.D. says a child will come down with measles, that child will come down with measles – and when an M.D. does eventually say that some child is going to come down with measles, we will infer that that particular child will in fact come down with measles. Is this inference to the best explanation? What current data of ours could possibly be explained either by the hypothesis that "when an M.D. does eventually say that some child is going to come down with measles, that child will in fact come down with measles" or by the claim that such and such a particular child is going to come down with measles?

Of course, neither of those hypotheses explains any of the current data. But the true explanatory pattern is easily revealed, once a tacit bit of deduction is reckoned in. A straight–rule induction can be chained with a syllogistic deduction, as follows:

> All observed predictions by M.D.s of a child's getting measles have been followed by that child's getting measles.
>
> ∴ All predictions by M.D.s of a child's getting measles are followed by that child's getting measles.
>
> An M.D. has just predicted that Jimmy will get measles. [Stipulated fact]
>
> ∴ Jimmy will get measles. [By deduction from the preceding two steps]

This is entirely plausible as an account of our tacit reasoning (even if we have serious trouble with the notion of "tacit reasoning"). We may call this compound pattern of inference "enumerative syllogism," since it is an enumerative induction elided with a simple individual syllogism.

But we have yet to deal with the hardest case, and I have no completely satisfactory treatment of it. Harman (perhaps inad-

---

3 The preceding alleged counterexample is misguided from the beginning: It ignores the obvious, and obviously intended explanandum, of the form that all *observed* Fs have been G. Ennis's remaining case is only a variation on the one that I am about to discuss in the text.

vertently) brings it up himself in his discussion of Ennis's third example, in which we see the control stick of an airplane pulled back and we infer that the plane's air speed will lower. The lowering of the air speed of course does not explain the previous pulling back of the control stick. Rather, says the explanationist, we have observed in the past that control-stick pullings are always followed by air-speed lowerings, and that observation is explained by the hypothesis that control-stick pullings are always followed by air-speed lowerings, and from the latter hypothesis we may deduce that the present pulling will result in yet another lowering. The trouble is that control sticks presumably have failed in the past, however infrequently, and so our initial statistical premise is not true. What is true is only that a vast majority of control-stick pullings have been followed by speed lowerings. And now we see a gross defect in our proposed explanationist reduction: Every one of our examples of "enumerative induction" has involved 100 percent of the sample. But enumerative induction is far more general:

N% of all the observed Fs have been G.

∴ [probably] N% of all Fs are G.

All, or 100 percent, is a very special case of N percent. Now, what happens to our earlier strategy if we grant that not all stick pullings have been followed by speed lowerings? We are left with a naked case of *statistical syllogism*. *Most* pullings have been followed by lowerings; therefore this next pulling will be followed by a lowering. The inference is of the form,

N% of Fs are Gs (where $N > 50$, by a good margin).

∴ The next F will be a G.

Such "myriokranic" or statistical syllogism is induction at its purest. It is very hard to see how to reconstruct it in terms of explanation. Let us take a look at Harman's response to Ennis.[4]

Harman thinks that we sometimes do explanatory inference in reverse and from A "infer A *explains* B and then infer B" (p. 530). That is, he says, in some cases of "inference to the best explanatory statement" we infer the truth of the explanandum as our final con-

---

4 Actually Harman has used the same ensuing move against Ennis's earlier examples as well. In those contexts is seems to me contrived at best; I am not sure why he prefers it to the more straightforward one I have provided.

clusion, rather than (as in the standard case of enumerative induction) the truth of the explanans. And he maintains that this is what is going on in the control-stick example. Fully spelled out, the reasoning about the control stick would take this form:

1. 99 percent (say) of As are Bs.

∴

2. The fact that 99 percent of As are Bs explains the next A's being a B (from step 1, by "inference to the best explanatory statement").

∴

3. The next A will be a B (from step 2 by deduction, since "explains," in step 2, creates a factive context).

The step from 1 to 2 is very peculiar. Notice that "inference to the best *explanatory statement*" is not the same as explanatory inference or inference-to-the-best-explanation, in our original sense, since no explanans is inferred. The idea seems to be just that one thing I would explain is the next A's being a B, and (Harman assumes) this is a *better* explanation than its competitors. What are its competitors? You would think that other explanations of the next A are potential explanations of the next A's *not* being a B. I find this quite counterintuitive, though perhaps it does not matter a lot.

We may also worry about uncritical appeal to statistical explanation, though we may have to resort to it eventually. I recognize no clear sense in which statements of the form of step 2 are true, though philosophers of science have worked on the notion of statistical explanation to some effect. There is at least a minimal sense of "statistical explanation" that is clear enough: Step 1 shows that the next A's being B *was to be expected*. But how does it do that? Normally we would say, by statistical syllogism. If so, our minimal sense will not help, since it renders our reduction of statistical syllogism to statistical explanation circular.

But no matter. My main objection to Harman's ploy is unrelated: It concerns the factivity of step 2 (i.e., the fact that 2 entails and/or presupposes the truth of 3). Step 2 does not mean simply that 1 "*would* explain" the next A's being a B, in our sense (= "would explain if true"), for then 3 would not follow; "explain," in 2, must be taken as a success-verb. But then we cannot infer 2 from 1 without already presupposing 3, and in this way the inference begs the question. One might try to say that 3 is not antecedently presupposed but is warranted by 1 at the same time 2 is, but the direct warranting of *3* by *1* is evidently just statistical syllogism, and we are back where we started.

Two things conspire to keep us from seeing the question-begging nature of the inference: (1) Our tendency, already encouraged by our original account of explanatory inference, to read "explains" as "would explain" and (2) an easy confusion of explanatory reasoning with *causal* reasoning. The confusion is illustrated by another example of Harman's (p. 530), of a person's present intention's "explaining" that person's subsequent action. Certainly we can infer that the person's intention will *cause* the person to perform the intended action (and thus that the action will be performed), but this is because *most intentions do cause the actions intended*; so it is a case of statistical syllogism itself, and as much in need of explanationist reconstruction as any.

Our problem is to see how statistical syllogism can be regarded as a special case of explanatory inference, *or of explanatory-inference-plus-deduction*. Let us turn to an alternative of my own that I think is more promising, though by no means invulnerable.

Suppose 99 percent of all *A*s are *B*s. There must be some explanation of why this is true: Why are so many *A*s *B*s? A likely hypothesis is that there is some reason why *A*s are normally *B*s unless something – perhaps some structural feature of *A*s interferes with them. This hypothesis recommends itself to us mainly because its natural competitor (that there is no general tendency for *A*s qua *A*s to be *B*s and that the high correlation just happens to obtain) does not satisfy our desire to make as many regularities as possible look nomological rather than accidental. (I assume here that "*A*" and "*B*" are replaced by "projectible" or at least uncontroversial predicates; if we were to consider "grue" predicates and the like, we could easily confute any scientific maxim to the effect that "we should make regularities lawlike when possible." I have already indicated the line I wish to take on "grue" predicates.)

Now, just as enumerative induction has its two associated fallacies, statistical syllogism has an associated fallacy that we may call the "fallacy of the atypical individual." It is cognate with "biased sample." Suppose you know that 99 percent of the students at Ronald Reagan College are men, and you know that Cynthia is a student at Ronald Reagan College. Do you infer by statistical syllogism that Cynthia is a man? Of course not, because we have

186

some advance information about Cynthia (namely, his or her name's being "Cynthia") that indicates that he or she is not a typical or representative member of the sample (a typical student at Ronald Reagan has a name like "Rock," or "Tab," or "Buck"), and the atypical trait is statistically gender-related. Statistical syllogism is an acceptable form of inference only when there is no reason to think that the next A to be observed is going to be atypical or unrepresentative. Thus, in a legitimate case of statistical syllogism we have reason to assume that the next A is a *normal A*. If so, and if we are right in hypothesizing that there is some reason why all normal As are Bs, it follows that the next A will be a B.

In this way we might subsume statistical syllogism under explanatory-inference-plus-deduction. But there are (at least) two objections.

Objection 1. Consider a random-distribution process.[5] Say a nucleus of some kind explodes and scatters particles randomly in all directions. The nucleus is inside a hollow sphere, and all the particles hit the inside of the sphere; they are more or less evenly distributed over the inner surface of the sphere. Now consider a large subregion of that inner surface (call it R); R is everything that is left over when we remove a small wedge from the sphere. By hypothesis, the vast majority of scattered particles landed in region R. And from this we would seemingly be justified in inferring of any given particle that it (probably) landed in R, provided it was not known to be atypical. But, by hypothesis, nothing about the particles themselves *makes* it true that most of them land in R; the scattering process was random. There is no obvious distinction, in this case, between "normal" particles and deviant ones.

Perhaps we should look not at the individual particles but at the system as a whole. By its nature, *it* has a propensity to scatter most of its particles in region R; whatever makes it random guarantees this. It is plausible to say that our datum (the fact that most of the particles landed in R) is best explained by the fact that R exhausts most of the sphere's inner surface and that the scattering process was random. But I see no obvious way of getting from this claim to the prediction that some *given* particle landed in R without appeal to statistical syllogism.

5 I think this case was first put to me by Joseph Tolliver.

Objection 2. My strategy may involve some tacit circularity as well. Consider the fact that nearly all the graduate students in the philosophy program at the Ohio State University are non-Filipinos. What explains that? Presumably just that the Philippines are very far away and that it is difficult and expensive for a Filipino to go to Columbus to study philosophy. *Normally,* students go to Ohio State only if it is relatively convenient for them to do so. Now, what about the next graduate student in philosophy to go to Ohio State? We assume that that student, whoever he or she is, will be "normal," since we have no reason to think otherwise. But here we must distinguish, as I did not in stating my proposal, between *not having positive reason to think that the student is not normal* and *having positive reason to think that the student is normal.* Which is required for nonfallacious use of statistical syllogism? I am not sure, but either gets us into trouble. Suppose we make only the weaker assumption. Then we do not get our deductive inference; in order to obtain our conclusion we must have the student's normalcy as a premise. But what would warrant the stronger assumption, that is, the positive assumption that the student is normal? Statistical syllogism, perhaps?

Possibly some ceteris paribus idea is associated with statistical syllogism, to the effect that things are normal until they are proved abnormal. And the reason we make a choice at all *may* be that otherwise we could not draw any conclusions (only a closer examination of the usual mechanics of statistical inference would resolve this). But these dubious suggestions remain to be shown.

I now think our best way of avoiding objections of the two sorts just described is to recast the argument in terms of objective (single-case) propensities of *systems* and accompanying propensity explanations, following recent writings of Trenholme (1978) and Fetzer (1981). This idea, however, will take some time to work out.

10

Reality

. . . the word "reality" is generally used *with the intention of evoking sentiment.* It is a grand word for a peroration. "The right honourable speaker went on to declare that the concord and amity for which he had unceasingly striven had now become a reality (loud cheers)." The conception which it is so troublesome to apprehend is not "reality" but "reality (loud cheers)." — Sir Arthur Eddington

Epistemology, explanationism in particular, has always instigated the question of the relation of beliefs and other representations to the external world. Indeed, epistemology explicitly asks whether we have any reason to believe in the external world at all, and as I noted in Chapter 7, explanationism has often been felt to raise skeptical questions parallel to those occasioned by Lockean representationalism.

I "REALISM"

On the question of the external world, I can be mercifully brief. Our reason for believing in public, middle-sized objects is of the same kind as our reason for believing in anything else: that that belief is entailed by what is by far the most satisfactory explanation of regularities in our experience, of ways in which we are systematically appeared to. To reject it would be to create intolerable mysteries. If the competing hypothesis is proposed that we are brains in vats – more properly, that *I* am a brain in a vat, the rest of you being only my mistaken explanatory posits – I grant that that hypothesis is perfectly coherent and logically consistent with the character of my current experience. But it raises vexing and unanswerable questions: Who is thus manipulating my mind? For what possible reason? Why and how did that person choose to produce in me just the particular sequence of experiences (as of my entire life to date, just exactly as it happens to have run) that he or she did? And so on and so forth. Moreover, from the principle of conservatism defended in Chapter 8 we can extrapolate a burden-of-proof doctrine to the effect that appearances should be taken at face value in the absence of any special reason to doubt them or reject them as misleading. Thus, if asked how I know I am not a brain in a vat, all I can say is that I have every explanatory reason to think I am not one and no reason at all to suspect that I am one. If it is then asked why I think that this is a good argument or why the considerations I have just mentioned should be taken to count against the vat hypothesis, I refer the questioner back to Chapter 7. Thus, explanationism does not in itself raise any proper doubt about the external world.

Readers of the current literature on "realism" and "antirealism," of lamentably various sorts, will know that the preceding argument does not even begin to address that literature. The ordinary philosophers' use of the term "realism" is now all but forgotten: You are a *realist about* Xs (about public physical objects, subatomic particles, numbers, moral properties, ...) if you believe that there really are Xs in some literal, face-value sense of that clause (as opposed to some revisionary, neologistic sense). There is nothing very interesting about "realism" when it is understood in that way; to deny realism about public physical objects is to be an idealist, or at best an eliminative phenomenalist of some sort, and thereby to incur all the appalling onus of defending such an uncommon-sensical and cranky position. But such is not the intention of contemporary "antirealists."

II TWO OTHER RECENT SENSES OF "REALISM"

Michael Devitt once wrote, "Between the two of them, Hilary Putnam and Michael Dummett have managed to shed almost impenetrable darkness on the notion of realism." Putnam (1978 and elsewhere) distinguishes between "internal realism" and "external realism," claiming to uphold the former while rejecting the latter as rather silly superstition. Dummett (1978) idiosyncratically means by "realism about Xs" something to the effect that statements about Xs are either true or false, and his judgment on such a point of truth-valuedness per se is guided by rather crassly verification-ist considerations. Moreover, Dummett's usage is ineliminably metalinguistic, having to do with *truth* and the nature of the truth predicate.

I have briefly addressed Dummett's problematic (1984a, Section II of Chapter 10), and I shall not repeat myself here.[1] But a few words on Putnam are in order, especially since his distinction just mentioned and his attack on "external" realism are widely discussed and thought important. The first thing to note is that his internal–external distinction is breathtakingly obscure. Sometimes (e.g., in Putnam [1981], Chap. 3), it sounds as though "external realism" is an outlandish straw man, something like the following view (a gloss of my own, not a quotation):

Everything exists entirely independently of human language and the human mind, including human language and the human mind. Moreover, there is an omniscient and omnipotent God Who has ordained a system of natural kinds quite independently of human perception or human purposes. More-over human beings can step out from behind their perceptual systems and conceptual schemes and eyeball naked reality without benefit of any such things. Moreover the earth sits on the back of a giant cosmic turtle, which is what holds the earth up.

Putnam is at pains to convince us that the view just stated (which we may call Turtle Realism) is false. He succeeds effortlessly, in my case; I have never been tempted by Turtle Realism. Nor have I ever known anyone who was.

Caricatures aside,[2] Putnam gives one clue to his internal–external distinction in his discussion of brains in vats (1978, 1981): At some points he seems to equate external realism simply with belief in the conceptual possibility that one is a brain in a vat, being globally deceived as by an Evil Demon. And along with other well-known twentieth-century philosophers, Putnam rejects that possibility; he thinks that in the end it is *not* conceptually possible for my experiences internally to be just as they are and yet also to be the mendacious products of the Demon's or mad scientist's dream ma-

---

1 See also Devitt (1983, 1984), which are as thorough and effective an exploration of the relation between Dummett's arguments and ontology as I think ever need be made.

2 The "aside" here is an ambitious one. The current realism–antirealism literature consists very largely of satiric metaphorical characterizations of the "realism" being attacked, followed (on the antirealist side) by appropriate scoffing. I invite any reader who has the stomach for it to cull the antirealist literature for (1) a crisp *literal* statement of the view being rejected; (2) documentary evidence that anyone since perhaps the seventeenth century has held that view; and (3) a crisp, literal, and convincing argument against it. I am not holding my breath.

chine, and he gives at least one very clear and explicit argument to that effect (1981, Chap. 1). Other prominent philosophers have given quite different arguments for the same conclusion: Carnap and Ayer, verificationist arguments; Wittgenstein, a criteriological argument (see Lycan [1971]); J. L. Austin (1962), an "excluded-opposites" argument; Jay Rosenberg (1980), a Kantian argument.

So there is, after all, a clear issue between Putnam et al. and actual comtemporary people who call themselves "realists" and who can claim the title of "external realist," even though "external realism," in the present sense, bears no relation at all to Turtle Realism and could not possibly be taken to deserve scoffing or deriding, even if one disagrees with it. "External realism" in this sense (call it "Vat Realism") is just the view that, consistently with the character of my present experience, it is conceptually possible that I am a brain in a vat, being deceived by some uncannily successful producer of lifelike illusions. There are plenty of Vat Realists around. I am one.

In defense of Vat Realism I can again be mercifully brief. *Prior to philosophical argument*, I think anyone – ordinary person or philosopher alike – would grant the bare possibility of having totally illusory experiences throughout one's life. Indeed, global deception is almost *technologically* possible; never mind fantasy and science fiction on the scale of time travel or alternative universes. That the possibility of global deception is still *technologically remote and fanciful* I grant, of course. Its remoteness and fancifulness are just what made me say, in Section I, that we have no earthly reason to entertain it. But the Evil Demon hypothesis is a powerfully entrenched modal intuition. (If it were not so powerfully entrenched, Descartes could not have succeeded in worrying hundreds of generations of philosophers about skepticism.) Thus, Vat Realism seems true, on its face.

Powerful "modal intuitions" have been mistaken before. For example, people thought for years that water might not be composed of H_2O, and some people still claim to find it obvious that the phenomenal states of conscious subjects could occur independent of the subjects' functional or physical states[3] or that Cicero might not have been Tully. But a modal intuition of possibility is a datum and demands to be explained away, even if, dialectically

3 For elaborate diagnosis of this tendency, see my *Consciousness* (1987).

speaking, it creates only a prima facie case for the genuineness of the possibility in question.

The arguments of the philosophers I have mentioned (Putnam, Carnap, Ayer, Wittgenstein, et al.), of course, constitute attempts to explain away the Vat intuition. Those philosophers contend precisely that the intuition is specious and confused. But I think it is clear that they bear the onus of proof. If they maintain of something that seems perfectly possible to ordinary people and to most philosophers that it is in fact *conceptually impossible*, we have to see and assess the argument. Absent a proof seen to be sound, our original possibility remains unscathed.[4] For this reason, such a proof would be a very exciting philosophical item, to be exclaimed over as if it were a new baby.[5]

I cannot here set out and rebut all of the arguments I have mentioned; let me just go on record as stating that no such argument that I have ever seen has succeeded. Each of the arguments relies on some substantive premise that is far from being a "conceptual truth": a meat-ax version of verificationism, or a claim to the effect that a substantive epistemological principle is analytic (when it is not), or a metaphysical or psychological premise about the nature of mental representation. A few of these premises may possibly be true and may even assist in showing that we are not brains in vats, but they do not thereby show that the Vat hypothesis is conceptually impossible or incoherent. It is not conceptually impossible or incoherent. Vat Realism is still rather obviously true.

---

4 "Proof" here need not be taken philosophically. E.g., the scientific identification of a natural kind will do, as in the discovery that water is in fact composed of H_2O.

5 For some of us there would be a downside, pointed out by Rorty (1973): If one could show a priori that most of our common beliefs about the external world must be true, and particularly if one could show that this guarantee holds in virtue of the meanings of words (à la Wittgenstein) or otherwise by convention, the victory is hollow, for a kind of linguistic idealism results. We would have thereby shown that external reality is partly constituted by human language and is not (as we commonsensically take it to be) entirely independent of the thought processes of conscious subjects. Putnam (as presently construed) is right: the Vat hypothesis is the key. With Rorty, I would say that the hypothesis must be at least conceptually, if not metaphysically, possible if any substantive form of realism is true at all. Putnam evidently disagrees on this last point, since he seems to think that his "internal realism" is worth saving and cherishing. But like many other readers of the realism–antirealism corpus, I do not see how one can reject Vat Realism without falling into the silly view that truth and reality are just what our friends will let us get away with.

Let us remind ourselves, especially if we have been rereading Putnam, Dummett, or another fashionable antirealist, that except on specific and idiosyncratic philosophical grounds we do not doubt the existence of floors, rugs, other people, other galaxies, or electrons. We accept all of those, and on more or less explanationist grounds. (Let us call this acceptance Basic Realism.)[6] And we are justified in doing so, though far from infallibly justified; such is the lesson of Chapter 7. The only occasion for philosophical concern about that justification would be a very hard-hitting philosophical argument specifically to the contrary.

I cannot easily think of an argument that does not essentially involve a combination of metaphor with sarcasm ("Oh, I suppose you think you can step out from behind your perceptions and conceptual scheme and just eyeball... [etc., etc.]"). "Arguments" of this type can be peremptorily dismissed; once genuine transcendental reasoning against Vat Realism has failed (assuming it does fail), the only argument worth considering would be one whose conclusion was that there *are not* really floors, rugs, or electrons and that the existence of those items is an illusion. Absent such an argument (or a good argument for a radical skepticism in epistemology, which skepticism is abhorrent to the antirealist), we are perfectly justified, *in the fullest accepted sense of "justified,"* in thinking that there are such things.

Many self-styled antirealists would agree with my claim, couched as it is in the object language, that there are floors and rugs and even electrons. Their disagreement locates itself at a higher level of discourse. It has to do with the meta–metalinguistic interpretation of notions of truth and reference or else with the proper understanding of scientific method. That there are substantive issues to be fought out in these areas I do not deny. My point is only that (1) those issues do not affect Basic Realism, which is the most important metaphysical issue, and that (2) these issues are quite

6 Basic Realism, coupled with the repudiation of any interestingly stronger thesis, is very close to what Arthur Fine (1984a, 1984b) calls the Natural Ontological Attitude, or NOA. I am sympathetic to NOA and more generally to Fine's elegant writings on this topic, but Fine sees NOA as an important species of antirealism ("Realism is dead" [1984b]), whereas I do not. (Both of us firmly reject Turtle Realism.)

remote from basic epistemology and the question of how our beliefs about the external world and so forth are justified. Our beliefs are justified in the way I have said they are justified. This has nothing to do with the ultimate nature of truth, with the semantical interpretation of anyone's words or thoughts,[7] with the nature of a conceptual scheme, or with any doctrine regarding natural kinds.[8] Those are different matters entirely, or at least, if someone disagrees about that, we would have to see an argument, clearly spelled out, that led from some set of premises regarding any such matters to a conclusion incompatible with any plausible account of epistemic justification, and I have never seen any even faintly convincing argument of this type. Certainly any number of views of truth, language, representation, natural kinds, and so forth are compatible with everything I said in Chapters 7 and 8.

I am (perhaps) assuming or presupposing something that some antirealist readers would not grant: that, as Quine has taught us, *there is no first philosophy*. A felicitous explanatory coordination of common sense and science is the only test of truth; as we saw in Chapter 6, there is no further external Archimedean standpoint from which an independent, peculiarly philosophical method could get a grip and critique common sense and science together at the same time. If an opponent thinks I am mistaken about this, let him or her produce such a method and show how it resists the Quinean argument I presented in Chapter 6.

IV   SKEPTICISM AND REALITY

I close this chapter by offering a quick diagnosis of the antirealism disease and repudiating one very common type of skeptical argument against explanationism.

The diagnosis of antirealism is simple, and rather than try to offer historical support, I shall leave my readers to confirm the diagnosis against their own textual experience. Bluntly, antirealism in most of its forms comes from *morbid fear of skepticism*. Scratch almost any antirealist argument or "argument," and you find a premise that

---

7 To quote Michael Devitt again (conversation): "When someone starts talking about 'interpretation', reach for your gun."
8 Of all things. Readers of the current antirealist literature will confirm how strangely the matter is mixed up with questions about natural kinds that have prima facie nothing to do with the issue of existence or reality.

is really a lemma; lurking behind it is an assumed conditional to the effect that if the premise were not true, then reality would be forever hidden from us, and we could never have any good reason to trust our senses, and so forth. Such background conditionals are rarely argued for, since they are rarely made explicit, nor in my experience can support be readily supplied once the conditionals are brought out into the open. I shall give two brief examples.

It is often objected against Locke's representationalist realism that Locke's view leads directly to radical skepticism; a Lockean subject is barricaded behind an impenetrable wall of ideas, and so forth, and so cannot know anything of the noumenal goings-on behind that wall. The first conjunct of the latter sentence is mere metaphor, and the second, intended as a justified intermediate conclusion, does not in the least follow from anything that the first might mean when taken naturally and literally. In particular, a Lockean representationalist might also be an explanationist, quite justifiably adducing hypotheses about the external world from regularities holding within the "wall of ideas" directly open to his scrutiny. Explanationism may not in the end be true, but it is not logically false; no one could rationally suggest that the Lockean view *entails* skepticism.

My second example is that of a kind of skeptical move often made against ampliative inference generally, and against explanatory inference in particular, already mentioned in Chapter 7. Suppose Jones claims that P. Smith, an ordinary person, demands to hear Jones's evidence. Jones provides evidence E, the sort of evidence we would normally take as virtually conclusive in support of P. Smith subsides. But Brown, a professional philosopher, demands to know by what right Jones holds *that* E *supports* P, stating or implying that if Jones cannot himself answer this metaquestion, his right to maintain that P is forfeit, or at least he cannot lay claim to a belief that "corresponds to reality." ("Yes, I know people cite things like E when making claims like P – that is our custom – but what evidence do you have that P is *really true*, in the sense of corresponding to reality?")

Brown's conditional is completely without motivation or force. Jones's failings as an epistemologist cast no reflections whatever on Jones's right to claim that P. If E *does* support P, and if Jones believes that P on the basis of E, then there is no further question of whether Jones is justified in thinking it is "really true" that P. To be justified

196

in believing that P is to be justified in thinking it is really true that P, really really true that P, really and truly really true that P, and as far down that road as anyone might care to go.

I have suggested that antirealist feelings are stoked by fear of skepticism. But if skepticism is entailed by a philosophical position, and if skepticism is bad, then perhaps the fear is reasonable and the ensuing antirealism warranted.

I am not sure skepticism is all that bad; it depends on how radically it is formulated. Probably some modest forms of skepticism are true, as Armstrong says. But in any case, as I have already intimated, it is hard to find a sound argument taking us from any common theory of epistemic justification, or for that matter any plausible set of premises, to a seriously skeptical conclusion (unless it is my own argument against Armstrong's particular theory, offered in Chapter 5). We are all well acquainted with skeptical arguments of the sort we examine in our graduate epistemology courses, and we are all well acquainted with the standard criticisms of those arguments: The arguments commit modal fallacies, beg the question, illegitimately presuppose the KK thesis, and so forth. Most have *multiple* flaws of a textbook nature. Now, if two thousand years of epistemology have failed to produce a plausible argument for skepticism, even in conjunction with an initially plausible theory of epistemic justification, then skepticism is surely nothing to get all upset about – certainly not to the point of abandoning the real world. At the very least, we should not even think of abandoning the real world solely on the basis of a *purely philosophical* argument. Electrons, rocks, and probably even cockroaches will be here long after all the philosophers are gone.

197

11

Moral facts and moral knowledge

Moral facts are right up there with Cartesian egos, moxibustion, and the Easter Bunny in the ranks of items uncordially despised by most contemporary philosophers.[1] This ostracism is historically the result of a confluence of several major currents in twentieth-century thought. (1) Logical Atomism, as so vividly manifested in Moore's Open Question Argument: Moral judgments are not analyzable in naturalistic terms. (This conclusion was felt to embarrass moral facts, even though Moore himself moved to defend them as non-natural).[2] (2) Verificationism, as the logical positivist theory of meaning: Moral judgments are not verifiable by observational test. (3) Ordinary-language philosophy's emphasis on the social use of language, as it issues in Richard Hare's prescriptivism: Moral judgments are used to prescribe or command. And finally (4) our own more up-to-date scientific naturalism: Moral "facts" are not even metaphysically reducible to configurations of quarks and leptons.[3]

---

1 With the exception of virtually all the participants in the Spindel Conference for which this paper was originally written (Memphis State University, November 1985). I found myself preaching to the choir.

2 For an example of atomist embarrassment, see Russell (1910).

3 Perhaps some readers will maintain that the scientific-realist era is already dead on its feet and that our historical resumé should include (5) a sort of pluralism of conceptual schemes, with no one scheme having the sort of priority to or preeminence over the others that philosophers like Quine, Smart, Sellars, Armstrong, and the Putnam of the 1960s claimed for the scientific view of the world. According to such a pluralism, each such scheme or perhaps language-game has its own internal warrant (in the sense of not needing to be "validated" or vindicated from the standpoint of any other scheme), and there is no fact of the matter as to a choice between any of the schemes. The metaethical import of this sort of pluralism is to dethrone science as the chief arbiter of truth and thereby, in particular, mute the demand that morality be vindicated with respect to science; thus the moral language-game may be held to be exactly as secure, in its way, as the practice of science is in its own way, however secure (and in whatever way) that may be. If correct, I think, this pluralist view would be a good thing for moral facts, since we would still want to speak of scientific facts, mathematical facts, and the like, even if we did speak so only with the vulgar and in the

So, in sum, moral judgments are to be patronized, and moral facts must be consigned to the flames (to quote the immortal W. C. Fields).

I maintain that this apparently robust consilience of the verdicts of successive schools of contemporary philosophy is fortuitous, and mistaken. As against it – and against all of twentieth-century philosophy reacting to Moore, Prichard, and Ross themselves – I propose to defend moral facts; at least, I shall argue that there is plenty of conceptual space for a sound notion of moral fact. Moreover, I contend that none of the three sorts of argument I have just mentioned is (on its own) *even faintly convincing*, and I would suggest that the almost universal acceptance of these arguments is a striking sociophilosophical phenomenon – inviting one or more nice historical treatments of how this acceptance could have come to pass. But in this chapter I shall only make the defensive case for moral facts and then turn to more subtle and more legitimately troubling questions of moral epistemology.

I UNBELIEVABLY BAD ARGUMENTS AGAINST MORAL FACTS

1. The Open Question Argument, and deriving "ought" from "is." Moore's Open Question Argument (1903, Chap. 1) was supposed to show that since moral predicates cannot be correctly meaning-analyzed in naturalistic terms, and since (not being meaningless) they express properties of some sort, they must express nonnatural properties. And since the predicate "good," in particular, cannot be analyzed in terms of other moral predicates either, it must express a *primitive* and sui generis nonnatural property. If we also plug in one or two well-known logical atomist principles of the period, we will then say that goodness must be detectable "by acquaintance" and not just knowable "by description"; for, like yellowness (to use Moore's own analogy), goodness cannot be come upon by any Russellian process of analytic decomposition. Thus, like yellowness, it must be known directly. And (although Moore himself wanted uncomfortably to back off at this point) direct acquaintance

---

patronizing tone of the philosopher who really knows better. Unfortunately for my own defense of moral facts, however, I am unpersuaded by the pluralist view.

with goodness seems to require a special quasi-perceptual faculty of moral sense, just as yellowness requires a faculty of visual perception. The form of epistemological intuitionism thus engendered has put off level-headed philosophers ever since, starting with the positivists.

Ironically, in attacking Moore and defending emotivism, A. J. Ayer (1952, pp. 104–5) appealed just as confidently to the Open Question Argument. But he insisted (correctly) that Moore had committed the fallacy of false dichotomy by dismissing the possibility that moral judgments are literally meaningless. Indeed, he thought, the Verifiability Principle provided independent proof that moral judgments *are* meaningless if they cannot be meaning-analyzed in naturalistic terms. Thus Ayer turned Moore's own Open Question Argument against him.

The evidence for Moore's (and Ayer's) major premise that moral predicates such as "good" cannot be analyzed in naturalistic terms was that for any naturalistic predicate F, simple or complex, the questions "Are F things really good?" or "What is good about F things?" make perfect sense; one does not, simply in asking them, betray one's gross ignorance of English word meanings. I am not entirely sure that the latter claim entails the former, because I am not sure that one might not sensibly ask, "Are G things really F?" even when the predicates F and G are in fact synonymous in English; but let us pass that by for now. My real complaint about the Open Question Argument is that it presumes that identification of properties must be motivated a priori, by the established synonymy of the predicates expressing those properties. And this presumption has been known to be false at least since the 1950s, on the basis of some very straightforward examples. Reacting against the apriorism of both the positivists and the ordinary-language philosophers, U. T. Place (1956) and J. J. C. Smart (1959) offered myriad instances of the a posteriori identification of properties: clouds, with masses of tiny water droplets; water itself, with H_2O; lightning, with electrical discharge; temperature, with mean molecular kinetic energy; genes, with segments of DNA molecules; and so forth. Each of these identities was discovered empirically; none has anything to do with the synonymy of terms; each leaves "open questions" with a vengeance. An argument precisely parallel to Moore's would show that clouds, water, lightning, temperature, and genes

200

were nonnatural phenomena also.[4] Thus, I contend, *both* Moore and Ayer were guilty of the fallacy of false dichotomy, having overlooked the possibility of a posteriori identity of properties (although Geoffrey Sayre McCord [1985, p. 88] has pointed out an interesting difference between their uses of the Open Question Argument). I suppose that this is what comes of thinking of properties as predicate meanings, pure and simple.[5] In any case, the Open Question Argument simply fails; it is bankrupt.

Note that similar considerations apply to Hume's famous observation that we cannot derive an "ought" from an "is." This dictum has been thought to rule against moral facts, partly in Moore's Open Question sort of way but also partly epistemologically; for, if one cannot deduce a moral judgment or principle from any body of factual statements, no matter how large, then one cannot in principle *justify* any moral judgment or principle, and the passions rule. But his latter concern too is misplaced. There is no more reason to expect that moral facts, if any, must be logically deducible from natural facts than there is to suppose that facts about clouds, water, lightning, and so forth must be logically deducible from facts about their constituents. Nor is there any very good reason to join Kant in supposing that ethics must be an (either synthetically or analytically) a priori discipline.[6] This point, of

4 The point has recently and independently been hit upon, or at least hinted at, by a number of writers including Campbell (1981), Putnam (1981), Boyd (1983), Sturgeon (1984), Post (1984), Tolhurst (1986), and Sayre McCord (in press).

5 That is the beginning of a sociophilosophical explanation. A closely related and still more significant factor is that the a posteriori identity of properties is a discovery of scientific realism and could have been hit upon only by philosophers attentive to science. It is noteworthy that the atomists, positivists, and ordinary-language philosophers were united in their view of science's separateness from, and posteriority to, metaphysics.

6 A certain kind of moral skeptic wants to be shown that it is *irrational* to accept certain maxims or moral permissions. This skeptic wants us to prove moral principles using only reason and uncontroversial premises that do not include substantive moral claims. Notice that this is to rank epistemic value above moral value: "I won't be confident that this sort of action is morally bad until you show me that it is epistemically bad." (I take "irrational," in the philosophical sense, to mean "epistemically bad.") That skeptical attitude is very peculiar. For one thing, I would think anyone who was skeptical about moral value would be similarly skeptical about epistemic value; they are both values, after all, and subject to parallel sorts of skeptical argument. For another, even if one is a realist about epistemic value it is hard to see why anyone would set it up as a gold standard against which moral value would have to be measured. After all, moral value is

course, leaves us with the question of what less demanding moral epistemology might serve; I shall address that question later in this chapter.

2. *Verificationism.* Ayer's verificationist argument against the meaningfulness of moral judgments may be cast independently of his appeal to the Open Question Argument. For we may plausibly (though not uncontroversially) grant that moral properties are not *observed* in the more or less direct way that colors, pointer readings, or explosions are. Equally, it seems that we cannot verify or falsify, confirm or refute, a singular moral characterization of an action simply by observing that action. And if not, then by any standard version of the Verifiability Principle it follows that singular moral judgments are not "cognitively meaningful," that is, that (at least) they do not state facts. And if singular moral judgments do not state facts, then, presumably, general moral statements and principles do not state facts either.

The troubles of the Verifiability Principle are well known; see, for example, Putnam (1975b). Two of its failings are directly relevant to Ayer's metaethical argument. The first failing was argued by Duhem (1906), acknowledged by Ayer with surprising meekness (1952, p. 12), and driven home by Quine (1953c). It is that individual statements *do not have* verification conditions. A sentence is held true or rejected only in the context of a surrounding body of other judgments, and this body may be quite large and heterogeneous. Thus an individual moral judgment might (for all that has been shown) receive or lose evidential support in the context of an overall view of individuals and society broadly considered. (The point is also made by Sturgeon [1984] and by Sayre McCord [in press].)

The second failing is closely related: There are quite a few state-

ostensibly overriding in conflicts with other values; in some sense it is more important to the world that one fulfill one's moral obligations than that one fulfill one's epistemic obligation (unless in context, such as when one is on jury duty, epistemic violations are tantamount to moral violations). Epistemic wrongs – even believing contradictions and the like – are peccadilloes compared to moral wrongs of comparable magnitude. This point is a bit hard to state precisely without trivialization (it is not just that moral obligations are *morally* more important than epistemic ones, and vice versa), but I find it peculiar that the moral skeptic would be more upset by being called irrational (epistemically bad) than by being called immoral.

ments that we now regard as being factual and objectively true or objectively false but that do not admit of the direct sort of verification demanded by Ayer's argument. Examples: "$^d/_{dx}{}^2 = 2x$"; "If I hadn't voted for Jim Hunt instead of Jesse Helms I'd have stayed away from the polls"; "Sherlock Holmes probably had no homosexual tendencies"; "That transmitter is giving off electromagnetic waves"; "There are electrons that move backward in time." Sentences like these are verified *in*directly, on explanatory grounds; we believe them, when we believe them, as the result of explanatory arguments that make them reasonable to accept *and to act on* as theoretically informed judgments, even though the arguments do not deductively "prove" the judgments to be true. This indirect sort of verification is enough, it seems, to make them statements of fact. Now, we have agreed for the sake of argument that moral judgments cannot normally be verified directly by observation. But what is to prevent their being justified indirectly by moral theories? If moral theories can themselves be indirectly justified on explanatory grounds, then they can be statements of fact too. And moral theories are indeed compared in regard to explanatory virtues; we see this both in syllabi for undergraduate ethics courses and in more sophisticated discussions that make use of (roughly Rawls's method of) reflective equilibrium. I shall explore some details of the process later in this chapter.

Note also that if we as observers have assimilated enough theory (on a given subject), we sometimes come to be able to verify *through observation* claims that we could not have approached observationally before. For example, if I know the theory behind the Wilson cloud chamber, I can say that I have *observed that* an electron is crossing the chamber when the bulb has been squeezed. The moral case seems parallel: If I have internalized a justified moral theory that entails that murder is wrong, then upon witnessing what is unmistakably a brutal murder I can claim to have *observed that* a vicious, immoral act has taken place.

3. "Ordinary-language" prescriptivism. The ordinary-language movement contributed what I take to be a significant improvement on the positivists' version of noncognitivism. Ayer's emotivism, in particular, seemed to entail that the superficial grammar and logic of moral judgments are completely spurious and grossly misleading, that moral judgments cannot properly embed in conditional or propositional-attitude contexts, that they cannot figure in genuinely valid arguments, and the like – all very implausible consequences. Those consequences may be defended after the fact, as Stevenson (1944) essayed to do. But Hare's (1952, 1963) prescriptivism has few such consequences in the first place. If (as a more refined speech-act theory of meaning suggests) moral judgments function in part as commands, then moral judgments may be admitted to have a syntax and a logic, even though (Hare says) they are not genuine declaratives and are not used to state facts; this avoids the standard objections to emotivism mentioned earlier. But there is still a prescriptivist objection to the claim that moral judgments state facts. It is that in practice they *are* used to express pro and con attitudes, to inculcate them in others, and (yes) to issue Harean prescriptions. None of these paradigmatic uses of moral language has anything to do with stating facts, and there is no other evidence that moral judgments do state facts. Therefore, we have no reason to believe in moral facts, even if we believe that moral judgments are sometimes (in some sense) warranted.

This argument pays lip service to Hare's syntactic and logical concessions, but it simply ignores epistemological considerations, and in doing so it commits the "speech-act fallacy": As stated, it infers, from the indubitable contention that moral judgments are used to perform speech acts X, Y, and Z, that moral judgments are not also used to perform acts of fact-stating. This inference is simply invalid, since one and the same utterance may be used to perform any number of speech acts simultaneously. Once again, we are left with a well-grounded invitation to supply an acceptable moral epistemology but without any principled objection to the notion of a moral fact.

4. *Scientific naturalism.* Our naturalistic problem might be thought to fill the gap here. It is that moral facts are (ostensibly) not reducible to configurations of quarks and leptons. But this depends on what one means by "reducible." If moral properties are *type*-identifiable with properties of a more or less nonevaluative sort, then it does not matter whether the latter properties are type-reducible to configurations of quarks and leptons; after all, biological properties and the teleological properties of artifacts are not type-reducible to configurations of quarks and leptons but are nonetheless real. Our main question is of the (a posteriori) type-identification of moral prop-

erties with nonevaluative properties, regardless of the level of nature at which those nonevaluative properties are located. And now let us say a bit more about the epistemology of reduction and supervenience.

II A POSTERIORI REDUCTIVE IDENTIFICATION

There are a number of different paradigms for a posteriori reduction, found mainly in work on the mind–body problem. (1) Some property identities can be observed to hold, as in the case of clouds and masses of water droplets (one can ride a balloon up into a cloud and discover the true nature of the cloud without theorizing in any very rarefied way). (2) Some property identities are hypothesized as being the best explanations of empirical "correlations" between their instances, as in the cases of lightning and electrical discharge, water and H_2O, and (science-fictionally) pain and C-fiber firings. (3) Some property identities are established by role-occupant reduction, as in the case of temperature and mean molecular kinetic energy and the case of genes and segments of DNA molecules. I think that none of these three paradigms will actually do for the naturalization of moral properties, but a sort of hybrid fourth may serve.

Paradigm *1* is inappropriate; we cannot see the wrongness of an action by looking *more closely* at those of its properties with which wrongness is to be identified. Paradigm *2* is not quite what we want either, since as moral theorists we do not establish correlations between natural properties and clinically observed instances of wrongness. Paradigm *3* is a possibility but not a strong one: We might type-identify wrongness with "whatever property it is (in the real world) that accompanies the deliberate causing of harm or degradation and also produces such and such a syndrome of feelings in normal humans [a familiar social constellation of indignation, blame, guilt, shame, . . .]" (note the intersubjectivity of this syndrome). But our first hypothesis as to what this property is would be a purely psychological one, having to do with socialization. *Perhaps* a deeper hypothesis would mix evolutionary and (somehow) rational considerations that were more distinctively moral, but probably not, especially if it turns out that morality is only a plot for the maintenance of the status quo.

In any case I am inclined to think that moral expressions are rigid rather than flaccid designators, as Tolhurst (1986) also suggests; wrongness, goodness, and so on do not seem to be "role" concepts whose occupants are the objects of scientific search. But if moral predicates are rigid, then what is a plausible epistemology for the identification of their referents with natural properties? Here things become murky but quite familiar: Rather than start à la paradigm 2, with an empirically established correlation between actually detected instances of our reduced and reducing properties, we allow thought experiments as well and appeal to modal intuitions, asking ourselves whether an item of such and such a description would count as a so-and-so. Yet we depart from the linguistic methods of analytic philosophy, in consulting what I shall call *empirically tutored* modal intuitions – intuitions that we come to have only after acquiring some brutely empirical knowledge. Kripke (1972) has provided our best-known examples: Once we find out that water consists of H_2O, we come to think that water could not have failed to be H_2O and that in no possible world is there water that is not H_2O; once we find out that this wooden table is made of cellulose molecules, we lose our ability to imagine *this very* table's being made of anything else, and conclude that a table made of anything else would not be *this* table but merely another very like it.

Our modal intuitions in such cases warrant supervenience claims. (A crude intuitive notion of "supervenience" will do for my purposes here.) For instance, substance properties – *being water, being gold*, and so on – supervene on chemical properties. But we also have modal intuitions about moral properties; we philosophy teachers spend a good deal of time, in our ethics classes, describing hypothetical situations and judging whether certain decisions taken and actions performed in those situations would be morally right or morally wrong. These are tutored modal intuitions, in that we have them as a result of experience of life rather than as part of our specifically linguistic competence, but equally they support supervenience claims; and for that matter, the *general* claim that moral facts supervene on nonmoral facts seems obvious to cognitivists and noncognitivists alike. Now, how are supervenience relations to be explained? Following Armstrong (1982), I suggest that in most cases the best explanation of a supervenience relation is a type-identity hypothesis: *B*-properties are felt to supervene on *A*-properties because they simply *are* *A*-properties. (Absent any special reason for thinking that *B*- and *A*-properties are distinct, Occam's

Razor at least strongly encourages the identification.) Thus in particular, if moral properties are found by modal intuition to supervene on facts about utility, harm, degradation, or the like, we would be justified in identifying them with complex natural properties involving those things.

The deliverance of modal intuition is a mysterious and, I grant, suspect thing. Once we give up the positivistic identification of alethic necessity with analyticity and the a priori, we have no idea where modal "intuition" comes from or why it should be regarded as reliable. Yet the supervenience of moral upon nonmoral facts has as much to be said for it as that of sociological and psychological facts upon physical facts, for only tutored modal intuition tells us that physics determines psychology, even if Cartesian dualism is true; for that matter, I am not sure that anything besides tutored modal intuition underwrites the supervenience of biology on physics.[7] The *Aufhebung* of empirical discoveries into modal claims is also poorly understood; yet it seems to happen, and it seems to be rational and warranted when it does happen. (One's instinctive resistance to it diminishes dramatically once one decisively gets over the positivists' epistemologizing of metaphysics.) If we do have good reason to accept the naturalization of psychology and the physicalization of biology, we may have the same sort of reason to accept naturalistic moral facts.

Let us get on to a more general epistemology of moral claims, normative as well as metaethical.

III   MORAL KNOWLEDGE

I shall set my discussion of moral knowledge within the explanationist model of epistemic justification that I defended earlier. As before, I hold that all warranted ampliative inferences are (perhaps enthymematic) types of explanatory inference and that all epistem-

---

7 Harman (1986) claims that when we justify a theory by appeal to reflective equilibrium between the theory and our intuitions about thought experiments, we are only studying our own habits of thought and so are doing (human) *psychology* rather than discovering facts of any other sort. I do not accept this. Although the business of modal intuitions is mysterious, appeals to them cannot (yet) just be written off as commonsense psychology, for parallel reasoning would also impugn syntactic, epistemic, logical, mathematical, and philosophical intuitions; this is too direct a route to psychologism regarding mathematics, for example. More on this later in this chapter.

ically justified reasoning increases the explanatory coherence of the subject's total belief system. Any epistemic move on the subject's part must contribute to a better overall explanation of the available data than does any competing move. But explanatory inference presupposes a set of data to be explained, and as in Chapter 8, one may well wonder two things: (1) Why should we accept any "data" in the first place, since data do not themselves explain anything and so must, on pain of circularity or regress, be justified on grounds other than their ability to explain? (2) Even waiving that question, just which data *are* the ultimate explainees that get the business of moral theorizing, in particular, under way?

The first of these questions is a pressing one for any explanationist, in any field of inquiry. I tried to answer it for general epistemological purposes in Chapter 8. To recapitulate: My idea is that at any given time we find ourselves with some "spontaneous beliefs," beliefs that force themselves upon us whether we will or no. These spontaneous beliefs are produced in us by a number of subsequently discoverable sources, most notably by our perceptual organs. Of course, our present, up-to-date knowledge of those sources rests on other data, other ultimate explainees, and so does not by itself justify the initial spontaneous beliefs. Rather, our retention and epistemic use of the spontaneous beliefs are justified by my separate principle of conservatism – that one should hold on to any belief one has unless there is some positive reason to reject it. (Against charges of bigotry, pigheadedness, and so forth, I have defended the principle as necessary to get any reasonable epistemology of any subject off the ground. Moreover, it has exactly the same sort of justification – I say an epistemic rule-utilitarian justification – as have appeals to simplicity, testability, fruitfulness, and the other explanatory desiderata we use in ordinary life and in science.) Once we have retained our spontaneous beliefs on grounds of conservatism, they become data for explanation and are candidates for absorption into an overarching belief system that mobilizes whatever concepts are needed to explain them along with all our other data. Of course, the warrant conferred by conservatism is initially weak and is overridden by almost any other evidential consideration; many spontaneous beliefs get knocked off or thrown out within nanoseconds as hallucinations, misperceptions, inaccurate memories, superstitious forebodings, déjà vu, or whatever. But spontaneous beliefs that pass minimal consistency tests and that continue to fit without other anomaly into our overall body of belief become what I have called *tenable* and enter more aggressively into our explanatory economy. The final test (or so I have argued) is a matter of bootstrapping: If our overarching total theory can explain not only one of our spontaneous beliefs but how it is produced in us, and if the latter explanation involves the truth of the belief, then the belief is fully justified, perhaps to the point of counting as an item of knowledge. It is in this way that an initial spontaneous belief gets swept up into a coherent global explanatory structure. If there is circularity here, the circle is large, satisfying, and anchored in experience.

Many spontaneous beliefs fail this last test of coherence. We can find no reliable mechanism that produces them. Either we cannot at all see where the "information" in question is coming from or (worse) we find positively discrediting evidence that the beliefs are the products of disorder. Beliefs thus discredited cease to be candidates for explanation; the ability of a hypothesis to explain one of them does not count in favor of that hypothesis.

But there are piquant borderline cases here – spontaneous beliefs that will not go away *and* that cannot be seen to be the products of disorder or malfunction but whose provenance is also obscure and certainly does not consist simply in the functioning of a salient, modular bodily organ. Logical "intuitions" are a nice example. So are *grammatical* and other linguistic intuitions, modal and other metaphysical intuitions, and epistemological intuitions. One who wanted to take a hard line on the coherence of spontaneous beliefs would discount all such intuitions on grounds of being unable to find (respective) organs that deliver them. But this seems premature; we feel that there may be more to be said in favor of the trustworthiness of such beliefs. (And to resort to an argument ad hominem, intuitions of these various sorts are the standard grist to the philosopher's mill; I should like to see a single piece of cogent philosophical writing that proceeded with no appeal whatever to any of them.) Although the source of these beliefs remains mysterious, we do not discount them but rely on them for our livelihoods.

Moral intuitions are in this same category. We have spontaneous moral beliefs. Gilbert Harman's cat example is again particularly poignant: Seeing the young hoodlums pouring the gasoline on the cat, "you do not need to *conclude* that what they are doing is wrong;

you can *see* that it is wrong" (1977, p. 4). In my terms, you have a very firm spontaneous belief that it is wrong. The belief meets our minimal tests of consistency and of incorporability into an overall body of theory. But it is not obviously the output of any particular reliable mechanism. As Harman says, we can discover no modular, Jiminy-Cricket–like moral sense that serves to deliver moral facts to our consciousness; so far as we now know, the property of feline immolation per se triggers nothing in our brains whose function is to detect moral wrongness. But if we find some plausible a posteriori reduction of moral properties to sociological and/or evolutionary ones, there may still be some explanatory system that sweeps up our moral intuitions and invests them with full coherence.[8] For evolutionary reasons there may be a way, albeit not a very modular one, in which our brains register morally significant sociological properties of actions; Mother Nature may be a moral as well as an epistemic rule-utilitarian.

Notice that we have no reason to assume that detectors must be modular. For it is already known that human beings have detectors of various sorts that are not modular but work in some ill-understood distributed (and, phenomenologically, gestalt) manner. For example, if we are normal, we can almost instantaneously detect bilateral symmetry around a vertical axis, even in very complex patterns (cf. Braitenberg [1984, Chap. 9]); and we have an uncanny ability to tell when someone else is looking at us, even if we are facing another way.

The entirely reasonable doubt we may have about the suggestion concerning Mother Nature's rule-utilitarianism helps to explain why cognitivism and noncognitivism about ethics are so controversial. If the doubt is borne out and there is simply no evidence of any brain detection of morally charged properties, then so much the worse for moral facts; we would have little reason to believe in them. But against this there is the *insistency* of spontaneous moral

8 D. M. Armstrong has suggested to me in conversation that in order to be vindicated as real, the moral properties would have to play their causal as well as their explanatory roles *qua moral*. I reject this requirement. Plenty of perfectly real properties have their supervenient causal powers only in virtue of laws applying to their realizing substrata or supervenience bases; for example, a watermelon dropped on a philosopher's head from a third-story window does not have its lamentable effect qua watermelon, or qua fruit. Of course, it is possible to argue that moral properties do have their effects qua moral; cf. Sturgeon (1984) and Railton (1986).

judgments. Such judgments are almost impossible to ignore. Moral intuitions can seem as hard to disdain or to write off as are perceptual sensings, and this sort of insistency is, in the case of perceptual sensings, felt to indicate the presence and activity of delivery mechanisms. As I have suggested, there may be good evolutionary reasons for the existence of a firmly distributed if not modular moral sense (a sense of utility and/or a sense of justice),[9] but this is by no means obvious, and so we think there may be no moral facts after all.

Our question (2) about moral data was this: Just which data or facts are the moral theorist's ultimate explainees? The obvious answer is *moral intuitions*, and the obvious explanatory method to invoke is that of reflective equilibrium. But any number of deeper interpretations of the former suggestion are available.

There are at least three avenues to explore, leading from differing conceptions of a moral datum. All three ideas may be construed as alternative conceptions of "moral intuition," *whether competing or complementary.* The first two are by now familiar: (1) What needs to be explained is the intuit*ings*: *the fact of our having* insistent inclinations to make certain moral judgments, or the fact that we do instinctively make those judgments and cannot be cured of doing so save by extraordinary means, even after sophisticated factual, scientific, and philosophical training.[10] (2) What needs to be explained is the intuit*eds*, the accumulated content of the judgments thus made; that is, the explananda are the propositions *asserted by* those moral judgments.[11]

Explanandum (1) is of little immediate help to the champion of moral facts. As Harman observes, the fact that we have the moral feelings we do may well be accounted for without any allusion to moral fact. It might be explained entirely in terms of socialization and, perhaps, Nietzschean weakness of character. Actually, this is not obvious: The sociological and/or evolutionary facts on which

---

9 I would go for utility; but see Gibbard (1982), who tries to find an evolutionary basis for the sense of justice.
10 Anyone who has ever taught an introductory ethics class knows how easy it is to get a self-styled student "amoralist" to loose a fusillade of moral judgments. To produce a genuine freedom from moral intuitions, one needs a steady diet of hard drugs or some other very powerful alienating force.
11 I borrow the -ing/-ed terminology from Sellars (1968), by way of Jay Rosenberg's Kant seminar at the University of North Carolina.

moral judgments supervene may figure indispensably in explanations of why we make the spontaneous judgments we do. And if there are such moral-fact–incorporating explanations, they will nicely complement the other explanations I shall discuss next. But (merely as philosophers) we cannot be confident of that. Avenue (2) is much more promising.

In everyday contexts and in science, we do not take our primary explananda to be *facts of observing*. Rather, we explain the purported facts that are observed. No scientist qua scientist explains why it *seems to him or her that* a spring stretched 15 centimeters; the scientist explains why the spring did stretch 15 centimeters or why there is a vapor trail in the cloud chamber. In the context of my conservative explanationist epistemology, this seems to license our treating spontaneous moral judgments analogously: What needs explaining is the wrongness of incinerating the cat, the wrongness of letting Tina hit other children when hitting is generally forbidden, the goodness of helping Katie when she has fallen and hurt her knee, and so forth. Here is where reflective equilibrium comes into its own. As always, one may have doubts about the ability of mere reflective equilibrium to deliver facts.[12] But if my background epistemology is right,[13] then spontaneous moral judgments are prima facie as worthy of respect as are perceptual judgments and wait only upon the discovery of a very diffuse sort of moral sense – no more modular than are our logical, grammatical, modal, or epistemic senses – for virtually complete vindication as delivering, or at least pointing toward, facts. Moral facts cannot yet be admitted to the country club, but they are not yet blackballed either.

In concentrating on intui*teds* as opposed to intui*tings*, I am being far less fierce an empiricist than is Harman. He demands that in-tui*tings* be explained by moral facts; only in this way are moral

12 In Rawls (1971), the choosers in the Original Position achieve their equilibrium in part through bargaining with each other. I do not incorporate this feature into my moral epistemology. The actual opinions of others count, as they also count in general real-world epistemology, but only as opinions. Norman Gillespie has pointed out in conversation that cultural diversity may here distinguish the moral case from that of perception or the like. But that is not a problem of principle for me, since I have the option of taking others' opinions more seriously or less seriously, depending on my perception and epistemic assessment of their cultural backgrounds. In any case, with very few exceptions (such as, perhaps, that of the Ik), people's spontaneous moral judgments, *given congruent factual beliefs*, do not differ dramatically, even across cultures.

13 It is.

beliefs "tested against the world."[14] But I have defended the epistemic value of explaining intuiteds as well. I suspect there may indeed be an epistemological difference here between ethics and science. (If so, the same difference holds between logic, mathematics, linguistics, the theory of modality, and epistemology itself and science.) But I do not grant that this difference impugns moral facts – or, if it does, then logical, mathematical, linguistic, modal, and epistemological facts are consigned to the same flames.

Let me now make a third and novel suggestion about the nature of moral data: that *desires* can serve as data just as beliefs can. If this idea seems anomalous or crazy, remember that *beliefs* are not the only mental states that function as epistemic reasons. Reasons are always states of believers, but sometimes they are perceptual states, memory states, introspected states, proprioceptions, or some other states; beliefs can be warrantingly *based on* such states as well as on other beliefs.[15] Indeed, the case of beliefs' being based on other beliefs, which is what we call inference, is only one type of putatively justified belief; most of our *paradigmatically* justified beliefs are based on states of other sorts, particularly perceptions and memories. Why, then, may spontaneous moral judgments not be beliefs based on more primitive states having motivational content – that is, on desires of certain sorts?

I have in mind particularly desires whose contents are not self-interested. It is a striking fact that we should have such desires at all, and this should prompt us to ask whether there are any more general features of the world to which such desires are responsive. Like the other nondoxastic states on which justified beliefs may be based, those desires may be products of mechanisms created in us by Mother Nature in her wisdom and in the interest of our collective survival and welfare. And the mechanisms that produce them may in some sense be called trustworthy, although this remains to be spelled out. If all these reflections are on the right track, spontaneous moral judgments are on as good a footing as are (say) beliefs based on memory.

The problem with this third notion of a moral datum is going to be the (alleged) lack of a causal notion of veridicality for desires.

14 See Harman (1977, and particularly 1986). I see no compelling reason to let Harman set the agenda in this way.
15 See Swain (1981b, Chap. 3), and my Chapter 5, this volume.

Desires are not normally regarded as true or false, and unlike perceptions and memories and introspectings, they do not *reflect* existing states of affairs, even though they have intentional content. For this reason, an epistemological reliabilist would disdain desires as reasons. But I am not a reliabilist. In earlier chapters I argued that reliability, in the truth-directed sense, has been overemphasized in recent epistemology at the expense of other sorts of cost-benefit, fitness-promoting values. And there is nothing anomalous in the idea that a belief whose content is itself a normative representation of a future state of affairs might be based (and rationally so) on the desire for that state of affairs to be realized.

Here too we must distinguish representings from representeds, but when we do, we find that desir*ings* are the more helpful. It is quite possible that some of our spontaneous desirings are explained by, for example, the badness of pain qua badness (although causation would have to be transmitted by way of its supervenience base, as usual);[16] evolutionary reasons for this are easy to envisage.[17] It is less easy to see how desir*eds* might figure as explananda, but this is not out of the question either. A person's desireds can be taken collectively as a description and prescription of part of a possible world; this desire-world could be tested for coherence of various kinds and then used as an element of a piece of practical reasoning, particularly if one takes practical reasoning to be a matter of "inference to the best means," analogous to inference to the best explanation,[18] although one would have to be careful in distinguishing specifically moral prescriptions from *mere* means of desire-satisfaction. If we could successfully invoke a kind of practical reasoning analogous to explanatory inference, this would finesse the objection that desires are not information-*delivering* states; for the intentional contents of the premises in a practical inference are not "reflected" information either. (Note that even epistemic reasons do not always "reflect"; otherwise there would be no knowledge of the future.) Moreover, if moral beliefs are based in part on desireds *or* desirings, this would help explain why moral beliefs

16 See Kim (1983) and Tolhurst (1986). The idea of supervenient causation goes back at least to Davidson (1970).
17 For a somewhat similar and better-articulated idea, see Railton (1986).
18 I believe the idea was originally Rawls's (1971), but see particularly Darwall (1976).

characteristically motivate and why "internalism" about moral motivation has seemed so attractive to some philosophers.[19]

My suggestion about "desireds" and practical reasoning is perhaps too cryptic even to be discussed. But I emphasize that it and the other, preceding conceptions of "moral data" are mutually independent and complementary rather than competing; even if any one of them should prove useless, the others may stand. My particular favorite, on which I pin my hopes, is that of the intuiteds; for if one wants to reject these as data, one will find it hard to countenance the very sorts of logical, linguistic, and epistemological facts that are most often appealed to in arguments against moral realism.

I do not contend that moral facts are assured of a bright future. After all, there are principled objections besides those I have considered here. I do maintain that if moral facts are in trouble, then so are facts of any other sort that seem supervenient but are not yet uncontroversially reduced – and that the prospects for moral facts are much brighter than twentieth-century philosophy has so far allowed.

19 Actually I have a separate but related response to the skeptical Argument from Motivation: Since a belief is a functional state of its subject and since (in particular) beliefs are typed in part according to their functional properties, I see no reason why some beliefs may not have conative features as parts of their functional profiles. Indeed, I see no reason why moral beliefs may not per se be simply those whose functional profiles are conative in a characteristic way; after all, we need to be able to say what it is that makes moral beliefs moral in kind, and a functional feature is the most likely candidate for *differentiam*. This motivational property may be metaphysically essential to moral belief, even if this is not a *linguistic* truth. But in any case, there is no reason to suppose, as Mackie (1977) does, that the motivating element must inhere – weirdly – in moral facts themselves rather than being properties of the corresponding moral beliefs. (I plan to develop this point in a separate paper.)

References

Abelson, Raziel. 1970. "A Refutation of Mind–Body Identity." *Philosophical Studies* 21, 85–90.

Alcock, J. 1979. *Animal Behavior: An Evolutionary Approach.* Sunderland, Mass.: Sinauer Associates.

Annis, David. 1977. "Epistemic Foundationalism." *Philosophical Studies* 31, 345–52.

Armstrong, D. M. 1968. *A Materialist Theory of the Mind.* New York: Humanities Press.

    1969. "Does Knowledge Entail Belief?" *Proceedings of the Aristotelian Society* 70, 21–36.

    1973. *Belief, Truth and Knowledge.* Cambridge: Cambridge University Press.

    1978a. "Naturalism, Materialism and First Philosophy." *Philosophia* 8, 261–76.

    1978b. *A Theory of Universals.* Vol. 2 of *Universals and Scientific Realism.* Cambridge: Cambridge University Press.

    1982. "Metaphysics and Supervenience." *Critica* 14, 3–17.

    1983. *What Is a Law of Nature?* Cambridge: Cambridge University Press.

Audi, Robert. 1982. "Believing and Affirming." *Mind* 91, 115–20.

Austin, J. L. 1962. *Sense and Sensibilia.* Oxford: Oxford University Press.

Ayer, A. J. 1952. *Language, Truth and Logic.* 2d ed. New York: Dover.

Bauerle, R., U. Egli, and A. von Stechow, eds. 1979. *Semantics from Different Points of View.* Berlin: Springer.

Bechtel, P. W. 1982. "Realism, Instrumentalism, and the Intentional Stance." Unpublished photocopy, Georgia State University.

Bennett, Jonathan. 1976. *Linguistic Behavior.* Cambridge: Cambridge University Press.

Bentham, Jeremy. 1789/1961. *An Introduction to the Principles of Morals and Legislation.* Garden City, N.Y.: Doubleday (Dolphin Books).

Bigelow, John, and R. Pargetter. 1987. "Functions." *Journal of Philosophy* 84, 181–96.

Block, N.J. 1978. "Troubles with Functionalism." In Savage (1978).

    1981. "Psychologism and Behaviorism." *Philosophical Review* 90, 5–43.

Boër, Steven. 1985. "Substance and Kind: Reflections on the New Theory of Reference." In Matilal and Shaw (1985).

Boër, Steven, and W. G. Lycan. 1975. "Knowing Who." *Philosophical Studies* 28, 299–344.

1976. *The Myth of Semantic Presupposition.* Bloomington: Indiana University Linguistics Club Publications.

1980. "Who, Me?" *Philosophical Review* 89, 427–66.

1986a. "Castañeda's Theory of Knowing." In J. Tomberlin, ed., *Profiles: Hector-Neri Castañeda.* Dordrecht: Reidel.

1986b. *Knowing Who.* Cambridge, Mass.: MIT Press (Bradford Books).

Bonjour, Laurence. 1980. "Externalist Theories of Empirical Knowledge." In French, Uehling, and Wettstein (1980).

Boyd, Richard. 1981. "Scientific Realism and Naturalistic Epistemology." In P. D. Asquith and R. Giere, eds., *Philosophy of Science Association 1980,* vol. 2. East Lansing, Mich.: Philosophy of Science Association.

1983. "How to Be a Moral Realist." Address delivered to the Seventeenth Chapel Hill Colloquium in Philosophy, October, 1983.

1985. "The Current Status of Scientific Realism." In J. Leplin, ed., *Scientific Realism.* Berkeley: University of California Press.

Braitenberg, Valentino. 1984. *Vehicles.* Cambridge, Mass.: MIT Press (Bradford Books).

Burge, Tyler. 1979. "Individualism and the Mental." In French, Uehling, and Wettstein (1979).

Butterfield, Jeremy, ed. 1986. *Language, Mind, and Logic.* Cambridge: Cambridge University Press.

Campbell, K. K. 1981. "Naturalism in Moral Philosophy." *Proceedings of the Russellian Society,* vol. 6. Sydney University.

Carnap, R. 1956. "Empiricism, Semantics, and Ontology." In *Meaning and Necessity.* 2d ed. Chicago: University of Chicago Press.

Cartwright, Nancy. 1983. *How the Laws of Physics Lie.* Oxford: Oxford University Press.

Castañeda, H.-N. 1966. "He*: A Study in the Logic of Self-Consciousness." *Ratio* 8, 130–57.

1967. "Indicators and Quasi-Indicators." *American Philosophical Quarterly* 4, 1–16.

1980. "The Theory of Questions, Epistemic Powers, and the Indexical Theory of Knowledge." In French, Uehling, and Wettstein (1980).

Chisholm, R. M. 1946. "The Contrary-to-Fact Conditional." *Mind* 55, 289–307.

1958. Contributions to "The Chisholm-Sellars Correspondence on Intentionality." In Feigl, Scriven, and Maxwell (1958).

1977. *Theory of Knowledge.* 2d ed. Englewood Cliffs, N.J.: Prentice-Hall.

1978. "On the Nature of Empirical Evidence." In Pappas and Swain (1978).

1980. "A Version of Foundationalism." In French, Uehling, and Wettstein (1980).

Churchland, P. M. 1970. "The Logical Character of Action Explanations." *Philosophical Review* 79, 214–36.

1979. *Scientific Realism and the Plasticity of Mind.* Cambridge: Cambridge University Press.

1982. "Is 'Thinker' a Natural Kind?" *Dialogue* 21, 223–38.

218

1985. "On Representation, Computation, and Implementation: A New Theory of How the Brain Works." Typescript, University of California at San Diego.

1986. "Some Reductive Strategies in Cognitive Neurobiology." *Mind* 95, 223–38.

Churchland, P. M., and P. S. Churchland. 1983. "Stalking the Wild Epistemic Engine." *Nous* 17, 5–18.

Churchland, P. S. 1980. "Language, Thought, and Information Processing." *Nous* 14, 147–70.

Cohen, L. J. 1981. "Can Human Irrationality Be Experimentally Demonstrated?" *Behavioral and Brain Sciences* 4, 317–31.

Collins, A. W. 1979. "Could Our Beliefs Be Mental Representations in Our Brains?" *Journal of Philosophy* 76, 225–43.

Cornman, James. 1966. *Metaphysics, Reference, and Language.* New Haven: Yale University Press.

1972. *Materialism and Sensations.* New Haven: Yale University Press.

1978. "Foundational versus Nonfoundational Theories of Empirical Justification." In Pappas and Swain (1978).

1980. *Skepticism, Justification, and Explanation.* Dordrecht: Reidel.

Cummins, Robert. 1975. "Functional Analysis." *Journal of Philosophy* 72, 741–65.

1983. *The Nature of Psychological Explanation.* Cambridge, Mass.: MIT Press (Bradford Books).

Darwall, Stephen. 1976. "The Inference to the Best Means." *Canadian Journal of Philosophy* 6, 49–58.

Davidson, Donald. 1968. "On Saying That." *Synthese* 19, 130–46.

1970. "Mental Events." In L. Foster and J. W. Swanson, eds., *Experience and Theory.* Amherst: University of Massachusetts Press.

1973. "The Material Mind." In P. Suppes, L. Henkin, A. Joja eds., *Logic, Methodology and Philosophy of Science,* vol. 4. Amsterdam: North-Holland.

1973–4. "On the Very Idea of a Conceptual Scheme." *Proceedings and Addresses of the American Philosophical Association* 47, 5–20.

1974. "Psychology as Philosophy." In S. C. Brown, ed., *Philosophy of Psychology.* London: Macmillan.

Davidson, Donald, and Gilbert Harman, eds. 1972. *Semantics of Natural Language.* Dordrecht: Reidel.

Dennett, D. C. 1969. *Content and Consciousness.* London: Routledge & Kegan Paul.

1971. "Intentional Systems." *Journal of Philosophy* 68, 87–106; reprinted in Dennett (1978).

1975. "Brain Writing and Mind Reading." In Gunderson (1975); reprinted in Dennett (1978).

1978. *Brainstorms.* Montgomery, Vt.: Bradford Books.

1981a. "Making Sense of Ourselves." *Philosophical Topics* 12, 63–81.

1981b. "Three Kinds of Intentional Psychology." In R. A. Healey, ed., *Reduction, Time and Reality.* Cambridge: Cambridge University Press.

1981c. "True Believers: The Intentional Strategy and Why It Works."

In A. F. Heath, ed., *Scientific Explanation*. Oxford: Oxford University Press.

1982. "Beyond Belief." In Woodfield (1982).

1983. "Cognitive Wheels: The Frame Problem in AI." In C. Hookway, ed., *Minds, Machines and Evolution*. Cambridge: Cambridge University Press.

de Sousa, Ronald. 1971. "How to Give a Piece of Your Mind." *Review of Metaphysics* 25, 52–79.

Devitt, Michael. 1974. "Singular terms." *Journal of Philosophy* 71, 183–205.

1981. *Designation*. New York: Columbia University Press.

1983. "Dummett's Anti-Realism." *Journal of Philosophy* 80, 73–9.

1984. *Realism and Truth*. Princeton: Princeton University Press.

Donnellan, Keith. 1976. "Speaking of Nothing." *Philosophical Review* 85, 3–31.

Dray, W. H. 1963. "The Historical Explanation of Action Reconsidered." In S. Hook, ed., *Philosophy and History*. New York: New York University Press.

Dretske, Fred. 1971. "Conclusive Reasons." *Australasian Journal of Philosophy* 49, 1–22; reprinted in Pappas and Swain (1978).

1975. Review of Armstrong (1973). *Journal of Philosophy* 72, 793–802.

1981. *Knowledge and the Flow of Information*. Cambridge, Mass.: MIT Press (Bradford Books).

Dreyfus, Hubert. 1979. *What Computers Can't Do*. Revised ed. New York: Harper & Row (Colophon Books).

Duhem, Pierre. 1906. *La Théorie Physique, Son Objet et Sa Structure*. Paris: Chevalier et Riviere.

Dummett, Michael. 1978. *Truth and Other Enigmas*. Cambridge, Mass.: Harvard University Press.

Ennis, R. H. 1968. "Enumerative Induction and Best Explanation." *Journal of Philosophy* 65, 523–9.

Fahlman, S. E. 1979. "Representing and Using Real-world Knowledge." In P. H. Winston and R. H. Brown, eds., *Artificial Intelligence: An MIT Perspective*. Cambridge, Mass.: MIT Press.

Feigl, H., and M. Scriven, eds. 1956. *The Foundations of Science and the Concepts of Psychology and Psychoanalysis*. Minnesota Studies in the Philosophy of Science, Vol. 1. Minneapolis: University of Minnesota Press.

Feigl, H., M. Scriven, and G. Maxwell. 1958. *Concepts, Theories and the Mind–Body Problem*. Minnesota Studies in the Philosophy of Science, Vol. 2. Minneapolis: University of Minnesota Press.

Fetzer, J. H. 1981. *Scientific Knowledge*. Dordrecht: Reidel.

Ed., 1984. *Principles of Philosophical Reasoning*. Totowa, N.J.: Rowman & Allanheld.

Field, Hartry. 1978. "Mental Representation." *Erkenntnis* 13, 9–61.

Fine, Arthur. 1984a. "And Not Anti-Realism Either." *Noûs* 18, 51–65.

1984b. "The National Ontological Attitude." In Leplin (1984).

Fodor, Jerry A. 1968a. "The Appeal to Tacit Knowledge in Psychological Explanation." *Journal of Philosophy* 65, 627–40.

1968b. *Psychological Explanation.* New York: Random House.

1975. *The Language of Thought.* New York: Crowell.

1978. "Propositional Attitudes." *Monist* 61, 501–23; reprinted in Fodor (1981a).

1980. "Methodological Solipsism Considered as a Research Strategy in Cognitive Psychology." *Behavioral and Brain Sciences* 3, 63–73; reprinted in Fodor (1981a).

1981a. *RePresentations.* Cambridge, Mass: MIT Press (Bradford Books).

1981b. "Three Cheers for Propositional Attitudes." In Fodor (1981a).

1986. "Banish DisContent." In Butterfield (1986).

1987. *Psychosemantics.* Cambridge, Mass: MIT Press (Bradford Books).

Foley, Richard. 1978. "Inferential Justification and the Infinite Regress." *American Philosophical Quarterly* 15, 311–16.

1983. "Epistemic Conservatism." *Philosophical Studies* 43, 165–82.

French, P. A., T. E. Uehling, and H. Wettstein, eds. 1979a. *Contemporary Perspectives in the Philosophy of Language.* Minneapolis: University of Minnesota Press.

1979b. *Studies in Metaphysics.* Midwest Studies in Philosophy, no. 4. Minneapolis: University of Minnesota Press.

1980. *Studies in Epistemology.* Midwest Studies in Philosophy, no. 5. Minneapolis: University of Minnesota Press.

1982. *Social and Political Philosophy.* Midwest Studies in Philosophy, no. 7. Minneapolis: University of Minnesota Press.

1984. *Causation and Conditionals.* Midwest Studies in Philosophy, no. 9. Minneapolis: University of Minnesota Press.

Garcia, J., B. K. McGowan, and K. F. Green. 1972. "Biological Constraints on Conditioning." In A. H. Black and W. F. Prokasy, *Classical Conditioning II: Current Research and Theory.* New York: Appleton-Crofts.

Geis, Michael. 1973. "If and Unless." In B. B. Kachru, R. B. Lees, Y. Malkiel, eds., *Papers in Honor of Henry and Renee Kahane.* Champaign: University of Illinois Press.

Gettier, E. 1963. "Is Justified True Belief Knowledge?" *Analysis* 23, 121–3.

Gibbard, Allan. 1981. "Two Recent Theories of Conditionals." In Harper et al. (1981).

1982. "Human Evolution and the Sense of Justice." In French, Uehling, and Wettstein (1982).

Gibbard, Allan, and W. L. Harper. 1981. "Counterfactuals and Two Kinds of Expected Utility." In Harper et al. (1981).

Gillespie, N., ed. 1986. *Moral Realism.* Proceedings of the 1985 Spindel Conference, Memphis State University. *Southern Journal of Philosophy* 24 (suppl.).

Goldman, A. I. 1967. "A Causal Theory of Knowing." *Journal of Philosophy* 64, 355–72; reprinted in Pappas and Swain (1978).

1975. "Discrimination and Perceptual Knowledge." *Journal of Philosophy* 73, 771–91; reprinted in Pappas and Swain (1978).

1979. "What Is Justified Belief?" In Pappas (1979).

1980. "The Internalist Conception of Justification." In French, Uehling, and Wettstein (1980).

Goldman, Alan. 1979. "Appearing Statements and Epistemological Foundations." *Metaphilosophy* 10, 227–46.

1981. "Epistemology and the Philosophy of Perception." American Philosophical Quarterly 18, 43–51.

Goldstick, Daniel. 1971. "Methodological Conservatism." *American Philosophical Quarterly* 8, 186–91.

1976. "More on Methodological Conservatism." *Philosophical Studies* 30, 192–4.

Goodman, Nelson. 1955. "The New Riddle of Induction." In *Fact, Fiction, and Forecast*. Cambridge, Mass.: Harvard University Press.

Grandy, Richard. 1979. "Forms of Belief." Paper delivered at the University of South Carolina Conference on Pragmatics, Columbia, April 1979.

Grice, H. P. 1975. "Method in Philosophical Psychology (From the Banal to the Bizarre)." *Proceedings and Addresses of the American Philosophical Association* 48, 23–53.

Gunderson, K., ed. 1975. *Language, Mind and Knowledge*. Minnesota Studies in the Philosophy of Science, no. 7. Minneapolis: University of Minnesota Press.

Gunner, D. L. 1967. "Professor Smart's 'Sensations and Brain Processes.'" In C. F. Presley, ed., *The Identity Theory of Mind*. St. Lucia: University of Queensland Press.

Hacking, Ian. 1982. "Experimentation and Scientific Realism." *Philosophical Topics* 13, 111–222. Reprinted in Leplin (1984).

Hare, R. M. 1952. *The Language of Morals*. Oxford: Oxford University Press.

1963. *Freedom and Reason*. Oxford: Oxford University Press.

Harman, Gilbert. 1965. "The Inference to the Best Explanation." *Philosophical Review* 74, 88–95.

1967. "Psychological Aspects of the Theory of Syntax." *Journal of Philosophy* 64, 75–87.

1968. "Enumerative Induction as Inference to the Best Explanation." *Journal of Philosophy* 64, 529–33.

1969. "An Introduction to 'Translation and Meaning': Chapter Two of *Word and Object*." In Davidson and Hintikka, eds., *Words and Objections: Essays on the Work of W. V. Quine*. Dordrecht: Reidel.

1970. "Knowledge, Reasons, and Causes." *Journal of Philosophy* 67, 841–55.

1973. *Thought*. Princeton: Princeton University Press.

1977. *The Nature of Morality*. Oxford: Oxford University Press.

1978. "Is There Mental Representation?" In Savage (1978).

1986. "Moral Explanations of Natural Facts – Can Moral Claims Be Tested against Moral Reality?" In Gillespie (1986).

Harper, W. L., R. Stalnaker, and G. Pearce, eds. 1981. *Ifs*. Dordrecht: Reidel.

Haugeland, John. 1978. "The Nature and Plausibility of Cognitivism." *Behavioral and Brain Sciences* 2, 215–60.

Hempel, C. G. 1945. "Studies in the Logic of Confirmation." *Mind* 54, 1–26, 97–121. Reprinted in *Aspects of Scientific Explanation*. New York: Free Press.

Henson, Richard. 1964. "On What We Say." *American Philosophical Quarterly* 2, 52–62.

Hill, C. S. 1976. "Toward a Theory of Meaning for Belief Sentences." *Philosophical Studies* 30, 209–26.

Hintikka, K. J. J. 1969. "Semantics for Propositional Attitudes." In *Models for Modalities*. Dordrecht: Reidel.

1975. *The Intentions of Intentionality and Other New Models for Modalities*. Dordrecht: Reidel.

Hunter, J. F. M. 1980. "Believing." In French, Uehling, and Wettstein (1980).

James, W. 1954. "What Pragmatism Means." In *Essays in Pragmatism*. New York: Hafner.

Kaplan, David. 1975. "How to Russell a Frege-Church." *Journal of Philosophy* 72, 716–29.

1979. "Dthat." In French, Uehling, and Wettstein (1979).

Kaplan, Mark, and L. Sklar. 1976. "Rationality and Truth." *Philosophical Studies* 30, 197–202.

Kilgore, Clyde, and W. Lycan. 1982. "Epistemological Relativity." Typescript, University of North Carolina.

Kim, Jaegwon. 1966. "On the Psycho-Physical Identity Theory." *American Philosophical Quarterly* 3, 227–35.

1979. "Causality, Identity, and Supervenience in the Mind–Body Problem." In French, Uehling, and Wettstein (1979).

1983. "Supervenience and Supervenient Causation." *Southern Journal of Philosophy* 22 (suppl.), 45–56.

Kitcher, Philip. 1980. "A Priori Knowledge." *Philosophical Review* 89, 3–23.

Kornblith, Hilary. 1980. "Beyond Foundationalism and the Coherence Theory." *Journal of Philosophy* 77, 597–612.

1983. "Justified Belief and Epistemically Responsible Action." *Philosophical Review* 92, 33–48.

Kraut, Robert. 1979. "Attitudes and Their Objects." *Journal of Philosophical Logic* 8, 197–217.

Kripke, Saul. 1971. "Identity and Necessity." In M. Munitz, ed., *Identity and Individuation*. New York: New York University Press.

1972. "Naming and Necessity." In Davidson and Harman (1972).

1979. "A Puzzle about Belief." In A. Margalit, ed., *Meaning and Use*. Dordrecht: Reidel.

1982. *Wittgenstein on Rules and Private Language*. Cambridge, Mass.: Harvard University Press.

Lazerowitz, Morris. 1955. *The Structure of Metaphysics*. London: Routledge & Kegan Paul.

1964. *Studies in Metaphilosophy*. London: Routledge & Kegan Paul.

Lehnert, Wendy. 1979. "Representing Physical Objects in Memory." In Ringle (1979).

Lehrer, Keith. 1974. *Knowledge*. Oxford: Oxford University Press.

1978. "Why Not Skepticism?" In Pappas and Swain (1978).

Leplin, Jarrett, ed. *Scientific Realism*. Berkeley: University of California Press.

LePore, Ernest. 1982. "Truth and Inference." *Erkenntnis* 19, 379–95.

1983. "What Model-theoretic Semantics Cannot Do." *Synthese* 54, 167–87.

LePore, Ernest, and B. Loewer. 1981. "Translational Semantics." *Synthese* 48, 121–33.

Levi, Isaac, and S. Morgenbesser. 1964. "Belief and Disposition." *American Philosophical Quarterly* 1, 221–32.

Lewis, David. 1972. "Psychophysical and Theoretical Identifications." *Australasian Journal of Philosophy* 50, 249–58.

1973. *Counterfactuals*. Cambridge, Mass.: Harvard University Press.

1979. "Counterfactual Dependence and Time's Arrow." *Nous* 13, 455–76.

1981. "What Puzzling Pierre Does Not Believe." *Australasian Journal of Philosophy* 59, 283–9.

Loar, Brian. 1981. *Mind and Meaning*. Cambridge: Cambridge University Press.

Loewer, Barry. 1982. "The Role of 'Conceptual Role Semantics.'" *Notre Dame Journal of Formal Logic* 23, 305–15.

Lycan, W. G. 1971. "Recent Work on Wittgenstein's 'Criteria.'" *American Philosophical Quarterly*, 109–25.

1973. "Davidson on Saying That." *Analysis* 33, 138–9.

1974. "Mental States and Putnam's Functionalist Hypothesis." *Australasian Journal of Philosophy* 52, 48–62.

1977. "Evidence One Does Not Possess." *Australasian Journal of Philosophy* 55, 114–26.

1979a. "Reliability, Laws, and Counterfactuals." Unpublished ditto, University of North Carolina.

1979b. "The Trouble with Possible Worlds." In M. Loux, ed., *The Possible and the Actual*. Ithaca: Cornell University Press.

1981a. "Form, Function, and Feel." *Journal of Philosophy* 78, 24–50.

1981b. "'Is' and 'Ought' in Cognitive Science." *Behavioral and Brain Sciences* 4, 344–5.

1981c. "Psychological Laws." *Philosophical Topics* 12, 9–38.

1982. "Notes on the 'KK' Thesis." Memorandum, University of North Carolina.

1984a. *Logical Form in Natural Language*. Cambridge, Mass.: MIT Press (Bradford Books).

1984b. "A Syntactically Motivated Theory of Conditionals." In French, Uehling, and Wettstein (1984).

1985. "The Paradox of Naming." In Matilal and Shaw (1985).

1987. *Consciousness*. Cambridge, Mass.: MIT Press (Bradford Books).

Lycan, W. G., and G. Pappas. 1976. "Quine's Materialism." *Philosophia* 6, 101–30.

Mackie, J. L. 1977. *Ethics: Inventing Right and Wrong.* New York: Penguin Books.

Marras, Ausonio. 1980. "Cognitivism and the Computational Approach." Unpublished photocopy, University of Western Ontario.

Martin, E., and D. W. Smith. 1974. "On the Nature and Relevance of Indeterminacy." *Foundations of Language* 12, 49–71.

Matilal, B.-K., and J. L. Shaw, eds. 1985. *Analytical Philosophy in Comparative Perspective.* Dordrecht: Reidel.

Mayo, B. 1967. "Belief and Constraint." In A. P. Griffiths, ed., *Knowledge and Belief.* Oxford: Oxford University Press.

Minsky, M. 1975. "A Framework for Representing Knowledge." In P. H. Winston, ed., *The Psychology of Computer Vision.* Englewood Cliffs, N.J.: Prentice-Hall.

Moore, G. E. 1903. *Principia Ethica.* Cambridge: Cambridge University Press.

Moore, J., and A. Newell. 1974. "How Can MERLIN Understand?" In L. Gregg, ed., *Knowledge and Cognition.* Potomac, Md.: Lawrence Erlbaum Associates.

Mucciolo, L. 1974. "The Identity Thesis and Neuropsychology." *Nous* 8, 327–42.

Neander, Karen. 1982. "Teleology in Biology." Typescript, University of Adelaide.

Nisbett, R. E., and L. Ross. 1980. *Human Inference: Strategies and Shortcomings of Social Judgment.* Englewood Cliffs, N.J.: Prentice-Hall.

Nisbett, R. E., and T. D. Wilson. 1977. "Telling More than We Can Know: Verbal Reports on Mental Processes." *Psychological Review* 84, 231–59.

Nozick, R. 1981. *Philosophical Explanations.* Cambridge, Mass.: Harvard University Press.

Pappas, G. 1979a. "Basing Relations." In Pappas (1979b).

Ed., 1979b. *Justification and Knowledge.* Dordrecht: Reidel.

Pappas, G., and M. Swain. 1973. "Some Conclusive Reasons against 'Conclusive Reasons.'" *Australasian Journal of Philosophy* 51, 72–6.

Pappas, G., and M. Swain, eds. *Essays on Knowledge and Justification.* Ithaca: Cornell University Press.

Partee, B. H. 1979a. "Montague Grammar, Mental Representations, and Reality." In French, Uehling, and Wettstein (1979a).

1979b. "Semantics – Mathematics or Psychology?" In Bauerle, Egli, and von Stechow (1979).

Perry, J. 1979. "The Problem of the Essential Indexical." *Nous* 13, 3–21.

1982. "Belief and Opacity in Situation Semantics." Talk delivered to the Workshop on Propositions, Propositional Attitudes, and Finite Representability, University of Massachusetts, February 1982.

Place, U. T. 1956. "Is Consciousness a Brain Process?" *British Journal of Psychology* 47, 44–50.

225

Pollock, John. 1985. "Epistemic Norms." Typescript, University of Arizona.

Popper, K. 1972. "Of Clouds and Clocks: An Approach to the Problem of Rationality and the Freedom of Man." In *Objective Knowledge: An Evolutionary Approach*. Oxford: Oxford University Press.

Post, John. 1984. "On the Determinacy of Valuation." *Philosophical Studies* 45, 315–33.

Powers, L. H. 1978. "Knowledge by Deduction." *Philosophical Review* 87, 337–71.

Putnam, Hilary. 1967. "Psychological Predicates." In W. Capitan and D. Merrill, eds., *Art, Mind, and Religion*. Pittsburgh: University of Pittsburgh Press. Reprinted in Putnam (1975b) under the title "The Nature of Mental States."

1975a. "The Meaning of 'Meaning.' " In Gunderson (1975), reprinted in Putnam (1975b).

1975b. *Mind, Language and Reality*. Vol. 2 of *Philosophical Papers*. Cambridge: Cambridge University Press.

1978. *Meaning and the Moral Sciences*. London: Routledge & Kegan Paul.

1981. *Reason, Truth and History*. Cambridge: Cambridge University Press.

Pylyshyn, Zenon. 1973. "What the Mind's Eye Tells the Mind's Brain: A Critique of Mental Imagery." *Psychological Bulletin* 80, 1–24.

1979. "Complexity and the Study of Artificial and Human Intelligence." In Ringle (1979).

1980. "Cognitive Representation and the Process–Architecture Distinction." *Behavioral and Brain Sciences* 3, 154–67.

Quine, W. V. 1953a. *From a Logical Point of View*. New York: Harper & Row.

1953b. "On What There Is." In Quine (1953a).

1953c. "Two Dogmas of Empiricism." In Quine (1953a).

1960. *Word and Object*. Cambridge, Mass.: MIT Press.

1969. "Epistemology Naturalized." In *Ontological Relativity and Other Essays*. New York: Columbia University Press.

1970. "Philosophical Progress in Language Theory." *Metaphilosophy* 1, 2–19.

1975. "Mind and Verbal Dispositions." In S. Guttenplan, ed., *Mind and Language*. Oxford: Oxford University Press.

1978. "Reply to Lycan and Pappas." *Philosophia* 7, 637–8.

Quine, W. V., and J. S. Ullian. 1973. *The Web of Belief*. New York: Random House.

Railton, Peter. 1986. "Moral Realism." *Philosophical Review* 95, 163–207.

Rawls, John. 1971. *A Theory of Justice*. Cambridge, Mass.: Harvard University Press.

Rescher, Nicholas. 1973. *The Coherence Theory of Truth*. Oxford: Oxford University Press.

1976. *Plausible Reasoning*. Assen, Netherlands: Van Gorcum.

1977. *Methodological Pragmatism*. Oxford: Blackwell.

1980. *Induction*. Pittsburgh: University of Pittsburgh Press.

Rey, Georges. 1980. "The Formal and the Opaque." *Behavioral and Brain Sciences* 3, 90–2.

Richardson, Robert. 1980. "Intentional Realism or Intentional Instrumentalism?" *Cognition and Brain Theory* 3, 125–35.

1981. "Internal Representation: Prologue to a Theory of Intentionality." *Philosophical Topics* 12, 171–211.

Ringle, M., ed. 1979. *Philosophical Perspectives in Artificial Intelligence*. Brighton, UK: Harvester Press.

Rorty, Richard. 1972. "The World Well Lost." *Journal of Philosophy* 69, 649–65.

Rosch, Eleanor. 1977. "Human Categorization." In M. Warren, ed., *Advances in Cross-cultural Psychology*. Vol. 1. London: Academic Press.

Rosenberg, J. F. 1974. *Linguistic Representation*. Dordrecht, Reidel.

1978. "Linguistic Roles and Proper Names." In J. C. Pitt, ed., *The Philosophy of Wilfrid Sellars: Queries and Extensions*. Dordrecht: Reidel.

1985. "Science and the Epistemic Authority of Logical Analysis." In N. Rescher, ed., *Reason and Rationality in Natural Science*. Lanham, Md.: University Press of America.

Russell, B. 1910. "The Elements of Ethics." In *Philosophical Essays*. London: Allen & Unwin.

1957. "The Relation of Sense-Data to Physics." *Scientia*, No. 4 (1914). Reprinted in *Mysticism and Logic and Other Essays*. Garden City: Doubleday (Anchor Books).

Savage, W., ed. 1978. *Perception and Cognition: Issues in the Foundations of Psychology*. Minnesota Studies in the Philosophy of Science, no. 9. Minneapolis: University of Minnesota Press.

Sayre McCord, Geoffrey. 1985. "Logical Positivism and the Demise of 'Moral Science.'" In N. Rescher, ed., *The Heritage of Logical Positivism*. Lanham, Md.: University Press of America.

In press. "Moral Theory and Explanatory Impotence." In a collection to be published by Cornell University Press.

Schank, R. C., and R. P. Abelson. 1977. *Scripts, Plans, Goals and Understanding*. Hillsdale, N.J.: Lawrence Erlbaum Associates.

Schmitt, Fred. 1981. "Justification as Reliable Indication or Reliable Process?" *Philosophical Studies* 40, 409–17.

1982a. "Knowledge as Tracking." Typescript, University of Illinois.

1982b. "Reliability, Objectivity, and the Background of Justification." Typescript, University of Illinois.

1983. "Knowledge, Justification and Reliability." *Synthese* 55, 209–30.

Searle, John. 1969. *Speech Acts*. Cambridge: Cambridge University Press.

Sellars, W. 1956. "Empiricism and the Philosophy of Mind." In Feigl and Scriven (1956). Reprinted in Sellars (1963a).

1958. August 3, 1956, contribution to the "Chisholm-Sellars Correspondence on Intentionality," in Feigl, Scriven, and Maxwell (1958).

1963a. *Science, Perception, and Reality*. London: Routledge & Kegan Paul.

1963b. "Some Reflections on Language Games." In Sellars (1963b).

1968. *Science and Metaphysics*. London: Routledge & Kegan Paul.

1969. "Language as Thought and as Communication." *Philosophy and Phenomenological Research* 24, 506–27.

1973. "Reply to Quine." *Synthese* 26, 122–45.

Sklar, Lawrence. 1975. "Methodological Conservatism." *Philosophical Review* 84, 374–400.

1981. "Do Unborn Hypotheses Have Rights?" *Pacific Philosophical Quarterly* 62, 17–29.

Smart, J. J. C. 1959. "Sensations and Brain Processes." *Philosophical Review* 48, 141–56.

1967. "Comments on the Papers." In C. F. Presley, ed., *The Identity Theory of Mind*. St. Lucia: University of Queensland Press.

1984. "Ockham's Razor." In Fetzer (1984).

Sober, Elliott. 1975. *Simplicity*. Oxford: Oxford University Press (Clarendon Press).

1978. "Psychologism." *Journal of the Theory of Social Behaviour* 8, 165–91.

1981. "The Evolution of Rationality." *Synthese* 46, 95–120.

1984. *The Nature of Selection*. Cambridge, Mass.: MIT Press (Bradford Books).

1985. "Panglossian Functionalism and the Philosophy of Mind." *Synthese* 64, 165–93.

Stack, Michael. March 1980. "Why I Don't Believe in Beliefs and You Shouldn't." Paper delivered at annual meeting of the Society for Philosophy and Psychology, University of Manitoba.

Stalnaker, Robert. 1968. "A Theory of Conditionals." In N. Rescher, ed., *Studies in Logical Theory, American Philosophical Quarterly* Monograph Series, No. 2. Oxford: Blackwell.

1978. "Assertion." In P. Cole, ed., *Syntax and Semantics*, vol. 9. London: Academic Press.

1979. "Semantics for Belief." Unpublished photocopy, Cornell University.

1980. "Thoughts." Typescript, Cornell University.

1984. *Inquiry*. Cambridge, Mass.: MIT Press (Bradford Books).

Sterelny, Kim. 1983. "The Language of Thought Revisited." Typescript, Australian National University.

Stevenson, Charles. 1944. *Ethics and Language*. New Haven: Yale University Press.

Stich, S. P. 1971. "What Every Speaker Knows." *Philosophical Review*, 80, 476–96.

1975. "Logical Form and Natural Language." *Philosophical Studies* 28, 397–418.

1978a. "Autonomous Psychology and the Belief-Desire Thesis." *Monist* 61, 573–91.

1978b. "Beliefs and Subdoxastic States." *Philosophy of Science* 45, 499–519.

1979. "Do Animals Have Beliefs?" *Australasian Journal of Philosophy* 57, 15–28.

228

1980. "Paying the Price for Methodological Solipsism." *Behavioral and Brain Sciences* 3, 97–8.

1981. "Dennett on Intentional Systems." *Philosophical Topics* 12, 39–62.

1982. "On the ascription of content." In Woodfield (1982).

1983. *From Folk Psychology to Cognitive Science: The Case against Belief.* Cambridge, Mass.: MIT Press (Bradford Books). '

1985. "Could Man Be an Irrational Animal? Some Notes on the Epistemology of Rationality." *Synthese* 64, 115–35.

Stove, D. C. 1986. *The Rationality of Induction.* Oxford: Oxford University Press (Clarendon Press).

Strawson, P. F. 1952. *Introduction to Logical Theory.* London: Methuen.

Sturgeon, Nicholas. 1984. "Moral Explanations." In D. Copp and D. Zimmerman, eds., *Morality, Reason and Truth.* Totowa, N.J.: Rowman & Allanheld.

Swain, Marshall. 1972. "Knowledge, Causality, and Justification." *Journal of Philosophy* 69, 291–300.

1981a. "Justification and the Basis of Belief." In Pappas (1981b).

1981b. *Reasons and Knowledge.* Ithaca: Cornell University Press.

Taylor, Richard. 1968. "Dare to Be Wise." *Review of Metaphysics* 21, 615–29.

Thagard, Paul. 1978. "The Best Explanation: Criteria for Theory Choice." *Journal of Philosophy* 75, 76–92.

Tolhurst, William. 1986. "Supervenience, Externalism and Moral Knowledge." In Gillespie (1986).

Tolliver, J. T. 1980. "Reasons, Perception, and Information." Ph.D. diss., Ohio State University.

Trenholme, Russell. 1978. "A Physicalist Analysis of Probability." *Nous* 12, 303–16.

van Fraassen, Bas. 1980. *The Scientific Image.* Oxford: Oxford University Press.

Van Gulick, Robert. 1980. "Rationality and the Anomalous Nature of the Mental." *Philosophy Research Archives* 6, 599–612.

Vendler, Zeno. 1972. *Res Cogitans.* Ithaca: Cornell University Press.

Vickers, John. 1969. "Judgment and Belief." In K. Lambert, ed., *The Logical Way of Doing Things.* New Haven: Yale University Press.

Wallace, John. 1972. "On the Frame of Reference." In Davidson and Harman (1972).

Walsh, Dorothy. 1979. "Occam's Razor: A Principle of Intellectual Elegance." *American Philosophical Quarterly* 16, 241–4.

Wimsatt, W. C. 1968. "Purposiveness and Intentionality in Nature." Unpublished photocopy, University of Chicago.

1972. "Teleology and the Logical Structure of Function Statements." *Studies in History and Philosophy of Science* 3, 1–80.

1976. "Reductionism, Levels of Organization, and the Mind–Body Problem." In G. G. Globus, G. Maxwell, and I. Savodnik, eds., *Consciousness and the Brain.* New York: Plenum.

Winograd, Terry. 1975. "Frame Representations and the Declarative-

Procedural Controversy." In D. Bobrow and A. Collins, eds., *Representation and Understanding*. New York: Academic Press.

1976. "Towards a Procedural Understanding of Semantics." *Revue Internationale de Philosophie* 30, 260–303.

Winograd, Terry, and D. B. Bobrow. 1977. "An Overview of KRL, a Knowledge Representation Language." *Cognitive Science* 1, 3–46.

Woodfield, A. 1982. *Thought and Object*. Oxford: Oxford University Press.

Wright, Larry. 1973. "Functions." *Philosophical Review* 82, 139–68.

Index

Darwall, S., 214n
Darwin, Charles, 158
Davidson, D., 4, 7–8, 25–53 passim, 214n
DDP, *see* doxastic decision procedure
deductivist metaphilosophy, 116–124
Dennett, D. C., 4, 5, 6, 9n, 12, 15–16, 22, 31, 33, 44–45, 48, 51, 54, 57n, 59, 61, 63n, 67–70, 76n, 79, 80n, 85n, 143, 145, 150–151
de re, see narrow vs. wide
Descartes, René, 3, 93n, 103n, 115n, 120, 136, 138, 162, 177, 192, 207
"de se," see self-regarding attitudes
desires as reasons grounding moral beliefs, 213–215
De Sousa, R., 54n, 56n, 57
Deutscher, M., 91
Devitt, M., 9, 13, 48n, 72n, 83n, 190, 191n, 195n
dispositions to judge, 54–71 passim
doxastic decision procedure (DDP), 131–133, 138, 172
doxastophobia, 4–6, 15n
Dray, W. H., 70n
Dretske, F., 92, 93n, 94–99, 101, 102n, 107, 108n, 110
Dreyfus, H., 63n
Duhem, P., 120, 202
Dummett, M., 137n, 190–191

Eddington, Arthur, 189
ego(s), Cartesian, 3, 198
elegance of hypotheses and "elegance principles" of theory acceptance, 113–127
eliminative materialism, 47, 67–71
emotivism regarding moral value, 128, 200–201
Ennis, R. H., 182–185
Evil Demon, 93n, 103n, 191–193
evolutionary theory, 45, 93n, 126–127, 139–153, 170, 210–211, 214
explanation
and explanationism, 93n, 105, 112–177 passim
and truth, *see* truth, explanation and
explanatory virtues, 112–177 passim
"explicit" as opposed to "implicit" or "tacit" belief, *see* tacit knowledge and belief
externalism in epistemology, 93, 110, 131, 138, 162n, 168, 173

"extrapolator-deducer" mechanisms, 16, 59–64, 66

Fahlman, S. E., 63n
family resemblances, 30–31
Fetzer, J., 188
Feyerabend, P., 121, 162–163
Field, H., 7, 9, 61–62, 67–69, 76–77, 79n
Fine, A., 194n
fitness, *see* evolutionary theory
flowcharts, 5–6, 33–35, 43, 50–51
Fodor, J. A., 5, 6n, 7–14, 20, 21, 33, 45, 51, 70, 73, 76–77, 79n, 80n, 145
Foley, R., 56n, 58n, 177n
"frame problem" in Artificial Intelligence, 63–64
"funsters" and funster algorithms, 174–175

Garcia, J., 151
Geis, M., 133n
Gettier, E., and "Gettier cases," 92, 131n, 180–181
Gibbard, A., 108, 151n, 211n
Gillespie, N., 212
Goldman, Alan, 165n
Goldman, Alvin I., 45, 59n, 93–94, 97, 102n, 105–106, 108, 110, 128n, 131–133, 138, 147, 171–173
Goldstick, D., 176n, 177n
Goldwater, Barry, 157
Goodman, N., 181–182
grammatical intuitions, *see* logical and grammatical intuitions
Grandy, R., 23
Green, K. F., 151
Grice, H. P., 50n
"grue" paradox, 39, 179, 181–182
Gunner, D. L., 113, 115, 141

Hacking, I., 154–155
Hare, R. M., 198, 204
Harman, G., 7, 13, 14, 20, 38n, 46n, 56n, 65, 68n, 76, 92–93, 96n, 120, 128n, 169, 178–188 passim, 207n, 209–213
Harper, William, 160n
Harper, W. L., 108, 151n
Haugeland, J., 5, 33
Heidelberger, H., 87n
Hempel, C., 182
Henson, R., 123n

Hill, C. S., 7
Hobbes, Thomas, 25
Homuncular Functionalism, or Ho-
  munctionalism, 5–7, 11–17, 27,
  33–37, 41, 43–44, 48–53,
homunculi, 79, 145
Hume, David, 126, 178–179, 201
Hunter, J. F. M., 56

iconic representation, 22–23
Identity Theory of Mind, *see* Type-
  Type Identity Theory
images, mental, 22–23
"implicit" belief, *see* tacit knowledge
  and belief
incorrigibility, 123–124, 136
induction, 119–120, 178–188 passim
inductive fallacies, 179–180
inference, 19, 59–65, 75, 97–98, 117–
  118
  to "best means," 214
  "immediacy" of, 60–62, 66
information, 6, 11–12, 35–36, 214
  Carnap and Bar-Hillel's notion of,
  as opposed to Shannon and Wea-
  ver's, 35n
"informational fitness," 140n
instrumentalism regarding belief, 67–
  71
intensionality, 39, 47, 53
intentionality, 3, 9, 20, 39, 47–48, 53,
  71, 76, 214
"internalism" regarding moral motivation, 215
interpretation, 27, 39, 195n
intuitions, *see* logical and grammatical
  intuitions; modal intuitions; moral
  intuitions

James, William, 161n
judgment as opposed to belief, 55–56,
  68

Kant, Immanuel, 192, 201, 211n
Kaplan, D., 85
Kaplan, M., 176n, 177n
Kearns, L., 71n
Keats, John, 134
Kilgore, C., 136n
Kim, J., 26n, 214n
Kitcher, Philip, 106n
Kiteley, M., 87n
"KK" thesis, 93, 110, 137–138, 197

knowledge, 91–111 passim, 135–139,
  154, 172
Kornblith, H., 109n, 173
Kraut, R., 8
Kripke, S., 9, 11, 57n, 72–76, 77n, 206
Kuhn, T., 121

language
  conditions for something's being,
  10, 17–20
  of thought, 1–87 passim
Laplacean demons, 80
Laudan, L., 121, 154n
laws of nature as applied to belief
  states, 25–53 passim, 91–92, 93n,
  96, 98–103
Laymon, R., 150n
Lazerowitz, M., 122
Lehnert, W., 63n
Lehrer, K., 65, 96n, 124, 128n, 142n,
  161–165, 167, 173–175
Leplin, J., 160n
LePore, E., 83n
Levi, I., 59n
Lewis, C. I., 165
Lewis, D., 25n, 31, 32, 38n, 51, 60,
  77, 79n, 98–100, 108
lexical presumption, 86
linguistic intuitions, *see* logical and
  grammatical intuitions
Loar, B., 79n
Locke, John, 105, 189, 196
Loeb, D., 130
Loewer, B., 83n
logical and grammatical intuitions,
  169, 209, 215
Logical Atomism, 198–201
Logical Positivism, 166, 198, 200, 202–
  203, 207
Lottery Paradox, 92, 105

McCord, G. S., *see* Sayre McCord, G.
McGowan, B. K., 151
Machamer, P., 154n
Mackie, J. L., 215n
Manfredi, P., 71n
Marras, A., 51
Martin, E., 46
materialism, 3; *see also* naturalism
Matthews, R., 68n
Mayo, B., 67n
Meinong, A., 25
methodological solipsism, 21–22, 77–
  84